Translating Growth Into Poverty Reduction

Beyond the Numbers

EDITED BY

Flora Kessy, Oswald Mashindano,
Andrew Shepherd & Lucy Scott

MKUKI NA NYOTA
DAR—ES—SALAAM

Mkuki na Nyota Publishers Ltd
P. O. Box 4246
Dar es Salaam, Tanzania
www.mkukinanyota.com

© Contributors, 2013

978-9987-08-226-1

Visit www.mkukinanyota.com to read more about and to purchase any
of Mkuki na Nyota books. You will also find featured authors interviews and news about
other publisher/author events. Sign up for our e-newsletters for updates on new releases
and other announcements.

Contents

Introduction—Translating Growth Into Poverty Reduction
    Oswald Mashindano and Andrew Shepherd

Understanding Structural Influences on Poverty Dynamics
in Tanzania—Using a Relational Life History Q-Squared Approach
    Kate Higgins and Lucia da Corta

PART 1: TANZANIA POVERTY ANALYSIS

Exploring Resilience Avenues for Managing Covariant and Idiosyncratic
Poverty Related Shocks
    Flora Kessy and Simon Vendelin Tarmo

The Rise in Women's Responsibility in a Context of Increased Poverty
in Tanzania
    Lucia da Corta and Joanita Magongo

Escaping Poverty in Tanzania—What Can We Learn From Cases of Success?
    Kate Higgins

Hidden Hunger in Rural Tanzania—What Can Qualitative Research Tell Us
About What To Do About Chronic Food Insecurity?
    *Andrew Shepherd, Kim Kayunze, Simon Vendelin Tarmo, Emily Darko,
    Alice Evans and Lucia da Corta*

List of Illustrations

Foreword

Tanzania is a much aided country which has been politically stable through several rounds of multi-party elections, has consistently grown economically during the first decade of the millennium, and has improved on its human development indicators, but has failed to make a significant dent in its extreme poverty, when all the signs suggested it should have been. This book is an attempt to delve into the reasons, and what can be done to improve the record. It is based on some largely qualitative research which was undertaken in 2009 and 2010 by the Chronic Poverty Research Centre (CPRC). While no doubt not this book is not the final word on this important topic, there are some significantly different conclusions to what is often repeated in the discourse on poverty in Tanzania, and internationally. It is hoped that these will inform the political and policy debates in Tanzania. But it is also hoped that Tanzania can stand as one example of a stable country which has grown but failed to really address its poverty problem. There are others, and this book may stimulate similar lines of enquiry in other countries.

Tanzanian poverty is widespread throughout the country, with extreme poverty concentrated in rural areas. A big policy and public debate was stimulated by the finding of the 2007 Household Budget Survey that the incidence of rural poverty had not reduced much over the 2001 figure, despite a good record on growth during those years, political stability and some progress on human development. A national panel survey is being undertaken over three years from 2008/9 to try and elucidate the reasons, and analysis of that data is still awaited. In the meantime, the CPRC identified Tanzania as a country which had a good recent national living standards survey, which could be used as the basis for qualitative data collection and analysis to investigate the same issue, and gain a better understanding of poverty dynamics in the country. This was achieved, although less use has been made of the quantitative data than was originally hoped. It was also hoped that a strong link could be forged between this work and that of the national panel survey, and attempts were made to provide results from the largely qualitative work to the National Bureau of Statistics so that it could be used in designing the annual panel surveys. In research terms this work of gaining an understanding of why growth has reduced rural poverty so little is very much work in progress, and awaits analysis of the panel data once it has emerged, as well as joining that up with this and further qualitative analysis in a genuine 'q-squared' approach.

Nevertheless, while the research reported here is not complete, it is substantial, and there are some unexpected findings. The emphasis on property-stripping and property-grabbing, alcoholism, old age, divorce, serial polygamy and selling labour on credit as major sources of vulnerability capable of keeping people poor as well as impoverishing them further is not something analyses of poverty typically draw out. Other impoverishing factors were more expected: bad weather and disease; casual wages failing to keep up with price inflation; and the negative effects of policies. Witchcraft was also reported as a source of vulnerability, and this is something which has not yet had a policy response. While poverty tends to be seen as attaching to smallholder agriculture, the research found that wage labourers were particularly vulnerable and food insecure. This, and the fact that many poor households in rural Tanzania now depend primarily on wage labour has been confirmed by other recent research in northwest Tanzania. Again, there has not yet been a policy response to the changing nature of poverty. The indepth findings on changing gender relationships are also challenging for policy makers. Women have clear responsibility for maintaining their children, and often other family members, but are increasingly facing difficulties fulfilling these responsibilities, in particular when they lose access to assets including land. The laws have been rewritten to safeguard their position, but remain unimplemented in many cases; and the traditional male supports are no longer seen to be as dependable as they were. This is the crisis facing not only the quarter of households which are women headed, but also others; and the dynamic development of savings and other groups is only partial compensation. These are some of the explanations for chronic poverty and deprivation, often inter-generational.

The other side of the coin is that there are simply not enough good opportunities to escape poverty. Doing well in agriculture is central to escaping poverty, and there remain many reasons why small farms do not thrive – these are mostly to do with the organisation of markets. Agricultural policy by contrast focuses mostly on production and inputs, though, with initiatives on contract farming (e.g. in cotton), value chain upgrading projects, and the older attempts to organise the cashew market through inventory credit, there is now be a much greater emphasis on markets. Key to success in agriculture is accumulating assets – land, oxen, and ploughs. Policies making acquiring land, for example, through renting, easier for poor households in an age when the wealthy and companies are investing in rural land as never before, are urgently needed, as are programmes which support the acquisition of other assets. The emphasis in agricultural policy on research and extension, while always welcome in itself, seems misplaced since the availability of good seeds is rarely the binding constraint on productivity. While agriculture is always mixed up in stories of escaping poverty, it is nonfarm employment or business which provides the tipping point for households. And underlying access to these opportunities lies a good education and often the opportunity to migrate. Education is especially important, and it is beyond primary education which matters: arguably getting one child in each household access to a full 10+ years of quality education would do more to assist escapes from poverty than any other single measure. Policies to address this crying need would include the current supply side improvements in the availability and quality of primary schools, but also specific demand-side measures to see children from poor households through education – the recently started school feeding programme; and scholarships and school feeding at post-primary levels. Access to electricity is also important, especially for generating those all important non farm enterprises and nonfarm employment, which are often the tipping factors for households escaping poverty.

While there are many good policy initiatives in place in Tanzania it is often poor implementation and governance which prevents them having greater impact. The suggestion in this book is that governance reforms need to understand what it is that makes a real difference to the chances of poor people escaping poverty or preventing impoverishment. Getting agricultural governance right and justice reforms which enhance poor women's access to justice are two of the issues needing attention.

These are just a few reasons why policy makers and development programmers should read this substantial book. Its rich concluding policy menu is based on indepth research, and in the case of several of the researchers' decades of experience of both Tanzanian realities as well as international poverty and policy responses.

The CPRC would like to thank its partners in Tanzania, the Economic and Social Research Foundation (ESRF), and its director Dr H. B. Lunogelo, for unfailing participation in and support for the project; Research on Poverty Alleviation (REPOA); the Universities of Dar es Salaam, Mzumbe, and Sokoine. In the UK the Overseas Development Institute has provided extensive support to ensure that the research came to fruition, in terms of data management as well as financial and administrative support. In particular, Julia Brunt's management of the data, and the assistance of Lucy Scott, who edited the chapters, and Emily Darko,. The research was supported by a larger grant from the UK Department for International Development to the Chronic Poverty Research Centre, as well as financial and other support from DFID in Tanzania. While the researchers are grateful for this support, they bear the entire responsibility for the contents of this book. The team of qualitative researchers assembled and trained under this project is quite possibly unparalleled elsewhere in developing countries, and has already been the basis for other collaborative work. Hopefully qualitative socio-economic research will gain a new momentum at least in Tanzania as a result.

Andrew Shepherd
Director, Chronic Poverty Research Centre (www.chronicpoverty.org)
Overseas development Institute

List of Contributors

FLORA KESSY is a Senior Lecturer in Development Studies at Mzumbe University, Dar es Salaam Campus College. She holds a PhD in Agricultural and Consumer Economics from the University of Illinois at Urbana Champaign, USA. She has researched and published widely on issues related to poverty (income and non-income aspects), gender and development, access to health, water and sanitation services, and HIV and AIDS financing. She has also provided services on poverty analysis to the Government of Tanzania including leading the team that drafted the second cluster (quality of life and social wellbeing) of the National Strategy for Growth and Reduction of Poverty.

OSWALD MASHINDANO holds a PhD in Economics from the University of Dar-es-Salaam, Tanzania (1998). He is currently a Lecturer at the same University. He also worked with the Economic and Social Research Foundation (ESRF) for 5 years as a Senior Research Fellow and Coordinator of Research and Monitoring Department. He has researched and published on rural and agricultural development. Other areas include growth and livelihoods; public expenditure; and public policy analysis. He has also provided technical support to the team that drafted the Zanzibar Strategy for Growth and Reduction of Poverty (MKUZA).

ANDREW SHEPHERD is a research fellow at the Overseas Development Institute, London. He was Deputy Director (2000-5) and then Director (2005-11) of the Chronic Poverty Research Centre (www.chronicpoverty.org) and is now a co-director of the Chronic Poverty Advisory Network. He has worked on poverty reduction and rural development since the 1970s, as an academic at Birmingham University, as a Unicef employee, and at ODI. He was Director of Programmes at ODI from 2003-2008.

KATE HIGGINS leads the Governance for Equitable Growth program at The North-South Institute, a Canada-based international development think-tank. She has researched and published on economic growth, trade, inequality, wealth redistribution and poverty dynamics. She also has a keen interest in global development frameworks, such as the UN Millennium Development Goals and the post-2015 development framework. She has provided policy analysis and advice to governments and international organizations on a range of development issues. She holds an M Phil in Development Studies from the University of Oxford, and a B Ec. (Social Sciences) (first class) from the University of Sydney.

LUCIA DA CORTA is a Research Fellow in Extreme Poverty at the University of Bath, UK. Over the past 20 years she has carried out research in and teaching of development studies at the Universities of Oxford, Manchester and the London School of Economics. She has researched and published widely on issues related to agrarian political economy, labour, gender, and chronic poverty in south India, Tanzania and Bangladesh. Currently she works through Bath University on a DFID challenge Fund called SHIREE in Bangladesh where she has designed and managed a qualitative monitoring system which makes extensive use of life histories and follows through tracking programme evaluation in order to understand extreme poverty and graduation therefrom in 12 regions of the country. She was trained at Cornell University in Agricultural Economics; the LSE in International Relations at St. Antony's College, Oxford in Agricultural Economics and held a Junior Research Fellowship at St. Anne's College Oxford.

VENDELIN TARMO SIMON is a researcher and lecturer in Anthropology at the University of Dar es Salaam, Tanzania. He holds a BA degree in Sociology and Anthropology from the University of Dar es Salaam, MA in Gender and Development from the University of Bergen, Norway and currently doing PhD studies in Switzerland. His research experience includes the areas of poverty, gender, health, globalization, and livelihood of the vulnerable groups. He has offered a professional service to a number of organizations that work with vulnerable groups in Tanzania including HelpAge International.

JOANITA MAGONGO is a researcher at the Research on Poverty Alleviation (REPOA), a research institution based in Dar es Salaam, Tanzania. She holds an M.A in Development Studies specializing in Local and Regional Development from the Institute of Social Studies Erasmus University Rotterdam, The Netherlands. She has researched on areas related to gender, local governance, democracy, local economic development, upgrading of farmers products through value chain, social service delivery, and revenue collection. She has also provided technical support to government by co-authoring a chapter of governance in Poverty and Human Development Report.

KIM KAYUNZE is a Senior Lecturer and a Poverty Analyst at Sokoine University of Agriculture, Morogoro, Tanzania. He holds a PhD in Rural Development from the same University and teaches poverty analysis and rural finance, among other courses. He has researched and published papers on poverty, including contributions of non-farm and farm enterprises to rural poverty alleviation; poverty disparities in small, large, male- and female-headed households; and credit enriching or impoverishing? He has also done a number of consultancy assignments in Tanzania including one on Systematization of Bukombe District Council's Socioeconomic and Revenue database.

EMILY DARKO works in the Agricultural Development and Policy programme at the Overseas Development Institute, London, where she has researched in various areas including rural poverty trajectories, livelihoods, migration and remittances, agricultural value chain upgrading, natural resource management and food security. She holds an MSc in Development Studies from the School of Oriental and African Studies.

FESTO MARO has a Masters degree in Agricultural Economics from Sokoine University of Agriculture in Tanzania. He has Post graduate Diploma in Poverty Analysis for Socioeconomic Security and Development from the International Institute of Social Studies of the Erasmus University of Rotterdam (The Netherlands) in collaboration with Economic and Social Research Foundation (ESRF) and Research on Poverty Alleviation (REPOA). He is UNCTAD-Vi trainee in Teaching and Research of Economic and Legal Aspects of International Investments Agreements. His areas of interests for research and consultancy are agricultural economics, regional trade, development economics, benefit incidence and program budget analysis. He has done consultancy work for the government of Tanzania, development partners and consulting firms in Zambia and Kenya.

ALICE EVANS is a PhD Candidate at the Department of Geography and Environment of the London School of Economics and Political Science, UK. Her research explores how men and women come to support gender equality in the Zambian Copperbelt.

LUCY SCOTT is a geographer and External Associate of the Brooks World Poverty Institute at the University of Manchester where she completed her PhD. Her research interests include how development interventions can reduce chronic and extreme poverty and she was involved in the work of the Chronic Poverty Research Centre as a Research Officer. She has field experience of mixed-methods research in Bangladesh and Tanzania.

ELIAB LUVANDA is a Lecturer in Economics at the University of Dar es Salaam (Department of Economics) where he teaches econometrics. His main areas of research include macroeconomic policy, poverty analysis, rural micro-finance, and program/policy impact evaluation/assessment. He has worked in collaboration with international organizations such as the African Economic Research Consortium (AERC), Institute of Food Policy Research Institute (IFPRI), Oxford Policy Management (OPM), and Overseas Development Institute (ODI) to carry out research, training and consultancy activities.

Acknowledgements

This book is a result of one year research project on Chronic Poverty and Research Development Policy in Tanzania. The research project was intended to undertake an integrated qualitative-quantitative (Q^2) research analysis in order to understand the reasons for chronic poverty (which is widespread in Tanzania), and for mobility into and out of poverty, particularly sustained mobility out of poverty; as well as to inform MKUKUTA review through the Research and Analysis Working Group (RAWG). As it has been the case with other many other initiatives to publish a book, this process was also demanding. To make it successful, support from different individuals and institution was inevitable.

In view of this support we would like to acknowledge with gratitude the contributions made by authors of the book articles for heeding to our request and invitation to contribute papers. These chapters were contributed by researchers from Chronic Poverty Research Center (CPRC) at the Overseas Development Institute, London – Andrew Shepherd, Julia Brunt, Emily Darko, Lucy Scott and Alice Evans; the Economic and Social Research Foundation (ESRF) – Mr. Festo Maro; ODI and the North South Institute – Kate Higgins; Mzumbe University – Dr. Flora Kessy, Research on Poverty Alleviation (REPOA) – Ms. Joanita Magongo; Bath University –Lucia da Corta; and University of Dar es Salaam (UDSM) – Dr. Oswald Mashindano, Dr. Eliab Luvanda and Mr. Vandelin Tarmo. They were able to get time to compose chapters, submit them and respond to all the comments from reviewers in time despite their busy schedules of work. They also managed to attend all local and international meetings, workshops and conferences and present their research findings as part of the review process. Their dedication during the process of publication of this book shows their passion for development studies and their determination to make contributions towards poverty reduction efforts in the country and the world at large.

We are also indebted to ESRF Executive Director – Dr. H. B. Lunogelo for hosting and overall guidance during implementation of the project. Our appreciations and gratitude also goes to Professor Andy McKay at Sussex University who worked very hard to summarize Household Budget Survey (HBS) regional data that was used to select enumeration clusters. We are once again grateful to Dr. Eliab Luvanda for undertaking quantitative analysis of the HBS clusters; Mr. Ahmed Makbel of National Bureau of Statistics (NBS) for offering

HBS data and working closely with the team; Dr Joachim de Weerdt and Dr Rose Mwaipopo for providing insights on the research methodology, Ms. Julia Brunt who was a Program Manager for the CPRC, based at ODI for overall coordination as well as collating all life histories and organizing them in a way that simplified the analysis; and to Anna Simmons for reviewing and editing preliminary chapters of the book.

The editors are also thankful for the constructive comments which were received during presentations of the papers at ESRF conference hall particularly the local staff of the DFID, World Bank, and Economic Development Institute (EDI). The papers were then presented at Manchester Conference on Ten Years of the War on Poverty, the UN Least Developed Countries Conference at Istanbul, and in Tanzania at the National Policy Dialogue Week and the REPOA Annual General Research Meeting. Comments received from those platforms were useful in improving the contents of this book. In addition, we are thankful to the external reviewers for sparing their valuable time to read and comment on the early versions of the chapters and ensure the main messages are clear and consistent.

Last but not least thank to District officials at Nkasi, Newala, and Magu for their facilitation role during the field surveys, and for organization of meetings with villagers. We are also thankful to the members of the communities from the sampled wards and villages in Nkasi, Newala and Magu districts for their valuable time spent during interviews. Their responses were the building blocks for this book and source of inspiration to the researchers.

Chapter 1

Introduction—Translating Growth Into Poverty Reduction
Oswald Mashindano and Andrew Shepherd

The fact that poverty is a multidimensional concept makes it difficult to define.[1] Much has been written about the meaning of poverty but, because of its complexity, many authors feel safer stating its causes or manifestations rather than analysing what it is. Variations in definitions complicate the design of poverty measurements and poverty reduction programmes as well as the assessment of the impacts of policy on poverty.

What we find in the literature and through frequent visits to poor communities is that poverty deprives people of their security and well-being;prevents people having access to safe water, adequate food, clothing and shelter, education and health care; takes away people's rights and their freedom, dignity and peace of mind; puts people's lives in danger; and robs themof their future.[2] In its broadest sense, poverty is defined as the inability to attain a minimum standard of living. It is caused by a lack of adequate resources and capabilities to acquire basic human needs.

Poverty is therefore a global concern which lies at the heart of development economics.[3] The situation is not better at country level. Tanzania remains one of the poorest countries in the world, and poverty reduction has been one of its main national development challenges. Poverty in Tanzania is a phenomenon primarily in rural areas, where a bigger proportion of the people live. Thus, since independence in 1961, the government of Tanzania has been preoccupied with combating especially rural poverty.

The country's development path and its history of poverty reduction interventions can be divided into three periods. First was the post-independence period (1961–7). At this time, Tanzania was characterised by an economic system inherited from the colonial regime. Economic performance was satisfactory in terms of growth but there was no explicit articulation of how the benefits of growth were to be shared within society. During these early years of independence, relatively little attention was paid to equity issues.[4] Second was the post-Arusha period (1967–early 1980s). Under the 1967 Arusha Declaration, Tanzania adopted a socialist model of development, relying on a strong state to deliver equitable benefits across society. This ideology was reflected in central government controls in key areas of the economy. Initially, socio-economic performance was satisfactory, judging from basic social indicators. However, the country's capacity to sustain the delivery of basic social services came under enormous strain. Some of its earlier gains in areas such as education, health services and water supply began to be reversed. It has been argued that the focus was on distribution at the expense of growth.

A series of crises during the 1970s almost led to economic collapse, with improvements in living standards and the achievements won in the initial period after independence coming under serious threat by the end of the decade. Macroeconomic imbalances further aggravated the situation, manifested through budgetary deficits, balance of payments deficits, a growing debt burden, increasing inflationary pressure and a weakening of the productive sectors, among other things.

Since the early 1980s, Tanzania has been taking a number of reform measures aimed at ending the crisis. Among other things, the country has resolved to continue with macroeconomic and sector-specific policy reforms as a long-term strategy for economic growth. These reforms aim to create an environment conducive to private investment, among other objectives. This objective is now a matter of consensus across the political elite and is considered a matter of priority if the country's initiatives to reduce poverty are to be realised.

After a decade of preoccupation with structural reforms and re-establishing macroeconomic stability aimed at creating an enabling environment for growth, Tanzania resumed its focus on poverty reduction during the 2000s. This is of course part of the global effort towards a sustained exit from the poverty trap, represented by pursuit of the Millennium Development Goals (MDGs). The government undertook various initiatives towards poverty reduction and the attainment of social and economic development, within a broad policy framework—the Tanzania Development Vision 2025—which established the vision, mission, goals and targets to be achieved with respect to economic growth and poverty eradication by the year 2025.

Efforts to address poverty in Tanzania started after independence, when the country's motto was to fight three major development enemies, namely, 'Poverty, Ignorance and Diseases'.[5] Among a series of programmes geared towards eliminating poverty were the improvement and transformation approaches; village settlements; agriculture-related campaigns and programmes; nationalisation and villagisation; and cooperative movements.[6] These were followed by economic and structural adjustment programmes, economic reforms, accompanying social action programmes and then poverty reduction strategies. These latter include the 1998 National Poverty Eradication Strategy, the 2000 Poverty Reduction Strategy Paper, the 2005 National Strategy for Growth and Reduction of Poverty (known as MKUKUTA I), the 2011 National Strategy for Growth and Reduction of Poverty (MKUKUTA II) and the most recent National Five-year Development Plan (2011/12–15/16). Whereas earlier efforts were home grown, these later, post-structural adjustment efforts have all involved Tanzania's donor community as central actors.

The National Poverty Eradication Strategy provided a framework to guide initiatives to reduce absolute poverty by 50 per cent by the year 2010 and to eradicate it by the year 2025. It targeted improved economic growth and people's incomes as a basis for poverty eradication. The Poverty Reduction Strategy Paper—the outcome of the Heavily Indebted Poor Countries initiative—had as its focus the priority areas of basic education, primary health, water, rural roads, agricultural research and extension, the judiciary and HIV and AIDS. MKUKUTA I and II adopted an outcome-based approach, with the twin goals of achieving and sustaining high economic growth and substantial poverty reduction. The recently launched Tanzania Five-year Development Plan is currently under implementation, as a formal implementation tool of the country's development agenda articulated in the Tanzania Development Vision 2025. Over the past decade, through MKUKUTA and the five year development plan, there has been a gradual shift in these strategies from a Millennium Development Goals-based concern with human development to a more central focus on economic growth.

Evidence from various studies, including MKUKUTA progress reports, reveals little progress (if any) in the area of income poverty during the period of these poverty reduction and more growth-oriented strategies, at least up to 2007,[7] although there are significant disparities across social groups, by gender and by geographical location. Growth in Tanzania has not translated into poverty reduction despite the fact that the economy recorded a significant increase in growth rates between 1991/92 and 2007.[8] Relying on growth alone to reduce poverty is therefore neither equitable nor efficient. In Tanzania, the critical question is, why has rapid growth in Tanzania not been accompanied by a corresponding fall in poverty? Why have the numbers of impoverished risen?

This book is intended to shed some light on these issues using the results of largely qualitative research based on life histories, focus group discussions and key informant interviews across several regions in Tanzania, complemented by some analysis of national household survey data. The book brings together a total of 11 chapters discussing different dimensions of poverty and analysing its functioning. The focus is on its multiple aspects, its manifestations and what government policies have contributed in terms of reducing it.

The book suggests there are both important macro-level causes (inflation combined with limited employment and wage growth and the sectoral composition of growth) as well as micro-level causes. It is on these latter that the book focuses, for the most part. These micro-level causes centre around a negative dynamic affecting a large number of poor households in which a widespread failure to provide for household food security undermines gender relationships and reduces the possibilities for saving and asset accumulation which are necessary to escape poverty. This results in very low upward mobility. At the same time, vulnerability is widespread and resilience against shocks minimal, even for many who are not absolutely poor. In this context, the authors explore what can be done to make growth more inclusive and the implications for governance and the state–citizen social contract.

The book is organised into three sections. Before Part 1, on the analysis of poverty in Tanzania, Chapter 2 discusses the somewhat innovative methodological approach adopted in this research and the utility of combining quantitative with qualitative approaches. In this case, the emphasis has been on the qualitative, because the facts are relatively well known whereas the causes remain something of a mystery. The prime utility of good qualitative research is that it helps to get at explanations, which quantitative survey-based research may struggle to do.

Part 1 focuses attention on poverty, through analyses of vulnerability, the interaction of gender relationships and poverty dynamics, the realities involved in escaping poverty and the struggle to provide household food security.

Within this, Chapter 3 identifies the major covariant shocks as related to weather and agricultural markets, witchcraft and the theft of agricultural produce while on the farm. Critical idiosyncratic shocks and stresses identified include property-grabbing after the death of a husband and property loss after divorce/separation, as well as alcoholism, old-age vulnerability, serial polygamy and selling labour on credit. The poor are also found to be vulnerable as measured by the number of meals per day: the destitute and very poor can afford only one meal a day, and even that is not always assured. Major avenues for coping with these shocks include the transfer of available physical and human capital and the formation of networks. That is to say, property transfers and investments in human capital are major ex-ante resilience-building processes. One major latent resilience avenue that needs to be activated involves leasing out land. This chapter recommends promotive and transformative social protection measures in the form of measures to increase productivity, as well as legal institutional reforms.

Chapter 4 builds a picture of evolving gender relationships, based on the same data. In Tanzania, liberalisation and de-agrarianisation have led to unequal growth; stagnating and in some cases increasing poverty; fragmented landholdings; and a rise in the cost of essentials. Local user costs also continue to cripple local populations, despite the government's commitment to eradicating these. Meanwhile, traditional gendered roles in rural households have changed, with longer-term de-masculinisation and corresponding feminisation of responsibility for family provisioning—both within marriage (contingent on a rise in male underemployment, despair and alcoholism) and through a rise in divorce, widowhood and single motherhood.

Women have been empowered particularly by their membership in female credit networks. In response, some men assault this freedom by marrying second wives, spending more money and time outside the home, labelling women prostitutes and perpetrating physical abuse. These issues have contributed to a rise in the number of female-headed households.

Meanwhile, widowed and divorced women are exposed to customary stripping of assets by husbands or husbands' kin. Women's statutory rights under land and marriage legislation are not enforced. Traditional support has also fallen, leaving women deprived of the means to support children's nutritional and educational needs in a time of rising costs, which may perpetuate intergenerational poverty in the coming decade.

We suggest further linking small female credit networks to cooperatives so they can access more capital; reworking and enforcing legislation; acknowledging women's role as key providers; and establishing gender-sensitive employment guarantee schemes, in part to help poor rural men emerge from poverty traps so they can contribute to the family provisioning.

Chapter 5 focuses on escaping poverty. It examines how and why people have experienced upward socioeconomic mobility, and in some cases escaped poverty, in a context where such cases have been few. Using a locally relevant but comparable well-being classification system, we find that poverty is entrenched across all research sites. The overwhelming majority of households ranked in this study—derived from a representative sample in each site from the 2007 Household Budget Survey—were identified by representatives in their community as being poor. In line with other analyses, we find that there has been little socioeconomic mobility across these sites over the past decade, and stubborn levels of poverty despite sustained economic growth nationally.

Through systematic analysis of the qualitative dataset, we find that agriculture is a key factor in supporting upward mobility. But, critically, we find that it is non-farm businesses, the accumulation of physical assets (such as land and housing), salaried employment and favourable marriage—some of which agriculture plays a role in supporting—which are most effective at moving people out of poverty. When it comes to moving beyond vulnerability, these findings hold. Those who manage to move beyond vulnerability often have multiple sources of income and own a number of valuable physical assets.

A range of broad policy conclusions are made. These include that agricultural development should remain a priority; rural industrialisation requires greater attention; asset accumulation needs to be promoted (and those assets need to be protected); access to credit, and business development, needs to be supported; and secondary and vocational training opportunities need to be made accessible for young people from poorer households.

Chapter 6 investigates the experience of hunger, its causes and consequences and the strategies people use to prevent it, and derives a set of policy implications. The most food-insecure people depend significantly (although rarely exclusively) on wage labour, so controlling food price inflation and improving wages and working conditions for poor casual labourers is a clear priority. Buffers against hunger can easily erode for vulnerable older people and separated, divorced or widowed women, who need to be protected against the possible loss of their assets or access to resources. Knowledge is also a powerful tool against hunger—people at local level could use more and better information about nutrition, suggesting that a revival of the once-successful community nutrition programme would help.

Part 2 focuses on economic growth and poverty reduction. Chapter 7 underlines the fact that agriculture is vital to Tanzania's achievement of its poverty reduction strategy goals. Growth in agriculture has made contributions to gross domestic product (GDP), foreign exchange earnings and income poverty reduction. However, the growth pattern in the sector (which employed about 70 per cent of the population between 1998 and 2009) is not reflected in poverty reduction, particularly in rural areas. Findings indicate that the pattern of economic growth in the past decade has been influenced largely by services and industry and less by agriculture, where annual growth has been slow.

The origin of the growth–poverty mismatch is puts down to demographic factors; limited investment in education and agriculture; and the rising cost of living, including rapidly increasing costs of basic necessities and of water, education and health care services. Meanwhile, the poor operate in labour, service and commodity markets which are oversupplied, and returns are low as a result. MKUKUTA II constructively addresses several of these agendas but has little focus on practical measures to improve labour markets for the poor. Given the strategy's reliance on commercialising agriculture and releasing labour to other sectors, this would seem to be a priority.

This chapter puts forward a number of strategies to overcome this mismatch: improving data collection, processing and management; improving governance to ensure better strategic resource allocation; reducing the supply of and increasing the demand for labour; checking momentum for accelerated population growth; raising the level of education of girls; increasing economic opportunities for women; focusing on agriculture as a priority sector, and especially on productivity-enhancing factors; and making financial services accessible by the poor and very poor. Meanwhile, policies which make land easier to rent (in and out) would be especially helpful, complemented by policies focused on helping poor people acquire or rent farm assets (e.g. irrigation and oxen) and non-farm business assets

Chapter 8 notes that agricultural growth has been consistently lower than required to reduce poverty significantly; the growth which has occurred has not 'trickled down' adequately to the poor. A number of bottlenecks are evident. These include low income generation, low capital investment, low productivity, diminishing livelihood sources, food insecurity and therefore intensive poverty and poor quality of life. This chapter identifies strategic interventions to stimulate agricultural growth as well as enable a significant reduction in poverty.

Strategic interventions to improve the functioning of markets can boost agricultural growth and render it more pro-poor. A number of policy measures need to be considered in this regard. These include improving market access and the functioning of value chains. More competitive export markets are needed in border areas and in basic staple crops. Markets often do not function transparently enough: top political executives should not be involved in crop marketing, for reasons of conflict of interest, and standard weights and measures are needed to counter widespread under-recording of farmers' crops. Improved market access also entails increased access to land, education and skills development and increasing productivity, particularly through input markets and agricultural extension. Efforts are needed in relation to new technology, secure markets, mixed farming (diversification of crops and livestock) and efficient institutions. This chapter describes the government's Warehouse Receipt Scheme (WRS) to illustrate the potential gains available from focusing on output markets although, if cooperatives are to be involved, they need access to adequate and timely liquidity. The priority given to improving road connections in MKUKUTA I should be continued in order to reduce transport costs and time.

For poor, vulnerable, rural households, the priority may be to ensure better risk management. Productive asset accumulation can lead to the growth of poor and very poor people's incomes, but also underlies resilience against shocks. Making financial services accessible to the poor and very poor is a priority (e.g. by linking them to Rotating Savings and Credit Associations (ROSCAs), which can then be strengthened by linking them to Savings and Credit Cooperative Societies (SACCOS) and securing appropriate safeguards). Measures which ease access to land, livestock and productive equipment include social protection but also specific policies such as soil and water conservation, price stabilisation schemes or insurance linked to financial services.

Part 3 focuses on governance and the social contract. Chapter 9 looks at poverty mobility and linkages with governance. MKUKUTA I sees governance as a key ingredient in poverty alleviation. However, decisions on and implementation of economic and social development activities have often been inefficient, associated with bribery, not transparent and inequitable. Meanwhile, there is an underlying governance agenda which is different from the wider governance improvements sought in Tanzania. This concerns the access of vulnerable groups (e.g. poor and single women) to justice, and to more transparent, accountable and participatory governance at local level. While aspects of bad governance for the poor have been removed (e.g. the development levy), a large number of issues remain.

This chapter identifies what governance issues really matter for poverty mobility in Tanzania. It finds biases in the provision of education, health and water services; bribery in the construction of classrooms and the allocation and transfer of teachers; limited access to justice for women and poorer community members; lack of transparency of expenditure of community money and allocation of materials (including medicines) in the education, health and water sectors in some areas; limited participation in decision-making, as many community members do not attend meetings at which decisions are made; and late completion of construction works and distribution of agricultural inputs. These problems all exacerbate poverty. As such, it is recommended that MKU-KUTA II give more weight to governance issues, including those listed above, lest they slow the pace towards attainment of the Tanzania Development Vision 2025.

Chapter 10 encourages the government to 'take the plunge' on developing a national social assistance programme to implement the National Social Protection Framework already devised. Social transfers can be an important part of a transformative approach to development which can interrupt the exclusion and adverse incorporation which characterises current patterns of development.

Insecurity and vulnerability are widespread in Tanzania. Many people are trapped in poverty, lacking the resources to participate in growth which has not reduced income poverty and increased upward mobility as expected. There are categories of people who are especially vulnerable, usually to several sources of risk, and who therefore need broad protection: households mainly dependent on casual wage labour; single adult women (unmarried, separated, divorced, widowed and bereaved) and their dependants; socially excluded women without children; orphaned youth-headed households; older people; the chronically ill; and carers of the chronically ill. Well-designed social assistance would support the greater involvement of these groups in growth and accessing health and education services, the latter being especially important for interrupting intergenerational poverty.

The many sources of risk and widespread vulnerability, together with the affordability and capacity contexts, create two difficult choices: between running one versus several programmes of social transfers and between categorical and non-categorical targeting. Social transfers should be able to support the risks poor people have to take to improve their livelihoods, escape poverty and contribute to growth. They should also be capable of addressing the main reasons for impoverishment, which include divorce and business failure. A non-categorical transfer targeted at poor households would be best as it would entail fewer exclusion and inclusion errors. Local focus group discussions have in some cases proven effective at identifying the poor, although safeguards against corruption would be needed if these are used to target any financial or non-financial incentive.

Politically, categorical transfers, such as pensions and child or disability allowances, combined with an employment guarantee might be most attractive, as these are simple to understand and easier to target. But, given the likely scarcity of financial resources for the long-term commitments required, as well as strained implementation capacity, one programme addressing many risks and funded from tax revenues would be optimal, at least until scale-up seems more feasible.

Chapter 11 draws the study to its conclusion and derives the main policy implications.

---

1   C.R. Laderchi et al. (2003); S. Likwelile (2000)
2   See, for example, F. Kessy et al. (2006); O. Mashindano (2007); L. Msambichaka et al. (2005); Revolutionary Government of Zanzibar (2009)
3   R. Kanbur and L. Squire (2001)
4   F. Kaijage and A. Tibaijuka (1995)
5   J.K. Nyerere (1998)
6   See A. Coulson (1982)
7   A.V.Y. Mbelle (2007)
8   See Chapter 4 and Chapter 7 of this volume

Chapter 2

Understanding Structural Influences on Poverty Dynamics In Tanzania—Using a Relational Life History Q-Squared Approach
Kate Higgins and Lucia da Corta

Introduction

This chapter outlines the research methodology for the study from which this edited volume derives. The study was titled 'Chronic Poverty and Development Policy: Q-Squared Research in Support of the 2010 Poverty Reduction Strategy in Tanzania.' The field research was conducted in three locations in mainland Tanzania between August and December 2009 and was funded by the Chronic Poverty Research Centre (CPRC).

This chapter outlines the unique Q-squared approach developed by CPRC and adopted in this study of chronic poverty in Tanzania. It focuses particularly on the qualitative methods designed to produce the empirical research on which the chapters of this volume are largely based. Following this introduction, it briefly outlines the Q-squared approach to understanding poverty dynamics developed by partners of CPRC and introduces the approach taken to the Tanzania study. It also covers the study's research objectives and questions, and then the design and field research approach in detail. It goes on to reflect on the research approach and methods, focusing on how the approach captured the structural influences of chronic poverty as well practical lessons for utilising such an approach.

Q-squared research: a legacy of CPRC

Q-squared research can be defined as research that generates and draws on quantitative and qualitative data in an integrated and synergistic way. In the field of poverty dynamics, it has often been conducted at the sub-national level. However, recently, under the direction of Andrew Shepherd, CPRC has encouraged the linking of a nationally representative survey (e.g. a household budget survey or a panel survey) with life history qualitative data from a sub-sample of households included in the survey.

Qualitative work adds substantial value to quantitative research by exposing the context and causes of what is observed quantitatively. For instance, if quantitative surveys reveal how much poverty is reduced, qualitative data can help us to understand *why* certain groups of people moved out of poverty, while others did not. It reveals *how* they moved out of poverty, which is crucial for policy- and programme-making. Qualitative research also sheds light on issues that are difficult to explore using household surveys, such as changes in power in relationships in markets, societies and polities, which are so crucial for sustainable livelihood changes. Qualitative data can also feed back into quantitative survey design, by revealing new categories or refined variables to include in the next survey.

Life histories are a longitudinal qualitative approach that can generate a very rich picture of the causes and experience of chronic poverty and poverty dynamics. They have been central to CPRC Q-squared efforts, used in Bangladesh,[1] Kenya,[2] Senegal[3] and Uganda.[4] Life histories map chronologically the lives of respondents, highlighting key social, political and economic events, processes, networks, relationships and norms—and the implications of these for levels of well-being. They seek to help us understand the multi-causal processes which affect well-being and focus particularly on *how* and *why* people move into and out of poverty. Life history interviews not only support and supplement aggregate data derived from conventional quantitative surveys, but also can add a longitudinal dimension to research where panel data are lacking.

Given the success of a Q-squared study conducted in rural Bangladesh, CPRC was keen to replicate the approach in a sub-Saharan African country. Tanzania was chosen for three reasons. First, Tanzania's National Strategy for Growth and the Reduction of Poverty (MKUKUTA) between 2005 and 2010, was coming to an end and was under review. We planned to use our study to evaluate the impact of MKUKUTA and earlier poverty reduction initiatives and to recommend priorities for MKUKUTA II. Second, Tanzania had a good recent Household Budget Survey (HBS), conducted in 2007 and based on a nationally representative sample of 10,466 households.[5] Third, until the commencement of the National Panel Survey in 2007, there were no nationally representative panel data in Tanzania.[6] Many developing countries lack panel data, and we hoped the study could examine the quality of data generated using one-point-in-time surveys, such as household budget surveys, with longitudinal qualitative tools, such as life history interviews.

Research objectives

A policy workshop was conducted in Dar es Salaam in August 2009. The objective of this was to introduce the study to a range of stakeholders, to identify the key questions on the minds of policy-makers and local research-ers and to gather information and input to support the research design. The workshop was attended by officials from a range of Tanzanian government ministries, non-governmental organisations, universities and donor agencies. It was followed by a research design workshop, also held in Dar es Salaam in

August 2009. This was attended by the research team, which comprised 11 researchers from a range of think-tanks and universities in Tanzania and the United Kingdom.[7]

'Ihrough the policy and research design workshops, three clear objectives for the study were identified. The first was to understand the reasons for chronic poverty in Tanzania, and for mobility into and out of poverty. We were particularly interested in why so many households were clustered around the poverty line, unable to move out of poverty, despite relatively strong and sustained economic growth in Tanzania and policy commitments to poverty reduction through MKUKUTA.[8] This influenced the second objective, which was to inform the review of MKUKUTA and the priorities of MKUKUTA II by disseminating the research findings widely in Tanzania. The third objective was to present the findings to a wide and varied international audience, as well as our reflections on the usefulness and applicability of the research approach for understanding poverty dynamics.

Research design and methods

Life histories have been used to investigate economic mobility in developing countries for some time.[9] Davis applied the approach to chronic poverty research by designing a life history method which sought to capture poverty dynamics through well-being trajectories.[10] The life history narratives generated through his research captured the dynamics of vulnerability and adverse coping sequences—for instance, the way in which illness leads to the loss of work, which leads to the sale of assets, which creates further vulnerability and a decline in well-being. He presented the narrative visually through life history maps, which comprised well-being on the y axis and time on the x axis, with a line representing the well-being of the respondent over their life-course. On the map, explanations are provided for a rise or decline in well-being. CPRC found that these visual representations, and the stories that accompanied them, appealed to decision-makers, policy-makers and programme managers. By taking this life history approach, and linking the life history analysis to large-scale surveys, Baulch and Davis' work in rural Bangladesh helped to take Q-squared studies out of academia into the purview of development policy analysis and programming.

Bird and Higgins adapted Davis' life history methods for chronic poverty research in Uganda and Kenya. A notable feature of this work was the tracking of intergenerational transmissions of poverty and resilience[11] by periodising life histories according to points in the life-course—childhood, youth and (young, middle and late) adulthood. Detailed life history narratives were documented, followed by graphic representations of changes in well-being over the respondent's life. In these research efforts, the respondent subjectively assessed their well-being at different points in their life (i.e. whether they were very poor, poor, average, rich or very rich).

In our study in Tanzania, we built on the life history methods adopted by Davis, Bird and Higgins and others, but sought to modify these approaches to consider more closely the terms of people's relationships with economic, political and social agents, events and institutions and the norms governing these relationships. Thus we pursued, through smaller 'n' research, more structural or relational conceptions of poverty.[12] This harked back to the original ideas behind CPRC,[13] which include social exclusion and adverse incorporation into markets, societies and polities and the norms governing these relationships,[14] as well as destitution.[15] Our approach was also informed by the thinking that contributed to CPRC's comparative life history project.[16] Drawing on experience, members of the research team had through their involvement in the World Bank's Moving Out of Poverty study,[17] we also paid greater attention to the role that macro events, policies and programmes play in determining poverty dynamics.[18]

Research sites

Quantitative analysis of the 2007 HBS informed the selection of research sites for the study. Six research sites, in three districts in mainland Tanzania, were selected, to reflect different regions of the country as well as different agro-ecological zones and associated livelihoods. All sites selected had relatively high levels of poverty. Further, according to the Tanzanian members of the research team, the sites were comparatively under-researched. Table 2.1 outlines the research sites and the rationale for site selection.

Table 2.1: Rationale for site selection

Site	District	Region	HBS characteristics	Rationale
Nchinga	Newala	Mtwara	Rural, coastal southern and western zone	Cashew nuts as traditional cash crop
Nkangala	Newala	Mtwara	Urban, coastal zone	Livelihood mix of fishing and farming cashews
Ndite	Magu	Mwanza	Rural, plateau zone	Mixed farming of cotton as traditional cash crop, plus livestock and fishing
Wazabanga	Magu	Mwanza	Urban, plateau zone	
Kayumbe	Nkasi	Rukwa	Rural, highlands and southern and western zone	Maize as main cash crop. A remote and marginalised area marked by poor markets
Kalesa	Nkasi	Rukwa	Urban, highlands zone	Market dynamics different from other regions owing to grain reserve policies which prevent export to the Democratic Republic of Congo

Research methods

The research approach comprised three field tools: focus group discussions, life history interviews and key informant interviews. Table 2.2 outlines the research sequence.

Table 2.2: Field research sequence

Steps	Research component
1	Protocol meetings at the regional, district, ward and village levels
2	Focus group discussion: knowledgeable people
3	Focus group discussion: well-being classifications and socioeconomic mobility
4	Life history interviews
5	Key informant interviews
6	Focus groups discussion: community feedback and action research

Protocol meetings

For each research site, we began with protocol visits at the regional, district, ward and village levels. At these meetings, we discussed the objectives of our work and the plans for our field research. These visits are standard practice for research in Tanzania, and ensured that sub-national administrations were aware and supportive of our research. Engaging with community leaders at the village level was critical and helped with the identification of research participants for the study. We were sensitive to the bias this could generate (i.e. community leaders selecting their family and friends as participants) and sought to manage this by speaking with a number of leaders and discussing the composition of selected participants with a range of members of the community.

Focus group discussion: knowledgeable people

The first focus group discussion was with a group of five to seven knowledgeable women and men from the community. The objective of this was to obtain insights into the economic, social and political history and context of the community. We sought to generate

- A community history, focusing on key events and explanations for mobility into and out of poverty within the community;
- A list of key institutions in the community, when they were set up and their functions;
- Location and distances to critical institutions from the community (health centre, school, district offices, major market centres);
- A list of major economic activities and sources of livelihoods in the community; and
- The value of key assets, wages and prices (e.g. prices received for crops at the village and major market).

We also gathered information about how different policy periods affected communities (e.g. crops, poverty levels, migration). The objective of this questioning was to get a handle on major historical trends. Periodisation was crucial to understand macro policy effects and to understand the influence of MKUKUTA on livelihoods and well-being compared with other policy periods. Periods we focused on were

- The period before and just after independence (1961–7);
- Ujamaa (the period of villagisation after the Arusha Declaration: 1967–86);
- Economic liberalisation, or sokohuria (the free market period: 1986–92);
- Political liberalisation (1992–2005) which overlapped with deeper sokohuria; and
- The poverty reduction strategy period (2001–4) and the MKUKUTA period (2005–10), which overlapped with further economic and political liberalisation.

Focus group discussion: well-being classification and drivers of socio-economic well-being

Developing the well-being classification scheme

At the core of our research approach was a system of well-being classification, developed to get a strong handle on well-being distribution within and well-being mobility among the community. The objective was to produce a well-being classification scheme which was conceptually coherent across regions and diverse research sites in Tanzania, but which could also retain local meaning and relevance at each site. We were eager to expand the range of indicators on which the well-being classification was based, and so developed a scheme that took account of

- Income and ability to save;
- Work capacity and dependency on others for support;
- Level of productive agricultural and non-farm assets;
- Security of consumption over the year (e.g. lean periods versus normal periods of consumption);
- Vulnerability to risk (and to downward mobility); and
- Power in market relationships (e.g. labourer, borrower or seller of crops compared with employer, moneylender or trader of crops).

The scheme included six well-being classifications, ranging from 'destitute' (1) to 'rich' (6). Table 2.3 outlines these classifications. We were interested in disaggregating the group of 'poor' people bunched around and below the poverty line and therefore established three 'non-poor' classifications. 'Destitute' was the classification for people who cannot work, who depend on social relationships of support or begging for survival and who tend to be socially excluded. 'Very poor' was the classification for people who have no productive assets and depend largely on labour and negotiating labour relationships. 'Poor' was the classification for people with some productive assets but not enough to escape labouring to make ends meet. This group also has to rely on credit and labour relationships. The conceptual thinking on poverty that underpinned CPRC very much influenced how the scheme was developed.

Table 2.3: Well-being classification scheme

1. Destitute = maskini hohehahe
Depends on others for basic needs
Cannot work
Tends to be socially excluded
2. Very poor = maskini sana
No clear livelihood source
No significant productive assets
Dependent on selling labour and/or scavenging
Erratic income and food access
Very vulnerable to becoming destitute with a shock
3. Poor = maskini
Access to limited productive assets (e.g. land and livestock)
Cannot earn enough from farming or trade to take family provisioning through the whole year so will reduce family food consumption
Cannot save much in good years
Must sell assets in order to cope in a crisis
Vulnerable to downward mobility to 'very poor' category but not to 'destitute' category
4. Vulnerable but not poor = tete ila siyo maskini
More productive assets which take the family through the year
During good times can save
During bad times will reduce family consumption
Vulnerable to downward mobility with a significant shock
5. Resilient = tajiri kiasi (mwenye uwezo)
Sufficient capacity (e.g. assets, social networks) to prevent significant downward mobility relative to overall productive wealth
May employ small amounts of labour on farm or be involved in small -cale trade
6. Rich = tajiri
Significant assets and local power
Involved in large-scale trade or employment of labour
Owns large scale non-farm assets
May lend money

Applying the well-being classification scheme

The second and third focus group discussions at each research site were with approximately eight women and eight men, selected during the focus group discussion with knowledgeable people. The research team requested that a cross-section of the community be represented. These discussions had three objectives. The first was to establish community specific well-being classifications. The well-being classifications developed by the research team, and indicators that accompanied them, were used as the basis for the stratification. But the *characteristics* that defined these were generated by the focus groups. The objective here was to understand the types of characteristics that defined these classifications in each community, while being able to aggregate and compare the data at a later stage. Unsurprisingly, given the diversity of the research sites, the characteristics attached to each classification and sets of indicators varied from community to community.

To illustrate this, Box 2.1 outlines the characteristics attached to the 'poor' classification by two well-being ranking focus groups.

Box 2.1: Characteristics attached to 'poor' classification in two research sites

IN NKANGALA, WOMEN DEFINED THE 'POOR'—WELL-BEING LEVEL 3—AS THOSE WHO	
• Could educate their children in government schools;	• Might own a cashew nut farm, but in most cases production would be very low owing to lack of necessary inputs;
• Paid school contributions with difficulties;	
• Were involved in work such as making cookies or carrying luggage;	• If they owned a house, in most cases it would not be well maintained;
• If a young woman, may be involved in sex for money;	• If they owned a house, there was a high chance that the house was inherited; and
• Owned 1 ha of land for maize, legume and cassava production;	• If a woman, would own a maximum of one pair of khanga (women's garments).

IN WAZABANGA, MEN DEFINED THE 'POOR' AS THOSE WHO	
• Owned small farms and few livestock (perhaps four goats and no cows);	• Gave up easily in life;
• Did not make much profit through cultivation and business and could not save;	• Were more likely to be suicidal (since they are used to not making it in life, they easily become disheartened and commit suicide);
• Did not have enough to take them through the year;	• Had a house with tin roofing and mud bricks;
• Were typically lazy and didn't work hard;	• Had two pairs of trousers, three shirts, a vest and one pair of underpants if a man; three pairs of khanga, three gowns and one pair of underpants if a woman;
• Were not smart about their cultivation practices;	
• Owned 2–3 acres of land that were never utilised—cultivated only a quarter of the land they owned;	• Might own a bicycle, used to carry water and other goods and to travel to the milling machine;
• Tended to have large families, as they do not follow family planning practices. They have eight or more children on average;	• Might send children to primary school, but cannot afford to pay the fees and for uniforms for secondary school.

Each focus group was also asked to identify the number of meals per day that people in each classification would eat, and what those meals would constitute. This enabled the research team to understand the food security context of each community and to make useful comparisons with quantitative surveys, such as the 2007 HBS.

Stratifying HBS households and documenting drivers of socioeconomic well-being

The second objective of these focus groups was to stratify the well-being of each of the twenty-four HBS households in the community in 1999 and 2009, according to the community-specific well-being classification system generated by the focus group.[19] We also sought to identify the reasons *why* socio-economic wellbeing had improved, declined or been stable in the twenty-four households. Among the six research sites, eight well-being rankings were conducted: four by women and four by men. In total, 144 households were ranked, although 192 rankings took place (in two clusters, both women and men ranked the households). This dataset served as a way to choose households for our in-depth life histories, as well as constituting a very useful medium dataset in which to contextualise our narratives.[20]

The final component of these focus group discussions was to facilitate a more general discussion about what the key drivers of upward and downward socio-economic mobility had been in the community ten years ago and now, and what the participants thought would be the drivers in the future.

Life history interviews

Based on the findings from the well-being rankings, the research team selected around ten of the twenty-four HBS households in each community for life history interviews. Households were selected to reflect patterns of upward mobility, downward mobility and stagnation which were found among the twenty-four HBS households. We were also interested in ensuring that different ages and genders were represented in the life history sample. At least five households selected were part of the National Panel Survey, to ensure that future longitudinal Q-squared work could be carried out using the latter and our qualitative dataset. Within each household, male and female household heads were targeted for interview. If there was only one household head (such as in the case of a widower), a second respondent within the household was identified, ideally to ensure gender balance (e.g. a female widow and her young adult son).

The life history interviews sought to map the lives of the respondents and to understand the economic, social and political factors that contributed to changes in their well-being. In the life histories, we paid close attention to the role and influence of macro-level events, policies and programmes on well-being and sought to compare people's experience with different periods in Tanzania's history. Importantly, the objective was to gather people's own narratives of events and relationships. To achieve this, the life history interviews commenced with open questioning (e.g. 'what happened during your childhood?'). Respondents were asked to give their story chronologically. Towards the end of the interview, structured questions were asked to follow up on issues the respondent had not addressed in their narrative. Box 2.2 outlines issues explored in life history interviews.

Box 2.2: Issues explored in life history interviews

- Genealogy of the family and family relationships;
- Livelihoods and income-generating activities over the life-course;
- Ownership: house and compound (homestead), productive assets (e.g. land, agricultural and non-agricultural equipment and assets, livestock, vehicles) and other assets (e.g. clothes, utensils, furniture);
- Key events (e.g. policy changes, drought, inheritance, marriage) and key processes (e.g. processes of liberalisation, decentralisation, commercialisation, market access, climate change);
- Agricultural changes (e.g. in climate, crops, agricultural extension and prices);
- Education and health of grandparents, parents, siblings, spouse, children;
- Migration patterns;
- Key relationships at different points in the life-course and the nature of those relationships (e.g. between men and women, different aged family members, friends, employers, traders, moneylenders, labourers);
- Important institutions at different points in the life course (e.g. schools, church, micro-credit schemes, non-governmental organisations, government agencies, banks, warehouse schemes, programmes, farming groups, rotating savings and credit associations, savings and credit cooperative organisations, burial societies)
- Urban–rural linkages (e.g. remittances, employment opportunities, trading opportunities)

At the end of each interview, the life history trajectories of respondents were mapped graphically against the six well-being classifications (y axis) to reflect changes in well-being over time (x axis). Figure 2.1 provides an example of life history map.

Figure 2.1: Example of life history map: Samweli Togoro, age 35, Kalesa Village

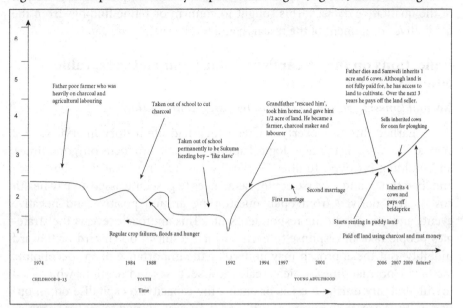

Key informant interviews

Key informant interviews were conducted to examine particular research themes in more depth. Respondents were selected opportunistically, based on issues and relationships highlighted in focus group discussions and life history interviews. Those targeted for key informant interviews included government officials, community leaders, crop traders, creditors, agricultural extension agents, teachers and health workers, warehouse scheme officials and heads of burial societies and financial institutions.

Focus group discussion: community feedback and action research

The fourth focus group discussion sought to confirm key findings, explore any outstanding issues and provide feedback to the community on our preliminary analysis. It typically involved up to fifteen people. The idea was to confirm findings and obtain clarity on issues we were grappling with. There was also an action research element, whereby we sought to elicit suggestions about potential changes the community themselves, as well as others, could make to address the challenges that had been identified through the research.

Quantitative analysis of the 2007 HBS

As has already been noted, analysis of the 2007 HBS was conducted to choose research sites. Households included in the HBS 2007 formed the basis of our well-being ranking in each community and the selection of households for in-depth life history interviews. Following the field research, quantitative analysis was conducted using the 2007 HBS, informed by preliminary analysis of the qualitative dataset. This sought to confirm or refine findings from the qualitative component of the research and to fill critical data gaps.

Reflections on the research approach and methods: value added and lessons learnt

Normal times: livelihoods, productive assets and relations

Earlier chronic poverty studies which had life history interviews as a central part of their methodological approach tended to focus on 'good times' and building on opportunities (e.g. using savings from wages to buy land) and 'bad times' and adverse coping sequences (e.g. selling assets to pay health costs). This derived from open questioning around positive and negative events and periods in the respondent's life. This approach reveals the strategies people take in response to events which result in downward or upward mobility. But the approach may underplay the importance of socioeconomic factors in 'normal times', which create the asset bases and relations which lead to vulnerability during a crisis or enable the capacity to capitalise on an opportunity. We were cognisant of this, and the research tried to capture people's experiences during 'normal' as well as 'good' and 'bad' times through the life history interviews.

Balancing actors' perspectives and broader relations, processes and events

A research approach that draws heavily on household survey analysis and life history interviews can be methodologically individualistic, focusing on the individual and the household without giving sufficient attention to powerful actors, meso and macro political and economic trends and intergenerational relationships. In this research, we sought to achieve a careful balance between the actors' perspectives and broader processes and events. We did this by exploring power relations in various institutional contexts, assessing magnitude where possible and paying attention to linking life histories to macro changes.

<u>*Exploring power relations in various institutional contexts*</u>

To move beyond individual narratives, we sought to capture how power relations operate in various institutional arenas, such as markets, societies, polities and domestic units. We also sought to understand how these relations enabled or constrained people's ability to take action to experience upward mobility. For instance, in the context of markets, a ability to command a good price for crops will be mediated by the bargaining relationship with cooperative officials. In the context of polities, a person's ability to access state benefits to which they are entitled (e.g. a fertiliser voucher or health access) may be thwarted by inability to pay a bribe. In the context of domestic units, norms governing gender and age relations influence, for example, a young married woman's right to control household resources.

We found that life histories were very good at capturing gender relations over time, especially between women and men in the same family. They were far less useful at capturing power relations between our life history respondents and actors outside of the households. We addressed this by linking life histories with key informant interviews. In practice, this meant exploring relationships between life history respondents and key external actors in the life history interviews and then, critically, following up with key informant interviews with the external actors. For example, when a respondent emphasised the importance of a relationship with a crop trader, we sought to interview the trader. Where a woman expressed difficulty accessing credit, we sought to interview representatives from the relevant microfinance institution.

Assessing magnitude

In field research on chronic poverty, there is often an artificial distinction: social and cultural issues tend to be examined at the micro level by anthropologists, sociologists and political scientists, while economic processes tend to be examined through meso- or macro-level quantitative analyses by economists. The meso and macro issues covered through these analyses, however, do not always capture the reality facing the chronically poor. For example, meso and macro prices, wages, costs and interest rates do not always accord with the prices, wages and interest rates that the chronically poor face. Power in economic relations is often reflected through these means (e.g. crop prices received by poorer farmers compare unfavourably with district level prices owing to desperation sales). It is therefore critical to capture them, as they directly influence income and a person's ability to retain assets. Capturing the real prices, wages, costs and interest rates that poor people face also enables comparisons (e.g. crop sale as a proportion of school fees) that offer the researcher insights into the magnitude of choices and events that an individual and their household face.

Related to this, it has been found that economic data gathered by enumerators can be less reliable than those gathered by qualitative researchers. This provides further rationale for assessing magnitude in qualitative research. Davis and Baulch found this through their research in rural Bangladesh. The field research for a recent study of contract cotton farming in Tanzania[21] yielded similar results: the research team found that collecting quantitative survey data *following* in-depth qualitative interviews yielded more accurate accounts of economic status (e.g. crop yields, land owned and operated, inputs used, diets). One explanation for this is that, after a long interview, a certain level of trust had developed between the respondent and the interviewer, and therefore more accurate information was shared. In addition, the qualitative interview captured much economic information, which could be used to triangulate the responses to survey questions and to clarify contradictions.

Linking micro experience to macro changes

As we have already outlined, through our research we sought to gener
ate a richer understanding of the link between individual decisions and macro
events, changes and processes (e.g. changes in commodity production processes, shifts in national and sub-national policies and programmes, changes
in legislation and changes in entitlements). This was achieved by making analytical links between individual experience and the macro phenomena, which
were identified through focus group discussions and key informant interviews.
In ideal cases, life histories were carefully periodised—based on these macro
events, changes and processes—which enabled direct linking through the life
history interview between individual experience and broader processes and
events.

Using senior researchers

The research team comprised senior and experienced researchers. This
meant that researchers were able to detect unspoken subtleties or contradictions when life histories did not 'add up'. An interview conducted by Joanita
Magongo with a thirty-eight-year-old woman in Ndite is illustrative.

When Jeska[22] married, she was a housewife because her husband did
not allow her to work. She became 'very poor' (according to the well-being
classification scheme) when her husband abandoned her after being excused
from duty owing to corruption allegations. While she owned assets which
could have been sold to enable her survival or to start a business to support
her children, she felt should do not do this because of traditions. This meant
she was forced to get support from her sister-in-law for some months. She then
finally decided to return to her mother's house, where her situation deteriorated more because she did not have enough land to increase production. Her
friend assisted her in migrating to Magu town and there she found a job in a
bar. She made enough money to rent a room, eat and send money home. Her
well-being improved.

Further exploration through the life history interview, and drawing on
Magongo's extensive field research experience, established that Jeska was supplementing her income through prostitution. Magongo realised this because
the money she was making as a bar maid did not match her expenditure or
the conditions she was living in. In addition, the nature of her job provided
room for prostitution. Magongo had interviewed women in similar situations
to Jeska before, so knew how to interpret the life history in its correct context.
A young, inexperienced enumerator may have taken the story at face value,
thinking that the job as a barmaid was lucrative and failing to capture what
young abandoned women are forced to do to support their families.

The cost effectiveness of the research approach

This research was inexpensive when compared with, for example, large-scale panel surveys or randomised control trials. Nevertheless, it still generated robust and useful data, in-depth and nuanced analysis and policy-relevant findings.

Cost issues matter deeply in developing countries and expensive approaches are not always feasible. Our research approach offers a lower cost alternative which, when conducted by senior researchers, can generate—as this edited volume demonstrates—the kind of detailed analysis and policy evaluations that governments need to help them to allocate limited resources and make difficult policy decisions.

Further work needs to be done to support the cost effectiveness and value of our approach. A useful methodological project would involve comparing the results achieved from two different Q-squared approaches. The first would involve a combination of a one-point-in-time survey and longitudinal qualitative tools (such as life histories). The second would involve a combination of a panel survey and longitudinal qualitative tools. The question for investigation would be: does panel data add to the knowledge base achieved by adopting the first (one-point-in-time survey plus longitudinal qualitative tools) approach? The answer could ultimately inform cost–benefit analyses at the country level about whether to panelise data or rather to supplement one-point-in-time surveys with longitudinal qualitative tools.

Conclusion

This chapter has outlined the unique Q-squared approach to poverty dynamics research that was applied in our study of chronic poverty and development policy in Tanzania. By outlining the methods we adopted, and the rationale for the approach, we have demonstrated how to go about applying the approach. Forthcoming chapters will show how the approach can provide deep insights into the structural relational bases of chronic poverty and poverty dynamics and promote more nuanced policy understanding and policy responses. We hope this, combined with the cost effectiveness reasoning outlined above, will compel others to conduct similar Q-squared studies of poverty dynamics and chronic poverty. The approach was recently applied in a more confined and evaluative mode—to evaluate contract cotton farming in Tanzania[23]—and yielded useful and policy-relevant results. We are confident that others will find the approach applicable, insightful and, above all, useful in determining strategies for combating chronic poverty.

---

1   B. Baulch and P. Davis (2008); P. Davis and B. Baulch (2011)
2   R. Miller et al. (2011a; 2011b)
3   A.S. Fall et al. (2011)
4   K. Bird et al. (2010; 2011)

5   National Bureau of Statistics (2008a)

6   United Republic of Tanzania (2010a)

7   In Tanzania, these included the Economic and Social Research Foundation, Research on Poverty Alleviation, Ifakara Health Institute, Sokoine University of Agriculture and the University of Dar es Salaam. In the United Kingdom, these included the Overseas Development Institute and the University of Sussex.

8   See Higgins and Mashindano et al. in this volume for evidence and analysis on this.

9   See, for example, L. da Corta and D. Venkateswarlu (1992); A. Rahman (1986); W. van Schendel (1981)

10   P. Davis (2009; 2011a; 2011b; 2011c; 2011d)

11   K. Bird (2010); K. Bird et al. (2010; 2011); K. Bird and I. Shinyekwa (2005)

12   D.K. Bagchi et al. (1998); L. da Corta, (2010); L. da Corta and D. Venkateswarlu (1992); S. Hickey and A. du Toit (2007); A. Shepherd (2007); Wood (2000).

13   See D. Hulme et al. (2001)

14   L. da Corta (2010); S. Hickey and A. du Toit (2007); A. Shepherd (2007)

15   M. Green (2009); see also B. Harriss-White (2002)

16   L. da Corta and K. Bird (2008)

17   D. Narayan and P. Petesch (2007)

18   F. Kessy et al. (2006)

19   See National Bureau of Statistics (2008a) for sampling approach

20   See Higgins in this volume

21   C. Coles et al. (2011)

22   The names of respondents have been anonymised in this chapter and the rest of chapters in this volume.

23   Ibid.

Part 1

Tanzania Poverty Analysis

Chapter 3

Exploring Resilience Avenues for Managing Covariant and Idiosyncratic Poverty Related Shocks
Flora Kessy and Simon Vendelin Tarmo

Introduction

This chapter identifies the major covariant and idiosyncratic shocks facing households and their main avenues for managing and coping with them, using analysis of focus group discussions and individual life histories from three districts in Tanzania, coupled with data from key informant interviews.

Risk is conventionally seen as the likelihood of occurrence of an adverse *exogenous*, or external, event.[1] However, not all potentially adverse events are exogenous. The occurrence of old age, and events such as weddings, for instance, can be adverse in nature, but are internal, or *endogenous*, generally being linked to the family life-cycle. Both exogenous and endogenous events can be either sudden onset ('shocks') or part of a longer-term cycle or trend ('stresses').

Risks are classified in many different ways. For instance, they can be acute (such as a disease epidemic) or chronic (e.g. the degeneration of resource productivity under increasing population pressure). They can be natural or manmade. They can also be *idiosyncratic*, affecting individual households or communities through, for example, personal injury or illness, or *covariant*, affecting a wide segment of the community or country, such as through drought. For covariant risks, insurance provision is costly and complex, and the capacity for informal compensatory transfers is destabilised.

Vulnerability, on the other hand, is the likelihood of being harmed by an adverse event. Chambers defines vulnerability as 'having an external side of risks, shocks, and stress to which individuals or households are subjected to, and the internal side which is defenceless, meaning a lack of means to cope without a damaging loss'.[2] Defined using a poverty lens, vulnerability is the increased probability of falling below the poverty line or, for those already under the poverty line, of remaining in, or falling further into, poverty. Vulnerability varies among individuals and households, according to their capacity to prevent, mitigate or cope with such events. Although conceptually distinct, risk and vulnerability are closely linked. For instance, a household negatively affected by a particular risk is likely to be more vulnerable to being harmed in the future by adverse events.[3]

Anticipated income or consumption changes are important to individuals and households before shocks occur—and regardless of whether a particular shock occurs at all—as well as after they have occurred. Vulnerability and the probability of falling into poverty are difficult to measure, but income and consumption dynamics and variability are potential proxies. Such analysis can be replicated for specific non-monetary variables, for example health status and asset ownership.[4] In the absence of cross-sectional surveys and panel data, qualitative data can support the analysis of vulnerability, uncovering households' participation in informal networks; patterns in household income and consumption (e.g. seasonal variations); people's perceptions of their vulnerability and its determinants; and the strategies that households have in place to reduce their vulnerability and whether these are depletive or not.

This chapter contextualises vulnerability by looking at the major covariate and idiosyncratic shocks (translation of risks) facing households and how these affect their well-being. It also discusses resilience and avenues for addressing shocks by drawing attention to the assets, endowments and capabilities, as well as the transforming structures and processes, which lead to improving, or declining, levels of well-being. People's resilience to poverty-related shocks depends to a large extent on their ability to mobilise, combine and transform livelihood assets, as presented in the Sustainable Livelihoods approach developed by the United Kingdom's Department for International Development:

> ... insecurity is a core dimension of most poverty. We are not talking about isolated events or occurrences but about a dynamic situation in which the poor are always on the brink of extreme insecurity, sometimes falling just below, sometimes rising just above. The SL [Sustainable Livelihoods] approach seeks to mitigate such insecurity through building up resilience.[5]

The Sustainable Livelihoods approach suggests that building resilience is key to tackling or preventing livelihood insecurity. Five livelihood assets are central: human capital (knowledge, education, physical condition for labour); social capital (membership in family, social networks, associations); natural capital (land, agricultural products, livestock); physical capital (buildings, equipment, transport); and financial capital (savings, cash, credit). Resilience-building means mobilising and transforming these assets and fostering policies, institutions and organisations to enable this. These livelihood assets, and the institutions that shape their transformation, constitute a livelihood system that provide people with 'layers of resilience' to cope with and buffer various disturbances.[6]

Resilience is seen to have two dependent features: one occurring *ex-ante* as a process and the other *ex-post* as either a process or a curative measure. Effective *ex-ante* interventions reduce the chances of a hazard occurring and the need for subsequent *ex-post* interventions.[7] The state has a role in both *ex-ante* and *ex-post* processes, but emphasis also needs to be placed on the agency of households and their potential, competence, capabilities and strengths in solving poverty-related problems.

Vulnerability and the main sources of risk in the research sites

Vulnerable groups

Not everyone is equally vulnerable to different risks, or, phrased slightly differently, is as likely to be harmed by an adverse event. Vulnerable groups are those that are more likely to be hit by covariant and idiosyncratic shocks (see next section) while also having the least capacity to manage these. These groups particularly comprise the elderly, youth and children. Aloyce, seventy-three years old, from Kalesa cluster, described her old-age vulnerability during a life history interview:

> I lost my husband in 2002, and I am now living with my children and grandchildren. There are times when my children support me but they are also busy with their own lives. As with many other young people in the village, they have no interest in the land and I have been fighting with them to buy one; no one listens. I own 2 acres which was left by my husband. I have difficulties to cultivate this land given my age and the fact that I always fall sick. I can't work on this land as I used to when I was young and this makes my family very poor and always desperate for a single meal a day.

Meanwhile, young people were described by some informants as 'a flag which blows according to the wind'. They move to and from any place at any time; they can attend three traditional dances at the same time at three different households; once they find out where mourning for a deceased person is going on they stay there even for a number of nights so long as there is food. Youths were also cited as being vulnerable because of their mentality: they need not farm since they have no family. As a youth in Nchinga, Mtwara, said, 'Why should I farm for only one stomach? I will eat at my parents, at my relatives or at my friends.'

Children's nutrition is dependent on the care they receive from parents or other relatives. While most families prioritise the needs of children and older people when there is not enough to eat, sometimes children can lose out if they are poorly cared for. Particularly vulnerable children include those whose parents have died and whose father's wealth has been taken by relatives (e.g. uncles or mistresses of their father). The most vulnerable children scavenge and beg from neighbours at an early age. During an interview with Sabrina, thirty-three years old and living in Nkangala, Mtwara, one of her children explained why they do not go to school:

> I left school as I always went with an empty stomach in the morning and when I came home for lunch there would be nothing, and sometimes we would have no dinner and would just sleep. After a year of being hungry, I decided to roam and scavenge, and some days I get TZS 100 which is enough to buy a biscuit or a bite to ease the pain of hunger.

When Sabrina's husband came back during the interview, she asked immediately if he had managed to bring any money; he said no, then she just put her head down.

Children are vulnerable in many situations. According to the 2004/05 Tanzania Demographic and Health Survey, 41 per cent of mainland children are deprived on at least three counts. While child survival indicators have improved significantly, and progress is 'on track,' child malnutrition is still widespread and children are vulnerable to shocks.[8]

People who rely on agriculture as their sole livelihood source are also particularly vulnerable, because of unpredictable weather conditions. Sometimes, they harvest nothing and so are unable to meet their immediate consumption needs. When there is a shock in the household, they often do not have any surplus to fall back on.

Covariant shocks

Table 3.1 summarises the major covariant shocks in the study areas. Those related to markets, weather and pests are examined elsewhere, and so are not the focus here.[9] Instead, this chapter focuses on two important and emerging covariant shocks: witchcraft and the theft of crops.

Table 3.1: Covariant shocks in the study areas in Tanzania

Type of risk	Rukwa district		Mwanza district		Mtwara district	
	Kayumbe village	Kalesa village	Wazabanga village	Ndite village	Nchinga village	Nkangala village
1. Market-related shocks, e.g. for cashews, cotton, maize	Major	Minor	Major	Minor	Major	Major
2. Market -related shocks (livestock)	NA	NA	Major	Major	NA	NA
3. Weather-related shocks, e.g. drought and too much rain (el Niño)	Minor	NA	Major	Major	Minor	Minor
4. Witchcraft	Major	Major	Minor	Minor	Major	Major
5. Shocks related to crop pests	Major	Major	Minor	Minor	Major	Major
6. Governance-related shocks e.g. theft of agricultural produce while on the farm	Minor	Minor	Minor	Minor	Major	Major

Witchcraft (*uchawi* in Kiswahili) featured in many of the life histories and was also one of the major shock/vulnerability factors cited in community focus group discussions in Kayumbe and Kalesa clusters. Witchcraft is associated with envy and household well-being, and is also used as revenge when there is conflict between households. It can have far-reaching consequences, including the death of people and livestock. Those interviewed believed that individuals who practise witchcraft are better-off than those who work hard, as they bewitch others to benefit from their crops and hard work. Such views were considered to have detrimental consequences on the community, as they discourage hard work and entrepreneurship, with some falling down the ladder and being labelled lazy or as beggars. Stories of bewitchment were quite rampant in Kalesa cluster. Albert explained during his life history interview that,

> Things of this place are very difficult to comprehend. Sometimes when you grow rice and you see that at least you will harvest 20 bags of rice, you end up harvesting 5 bags only. This is caused by the very common tendency in the area where people apply witchcraft to make crops thrive well in their own farms at the expense of your own crops in the farm. I believe that at least 70 per cent of the farms are not spared this practice. This has made some people despair and stop working hard in the farms for fear of producing too little because of witchcraft.

Respondents also alluded to what could be described as a 'witchcraft–poverty nexus', whereby witchcraft may prevent risk-taking, entrepreneurship development and displays of wealth (people have to leave a community if they become too wealthy and people who have left for the towns never return to visit the village after becoming rich).Some of those interviewed did not aspire to improve their life for fear of being bewitched. Members of a Kalesa focus group discussion explained that,

> People in this village are 90 per cent sure that Mzee Maswile was killed in 1966 and Mzee Mchimbamawe lost his life in 1968 because they were constructing modern residential houses. Prior to their deaths, many people were cautioning and warning them publicly not to involve themselves with such projects.

Witchcraft may impoverish households that are 'doing well', and some people residing in town never visit their relatives in the village because they fear being bewitched. Households reported that school children, particularly those at secondary school level, had been a target because education is considered a way out of poverty. When a child is bewitched, the household must sell assets in order to access care from witchdoctors. In most cases, these children either die or become psychiatric cases. A typical example of a victim is Angelina, twenty-five years old from Kalesa village. Angelina is a petty trader and is married to a fisherman. She completed primary education and passed her exams to carry on to secondary education. Unfortunately, her parents denied her the chance to do this for fear of her being bewitched and killed. Their concerns were both for Angelina and for the entire family, as they all might perish if they supported her education.

Anna, forty-seven years old from Kayumbe village, explained that witchcraft always followed someone getting a good job or harvest. Her life history illustrates how it can be a major cause of downward mobility. Major shocks in her household are related to the ailment of her children. In 2002, one of her sons finished secondary education (Form 4). He went to a teachers college in Mtwara in 2003. He was in the college for about a month when he started getting sick. He suffered from headaches and eye pains but later on the case turned into a psychiatric one. Her husband had to travel to Mtwara to bring him home, after which the economic situation of the household began to decline, as they sold one asset after another in order to take care of him. They initially took him to hospital as they suspected malaria, but it was later confirmed that he had psychiatric problems. This was when the household started visiting witchdoctors.

Anna's son was first sent to a witchdoctor's home in Sumbawanga, with treatment costing about TZS 2 million. The household sold 2 bags of maize at TZS 15,000 each, 5 cows (Anna could not remember the price), 3 goats and a 15-acre farm. Despite the treatment, her son did not get better. By then, her husband had had to quit his work so he could stay with his son in Sumbawanga. In 2006, Anna's younger son had to stop going to school so that he could travel to Sumbawanga to assist his father in taking care of his elder brother at the witchdoctor's home.

The elder son was moved to another witchdoctor around September 2006. This one demanded 3 cows, 3 goats, 1 cock and TZS 100,000 in cash. Her son got a little bit better but around Christmas time of the same year fell sick again. Her husband took him to another witchdoctor, while the younger son had to go back to school and repeat the year that he had lost at school. This witchdoctor demanded 1 cock and 1 sheep or the equivalent of TZS 45,000 and TZS 15,000 in cash.

Despite all these efforts, Anna's son did not get better. They decided to take him home in 2009 and, at the time of this study, he was going to the psychiatric clinic at the district hospital in Nkasi. He is always sedated; sometimes, he becomes aggressive and bites his father. The household has resumed its daily activities and Anna's husband is planning to restart his business.

The major covariant shock in Nchinga and Nkangala clusters is the theft of cashew nuts while they are still on the farm. Abdulrahman (forty four, Nchinga village) explained that thieves invade farms at night or very early in the morning and collect all the fallen cashew nuts. This means that households are deprived of their long-awaited harvest. Joanita (sixty, from Kayumbe village) recalled that thieves had come at night and stolen all her 150 goats and 70 cows. This incident meant that her family suddenly went from being very rich to extremely poor, and she and her family had to start work as labourers. Abdul, a key informant in Nchinga village, explained that,

> Theft is a big problem. For example, from one farm they can steal up to 30kg of cashew nuts, which is much. If we arraign them in the court of law, they are imprisoned for only two to three months. If the punishment was bigger than that, I believe most of the thieves would be scared and stop stealing.

No solution has been found for this community-wide problem. This type of theft also spirals households into poverty because people spend time guarding farms instead of participating in productive activities—they watch their farms all night and sleep in the day. Moreover, even staying awake all night, it is not possible to keep an eye on the whole farm.

Idiosyncratic shocks

Life history interviews identified several idiosyncratic shocks, ranging from morbidity and mortality shocks to behaviour-related shocks. This section emphasises behaviour-related shocks (see Table 3.2), since these pose a particular challenge to the formulation of policy, legislation and programmes in the form of social protection measures. However, life history interviews also identified several non-behavioural idiosyncratic shocks resulting in the downward mobility of households. These include failure of non-farm business, such as through closure by the government, illness, accident or death of a household member and associated medical costs; rising costs of living relative to income; loss of a salaried job; failure of agriculture or fish farming; and livestock disease.

Table 3.2: Idiosyncratic shocks in the study areas in Tanzania

Type of risk	Nkasi district		Magu district		Newala district	
	Kayumbe village	Kalesa village	Wazabanga village	Ndite village	Nchinga village	Nkangala village
1. Property grabbing	Major	Major	Major	Major	Major	Major
2. Alcoholism	Major	Major	Major	Major	Major	Major
3. Old-age vulnerability	Major	Major	Major	Major	Major	Major
4. Divorce and serial polygamy	Minor	Major	Major	Minor	Major	Minor
5. Labour market risks	NA	NA	NA	NA	Major	Minor

Property-grabbing

Widowhood was not necessarily associated with a downward spiral in well-being, except in cases where property had been grabbed by widows' relatives, in some cases even by their own children. Property-grabbing after the death of the husband was reported in a few instances in Wazabanga cluster, as described during a female focus group discussion:

> After the death of my husband, there was a family meeting that made me lose every bit that I owned with him. The brother-in-law took the house we were living in and moved in with his mother. They also grabbed the farm, land and assets I had accumulated with my husband through his income and by selling fish. After the death of my husband the in-laws also despise me.

Property appropriation by the husband after separation or divorce was reported in every research site, and was attributed mainly to the ignorance of women about divorce laws. Divorce and separation are caused by several factors, including husbands finding another wife and infertility. Fatuma from Nchinga cluster explained during a female focus group discussion how her husband had divorced her after she did not conceive for nine years after the birth of her first child:

> My husband said, 'I am capable of reproduction but you are not conceiving' ... Then he brought another woman in the same house and sent me back to my parents with a document authenticating that he had divorced me. I was ignorant of alimony and wealth-sharing at divorce; I just took the paper he gave me and travelled from Dar es Salaam to Newala to my parents. That was the end of my married life.

Failure by women to retain a share of the property after divorce was echoed throughout the key informant interviews and focus group discussions. Women in a focus group in Nchinga village explained that, 'if I contributed to the generation of the wealth so much and he gives me nothing, *basi*,which means "that is it!" I leave the case to God to punish him.' A key informant in Nchinga village concurred: 'if a man divorces his wife, most of the wealth is taken by the man. If the woman believes she has been given too little or nothing, she normally says "*basi*". This is notwithstanding the fact that women contribute substantially to the generation of household wealth, and even work harder on the farm than men. A key informant in Nchinga village said that men worked for about 3 hours per day on the farm whereas women worked for about 5. Men go to the farm for about 5 days per month, but women go for about 20.

Alcoholism

Alcoholism was also mentioned in every cluster. Some women, such as Mariam, fifty-three years old and living in Kayumbe Village, are able to make local beer-brewing a profitable venture. Mariam ferments maize every month by soaking it in water, which she gets from a shallow well close to her house, then drying it and sending it to the milling machine—finally making the brew using the flour. This is a profitable business for her. She buys 1 tin of maize for TZS 3,500 and the price to mill that is TZS 700. From 3 tins of maize she can make 7 to 8 tins of local brew, with one of these selling for TZS 3,000. With 3 tins of maize then, Mariam can make a profit of TZS 8,400-11,400, although this calculation does not speak to the opportunity costs of her time. So depending on her efficiency including time utilization, it takes her a month to make the profit of TZS 8,400-11,400. If she had wanted to do this business on weekly basis, she would have earned this profit in each week.

For most households, though, alcohol has brought harm, including bankruptcy and misery, driving people into poverty and contributing to the intergenerational cycle of poverty. Joyce is fifty-nine and lives in Wazabanga village. She and her husband enjoyed a harmonious relationship just after their marriage. They had a kiosk, which later became a shop, and also farmed cotton, maize, rice and beans. They ate three meals a day and Joyce always got what she wanted from her husband: clothes, lotion, etc. However, after a few years, her husband became an alcoholic and took mistresses, whom he spent money on. His drinking habit and misuse of resources continued until they had to close the shop, selling all its contents in order to be able to afford some basic necessities. Joyce then separated from her husband. He eventually died after losing his way in life: he wandered around, often sleeping in the open air, and his mistresses lost interest in him. To Joyce, separation meant losing the clan's farm which, when with her husband, she had relied on. Due to her economic downturn, Joyce was not able to hire out the extra 4 acres where they had been growing cassava, maize, millet and beans.

Alcoholism was associated with the erosion of household resources, including a failure to send children to school (low investment in human capital, which can lead to the intergenerational transmission of poverty) and to give the family a decent life (stagnation or moving into poverty). In particular, community members were concerned about the number of people using staple food grains after harvest to make local brew, thus putting the food security of their family at risk. Some community members sell their grain to buy local brew. Alcoholism is also leading to reduced agricultural production in some cases: if people find local brew on their way to the farm they forget the actual reason they left the house. Delays in tillage, planting and weeding are therefore very common, leading to low harvests. Such families were said to end up being food insecure and to suffer from internal conflict.

Alcoholism was also associated with family disintegration and divorce. Husbands who drink excessive alcohol are frequently violent and hit their wives. They also sometimes migrate for long periods of time without supporting their family. This violence often extends beyond the household, contributing to instability in the community. In Wazabanga cluster, the village authorities have had to establish a police post to provide order in the conflicts which happen every afternoon and evening when many men are drunk. The auxiliary police either punish the drunks or detain them in a room for 12 hours or until they are sober again.

Excessive drinking was also associated with multiple partners and increased incidence of HIV infection.

Serial polygamy

Linked to divorce and separation is serial polygamy. This was very evident in Kalesa, Nchinga, Nkangala and Wazabanga clusters, where it had resulted in family disintegration and loss of family property. The motivation of second wives is frequently to obtain economic security; many are attracted to men with off-farm income-generating activities, including ownership of a kiosk, fishing or fish-mongering or cultivation of a large amount of cashew nut trees. In the life histories there were examples of men replacing their first wives with new ones but either returning to their first wives after becoming bankrupt or being left by their second wives, as with Joyce's story above.

Old-age vulnerability

Elderly people (sixty years old and above), in particular those who are too weak for manual labour, are frequently ill or have impaired vision, and so experience declining income from employment, are particularly vulnerable. Their vulnerability is also related to dysfunctional institutions that do not enable them to access retirement benefits (and social services such as health), and a lack of support from their family, including through remittances. Until recently, family networks have proven a reliable support institution during old age. Now, though, elderly people are often left unattended to and struggle on their own, as younger family members have migrated to urban areas or are negligent in their responsibilities to the elderly. In Newala district, elderly people with large cashew nut trees are not necessarily poorer, since they can hire labour to manage their farms and pay them after the harvest. However, the typical situation, as told through life history interviews with 22 elderly people, is one of a decline in well-being during old age. Widows or widowers who recalled having the support of a partner during adversities in the past had experienced a greater decline in conditions. Nelson, seventy-one years old from Kalesa cluster, lamented,

I miss the company and support from my wife who died on 9 November 2008. I am now living alone and have no one to cook or wash for me. She left me with psychological depression and I know if she were alive we would be growing cassava and maize and not experiencing hunger and would be assured meals daily. Since I lost her, my well-being has become unpredictable and I see myself under Category 2, which is very poor, and soon will become destitute.

Labour market risks

The growing numbers of households dependent on wage labour are particularly vulnerable to a range of risks. In general, rural and agricultural growth has been hesitant; where it has been strongest, poor people have participated as labourers in oversupplied and low-return markets in areas such as petty trade, casual labour, brewing and subsistence food production. The worst form of 'undecent labour' is where the employer contracts a worker to provide their labour on credit—an arrangement based on trust, with no formal contracts. Labourers work under the agreement that they will get paid a lump sum after the harvesting and sale of cashew nuts, for example. Poor labourers have to enter into these arrangements through necessity. Being compelled to provide labour on credit is possible only where the labour market is oversupplied and under-regulated.

Hawa, forty-seven years old from Nchinga village, explained that selling labour on credit is a common practice there and that it can drive people into poverty. Hawa had had the bad luck not to have been paid over half of what she was owed in the 2009/10 season. This was because landowners said they had not got a good harvest and as such could not pay their debts. Some of them were trying to pay little by little, which was satisfactory, but being paid in a lump sum would have enabled Hawa to make substantial investments in necessary items: if the debt is paid piecemeal it ends up being consumed. In the 2008/09 season, Hawa was paid only TZS 25,000 as a lump sum; the balance of TZS 20,000 was paid piecemeal, in amounts of TZS 500, TZS 1,000 and TZS 2,000. According to her, this money just evaporated, meaning she was just spending it on small consumptive necessities.

Consumption measures of vulnerability

Current acute food insecurity levels can be used as one measure of vulnerability to future declines in poverty status. Number of meals per day—one measure of food insecurity—can be used as a proxy for the adequacy of household members' caloric food intake. However, while this indicates roughly the amount of food consumed, it is not sensitive to the quality of that food and any nutrient deficiencies.

Qualitative consumption data are available only for the number of meals per day at the time of the survey (Table 3.3).[10] In Kayumbe cluster, the majority of households eat one meal per day, most households in most other communities survive on two meals per day (in Nkangala cluster, the proportion is the same for each category). Detailed information on the type of meals was not collected, but during additional discussions it was apparent that sometimes this meal comprises just cassava stiff porridge and tea (Newala cluster), maize porridge (Nkasi cluster) or sorghum/maize porridge (Magu clusters). In focus group discussions, the poor but not vulnerable group and the rich were said to consume diverse food, including 'food from industry' (e.g. bread, soft and hard drinks), 'delicacies' (such as milk in Newala) and 'delicious foods'. Being able to consume such foods placed these households in a higher well-being category.

Kayumbe village has the highest proportion of households consuming more than three meals a day. This is reflecting the maize economy in the area—households produce a lot of maize which is used for household consumption (Kayumbe community is located in Rukwa region which is one of the grain basket regions in Tanzania). Wazabanga and Ndite have a market economy led by cotton, but the cotton industry has collapsed.

Table 3.3: Number of meals per day in households in the study areas in Tanzania

Cluster	No. of meals per day				
	1	2	3	>=3	Missing data
Nchinga	4%	38%	29%	8%	21%
Nkangala	29%	29%	21%	0%	21%
Kayumbe	33%	17%	17%	29%	4%
Kalesa	17%	58%	13%	4%	8%
Ndite	8%	33%	4%	0%	54%
Wazabanga	21%	33%	13%	4%	29%

Note: The percentages represent the number of meals per day as consumed by all household members; missing data—e.g. 54% of respondents in Ndite community didn't provide information on number of meals consumed per day.

Quantity of food intake is only one aspect of food security. Another important dimension is how food is obtained. This is particularly important for people who are in the 'destitute' and 'very poor' categories. Box 3.1 presents the characteristics of these groups based on a female focus group discussion in Nkangala cluster (other focus group discussions did not detail the number of meals very poor people take each day).

Box 3.1: Characteristics of destitute and very poor groups in the study areas in Tanzania

DESTITUTE	
• Recipient of aid and other material from others	• Very poor
	• Look dirty
• Cannot drive themselves to work	• Do not have entrepreneurial thoughts
• Cannot afford health services, education and accommodation (sleep in ruins)	• Do casual labour: sifting grain at milling machines, selling fallen branches as firewood, making and selling rope (used in construction), digging pit latrines, grinding maize/cassava or washing clothes
• Do not think about development	
• Drink excessively	
• Are very old and could have psychological problems	
• Often have or are vulnerable to tuberculosis, asthma, HIV and AIDS	• Have one meal a day; other meals not assured

Members of the Nkangala female focus group discussion said that destitute people would eat one meal per day (most of the time assured) by begging from relatives and friends. Very poor people are not assured one meal per day and sometimes end up eating maize stems or local brew. The poor mostly eat one meal but this meal is assured.

Sometimes, even one meal a day is not assured; on other days, the poorest may eat three meals a day. The female focus group explained that destitute people, 'can eat even more than three meals per day because people in this group carry their mouths wherever they go', meaning that they eat at relatives' and friends' houses. This contrasts with households in the 'resilient' and 'rich' categories, which obtain food through their own efforts and do not like eating at other people's places, even when invited to. This may signify a pride in their self-sufficiency.

Avenues of resilience and coping

This section explores the ways in which poor individuals and households mitigate and cope with risks. People are social actors who use a range of means and livelihood capitals to manage poverty. Despite facing a range of risks and being affected by system failures, such as poor governance (see Chapter 9), life history interviews and focus group discussions highlighted poor people's efforts to survive livelihood shocks and to explore human, social, natural, physical and financial capitals. However, people are not always successful in managing risks and are sometimes forced to adopt coping strategies that are depletive, with negative consequences for the individual, household or community.

Ex-ante resilience building

Investments in children's education and property transfers are major *ex-ante* resilience-building processes. Free education can enable the son of a vulnerable, but not poor, farmer to secure a salaried government job which provides resilience and upward mobility into resilient and rich categories over his lifetime. Selemani (fifty years old, from Nkangala) noted that his father valued education highly; school was free and the family was resilient enough that Selemani did not need to work on the farm. Being able to secure a job also means a family will have collateral to use in obtaining a loan, which generates extra security.

Inheritance systems that allow a person to obtain a piece of land after marriage is another *ex-ante* resilience-building process. Such a piece of land acts as a fallback in case a woman is divorced or if her husband dies and the property is grabbed by in-laws.

Employment creation is another *ex-ante* measure. In rural areas, agricultural employment opportunities could be created through mechanisation, agro-processing and the introduction of mechanic shops. These not only create jobs but also are important for achieving the mechanised agriculture, irrigation systems and agro-processing envisaged under the government's Kilimo Kwanza initiative, designed to transform Tanzania's agriculture sector. In line with this should be the extension or establishment of energy sources in rural areas to provide power for agro-processing industries and mechanics shops.

The potential for poor people to improve their well-being is not limited to farming and entrepreneurship. People in the research sites have also utilised networks and relationships as *ex-ante* means of building resilience. These relations range from employers *vis-à-vis* employees to credit schemes *vis-à-vis* those with an interest in taking loans. At times, they are intertwined with a sense that the performance of one actor in one place affects the performance of another actor in another place.

Burial societies in Kalesa were reported to cushion most shocks for their members. Thirty-year-old Restituta explained how such a society, through which women save to cover future events such as funerals, among other things, is designed to enable members to cope with different risks at the household level. Most women fund their deposits through savings from agricultural labour. However, the small size of donations and loans means that, while these societies prevent downward mobility, they are often insufficient to enable women to invest in livelihoods which could facilitate their escape from poverty. Linking these burial societies to savings and credit cooperative societies could treble the size of the loans given.

Ex-post responses to shocks

Selling agricultural produce, non-agricultural products (e.g. charcoal and firewood) as well as labour are all responses to shocks. Given the limited opportunities for diversification in rural areas, all types of households, including those comprising single women, sell similar produce, including casual labour. While these strategies enable households to cope with a shock, they do not necessarily build their resilience and could involve depleting the household asset base.

In particular, households are sometimes forced to sell agricultural produce at distress prices, below the market rate, in order to respond in the immediate aftermath of a shock. In Magu district, community members noted that, when a family is desperate for cash, they may sell a sack of rice for TZS 20,000, when the actual price ranges from TZS 30,000 soon after harvest to TZS 80,000 during the dry season.

In Newala, communities have to use the *kangomba*, a small weighing container for the sale of produce by the kilogram: the buyer profits because the weight of 3 *kangombas* is equivalent to 4kg and farmers end up cheated. They continue to sell in this way, though, because if they harvest only a small amount,[11] it does not make sense to queue at the warehouse. Even farmers who harvest more do not receive all the money at the same time and have to wait for a second payment and bonus, the values of which are uncertain. Another reason for farmers selling on a *kangomba* basis relates to the opening times of the warehouse. During the 2009/10 season, for instance, the warehouse did not open until early November; households required cash before this to manage their expenditure in the aftermath of household-level shocks. Because of this, they had to start selling by *kangomba* as early as late August.

Women consider making local brew a coping strategy. However, this is erosive, in that, while it enables one household to manage in the aftermath of a shock, and even to move a step up the ladder, it can pull other households down. A number of households mentioned that excessive drinking by husbands had resulted in their impoverishment. Begging for food is another response to shocks, although it does not enable an escape from poverty.

Discussion and conclusion

This chapter has analysed the vulnerability of poor people, in terms of covariant and idiosyncratic risks and shocks. Risks through several mechanisms, including low prices for agricultural product, trade entitlement failures and drought, can result in a reduced number of meals being consumed per day. Increasing the number of meals a household consumes per day requires measures that address the whole agricultural production and market chain. In addition, policies and interventions must address the individual risks that have far-reaching consequences for specific households.

The destitute and the very poor largely comprise the elderly and people living with disabilities. In 2008, disability prevalence in Tanzania was estimated to be 7.8 per cent.[12] This is higher in rural areas (0.3 per cent) than urban ones (6.3 per cent) and tends to increase with age. Common forms of disability include impaired vision (3.7 per cent), hearing difficulties (1.9 per cent), impaired mobility (3.1 per cent) and reduced cognition (1.5 per cent). Destitute and very poor people face two types of vulnerability: vulnerability to reduced consumption and vulnerability to reduced production. While the elderly and disabled people often lack the capacity to produce, alcoholics and people living in despair frequently lack entrepreneurial or development ambitions. Specific measures are needed to address the vulnerability of each of these sub-groups of the destitute and very poor.

Property-grabbing has been reported across Tanzania.[13] Some widows have lost property to their in-laws and have been asked to leave their nuptial home. Those who cannot leave have succumbed to the levirate system, whereby they are inherited by one of their in-laws. For most widows, being inherited is a matter not of choice but of convenience, as it means they will be able to safeguard their property and take care of their children. Despite any good intentions of the levirate institution as a social security system, its impacts must be examined closely in the context of HIV and AIDS and amid the rapidly changing societal values and norms fuelled by globalisation.

On the basis of participatory poverty assessments, it has been argued that the real concern of the poor in Tanzania is not their lack of income, consumption or assets, but rather insecurity, that is, the imminent likelihood of, or actual experience of, a sudden sharp reduction in any one of these. It is poor people themselves who must provide their basic socioeconomic security. Members of focus group discussions confirmed the insecurity facing the destitute and very poor in terms of daily food intake, with poor people always worried about where their next meal will come from. For resilient households, the issue is not how many meals they can afford per day but how to 'eat well today, tomorrow and the day after'.

Witchcraft is part of daily life in all social settings throughout Tanzania. Although its specific manifestations vary in each community, *uchawi* has certain characteristics and attributes that allow for intelligibility between various witchcraft traditions. Discourses on witchcraft in Tanzania consistently address themes of envy, greed, consumption, cannibalism and death.[14] While some studies in Tanzania show that witchcraft can be a path to accumulation—traditional healing, for instance, can provide a significant source of rural economic growth[15]—this study points to witchcraft causing more harm than benefits. Despite being rampant, it has not been debated as a policy issue because of difficulty in proving evidence on acts of witchcraft.

Vulnerability limits economic growth in that households cannot accumulate sufficient assets to consume and reinvest. As noted above, most *ex-post* resilience and coping avenues maintain households only at 'survival' level. Adopting these types of coping strategies means households may fall into chronic poverty in the instance of single or multiple shocks. Well-designed social protection measures can mitigate risks and vulnerability by contributing directly to economic growth and poverty reduction through redistributive transfers that raise the incomes and smooth the consumption of the poor. This would also allow them to engage in moderate risk-taking and to protect rather than erode their assets when confronted by livelihood shocks.[16] Transformative social protection measures are also relevant in addressing the regulatory and legal aspects that are pushing people further down the ladder.

The policy implications of the findings in this chapter revolve around measures to help households to build their resilience in the face of risks. Through this, they can accumulate assets to invest in more remunerative livelihood activities, thus addressing vulnerability. This may include adopting a holistic approach in terms of social protection measures that address specifically vulnerable groups such as widows, divorced women, abandoned families and the elderly.[17]

While making a nationwide policy/law on alcoholism may be a challenge, local-level remedies to this issue could involve forming village-specific bylaws on drinking habits. Examples can be drawn from villages in northern Tanzania, where local brew bars are open only for a few hours in the morning and then closed until 2:00pm, when everybody has done enough work. A functional legal system at the local level needs to be built to address the problem of theft, and witchcraft should be discouraged through speeches in village meetings and use of media, especially radio and television.

The economic empowerment of women through participation in off-farm income-generating activities is important to cushion against shocks such as abandonment, divorce and serial polygamy. Economic empowerment can be achieved through access to, and ownership of, land, and through enhancing access to capital for investing in agriculture and off-farm income generation. The introduction of mechanics shops and sources of energy in rural areas is also important to create more jobs for vulnerable youth and to maintain the machinery envisaged under the Kilimo Kwanza initiative.

Creating awareness about the legal rights of widows and divorced women is also important. Further, knowledge about legal contracting is needed to make people aware of their rights when selling labour or other products on credit. One latent resilience avenue which needs to be activated relates to the leasing-out of land. Currently, many of Tanzania's poorer farmers can afford to cultivate only a portion of their land but are unwilling to lease out the other part because of a lack of legal security in this regard: those who cultivate their land on lease may later claim it as their own.

1   J. Farrington et al. (2004)
2   B. Chambers (1989), p. 1
3   J. Farrington et al. (2004)
4   World Bank (2011)
5   Department for International Development (2000), p. 1
6   B.C. Glavovic et al. (2003); B. Obrist et al. (2010)
7   M. Wuyts (2006)
8   National Bureau of Statistics and ORC Macro (2005)
9   See O. Mashindano et al. (2010)
10 Seasonal variations in number of meals per day were not taken into consideration.
11 It is common to harvest just a few kilograms of cashew nuts, because of crop pests, because of old trees or because of the small size of the farm
12 National Bureau of Statistics (2008b)
13 F. Kessy et al. (2010)
14 A. Green and S. Mesaki (2005)
15 Ibid.
16 J. Omiti and T. Nyanamba (2008)
17 See A. Shepherd et al. (2011a) for social assistance options in Tanzania

Chapter 4

The Rise in Women's Responsibility in a Context of Increased Poverty in Tanzania

Lucia da Corta and Joanita Magongo

Introduction

In 1999, Deborah Bryceson argued that,

> The disappearance of agricultural subsidies amidst increasing commoditisation of rural life has engendered a cash crisis in domestic household units, forcing virtually all able bodied adults as well as many children to seek different forms of income. The individualisation of economic activity and the increasing tendency to engage in non-agricultural income earning *have had a dissolving force on long standing agrarian division of labour as well as economic rights and responsibilities within rural households* [our italics].[1]

This chapter examines the effects of the past decade's experiences of poverty reduction and women's rights on the evolving roles (livelihoods), rights and responsibilities of rural men and women. It looks carefully at processes of individualisation and their impact on women's ability to move their dependants out of poverty.

That unrestrained neo-liberalism was not the solution for the rural poor in Tanzania was first recognised officially in the late 1990s, in a series of documents that stressed that national economic growth was not producing the expected proportionate fall in poverty in Tanzania.[2] The response to this was a series of poverty reduction strategy papers, the first of which ran from 2000 to 2003/04. Its approach was conceptualised in terms of the Millennium Development Goals and it focused on enhanced service provision to the poor (e.g. education, health, water supply, rural roads and the judiciary). In 2005, the strategy was broadened through Tanzania's National Growth and Poverty Reduction Strategy (known as MKUKUTA, running from 2005 to 2010), which focused on growth in order to generate sufficient resources for poverty reduction, enhanced social services and improved governance—understood as three interlinking areas contributing to poverty reduction.[3] Yet in 2009 the government review of MKUKUTA I criticised the approach for its continued failure to reduce poverty in line with the impressive rate of national growth of between 6 and nearly 8 per cent in previous years.[*]

The question in the minds of academics and policymakers alike is, why did fairly healthy growth in Tanzania not correspond to a fall in poverty: why did the number of those in poverty increase by 1 million in 2001–07? This chapter argues that one important reason for the persistence of poverty into the first decade of the new century was the effect of unequal rural growth and the scramble for jobs among poor men and women on the norms governing traditional gender roles, responsibilities and rights—gender dynamics—which served to deepen poor people's inability to move out of poverty. Gender dynamics are defined as, for instance,

- Who does what work (family/household division of labour)? How much?
- How is responsibility for family maintenance (including education and health care costs) shared between men and women?
- Who has what rights—freedom to be employed, mobility and control over earned and joint income—to family assets?
- Who has power over people: (1) power in the household or clan and (2) actually enforced legal rights within the larger community?

These dynamics work on norms governing relations between men and women who are married (conjugal contracts); between parents and children (e.g. education in return for support: a gendered version might be 'I will accept your bridewealth when you get married but if you are abandoned I will accept you and your children back into my home'); and between, say, parent, abandoned daughter and brother ('your brother will get preferential access in education and you might work to help fund him, but in return he will look after you if your husband dies or abandons you').

Although the feminisation of responsibility without corresponding rights has tied women's hands, this chapter also identifies one area where improvements in women's ability to manage the rising burden are beginning to show.

Contesting gender dynamics in the context of 'the hardship of life'

This section examines how traditional gender relations are being contested fiercely in the context of a scramble for jobs, increasing land scarcity and rising costs—what respondents often refer to as 'the hardship of life'. Men and women are contesting who does what work, who has what share of the responsibility for family maintenance and who has what rights over assets, power and social protection in kin networks. A shift in responsibility for family provisioning onto women in the context of rapidly rising costs relative to earnings and their falling rights over assets and to kin social protection is intensifying their own poverty and that of their dependants. This does not bode well for their escape from poverty.

The de-masculinisation of traditionally male rural livelihoods

In order to understand changes in the gendered roles and responsibilities of women, it is first necessary to look at how men's roles and responsibilities have changed since independence.

It is extremely difficult to generalise about any 'traditional' gender division of labour, but it can be said that, compared with other continents, women in many parts of sub-Saharan Africa have spent considerably more time on the family farm than men in addition to their other duties. Bryceson and McCall trace the thinking on the source of women's role in farming from writers who suggest that the division goes back to hunter-gatherer societies, when men were largely involved in hunting-warrior activities and women daily plant-gathering. Men's hunting and warrior activities were largely eliminated under colonial modernisation, but women's role in cultivation rose as agriculture was intensified and fallow periods shortened. Women were forced to assume farm work because, under polygamy, men controlled the labour of multiple women as essentially forced labour through marriage payments.[5]

Bryceson and McCall suggest that this division between men and women's work was reproduced during the colonial period, but for different reasons. Men's work was siphoned off as forced labour in mines and on plantations, whereas women stayed in the villages. 'Men's physical absence served to make the sexual division of labour more rigid in terms of women's involvement in rural subsistence production and men's dissociation from it', creating taboos about men's involvement in the cultivation of certain crops, as well as other domestic and processing activities.[6] Colonial rule was indirect, through tribal leaders, and forced labourers were bachelors supposed to return home (circular migration, bachelor wages) to renew social bonds and avoid instability. However, by the end of the 1930s, it was understood that circular migration had led to abandonment as men found new wives in the vicinity of their workplace. The statutory urban minimum wage in 1957 reinforced urban migration and processes of urbanisation.

In the 1960s, the new nationalist government became concerned with creating opportunities in villages to deter migration and rapid urbanisation, by building institutions to raise productivity and provide local services and thereby enhance peasant production and rural livelihoods. Men returned home and 're-tribalised': in the decades after independence, their residence became relatively more local and participation in the production and control of the proceeds from the sale of cash crops rose (although women continued to work on the cash crop farms of male kin). Agricultural subsidies on inputs and a territorial producer price on food crops—despite 'sources of waste and corruption'—promoted crop production successes, such as maize in southwest and southern Tanzania.[7] Cashew production per capita in the mid-1960s was treble the size it was in 2007.[8] What we see, then, is that today's post-liberalisation feminisation of villages, of rural work and of female responsibility for provisioning through farming and farm labour is not far from the norm in Tanzanian history. The period of resident male cash crop farmers, associated livelihoods and traditional responsibility for maintenance was actually the exception and operated only from independence to mid-1990.

After liberalisation, men's livelihoods in cash-cropping in traditional exports, fishing, hunting and pastoralism began to perish. While there is disagreement as to the causes of this,[9] there is agreement that overall production began to decline in some traditional crops (such as the cashews and cotton grown in the study regions) as people diversified into other crops—cash crops such as paddy, vegetables, pulses and oilseeds and consumption crops like maize and cassava. Over the period 1991/92–2007, the proportion of rural incomes from the sales of cash crops fell steeply relative to other sources, from 25.6 to 15.3 per cent of household income, with a minor rise in income from sales of food crops (48.5 to 50.4 per cent).[10] This fall in traditional cash-cropping relative to food cropping has moved some observers to suggest that this is a response by farmers to the vulnerability of liberalisation: replacing cash crops which face erratic markets with more secure food production for subsistence and 'scrambling' for alternative non-agrarian sources of income.[11]

Some of this price variability resulted because liberalisation led to erratic prices for small, risk-prone cotton farmers, despite a rise in the number of traders entering the market. One focus group discussant in Ndite argued that markets for cotton were declining. He said that, in 1974, cotton production was the most profitable venture. In 1980, farmers sold their crops on credit to the government and to private traders (Nyanza Cooperative was flailing and collapsed in 1985). By 1995, private traders dominated the market (a certain business tycoon was mentioned). From this point, cotton prices never improved, and it was no longer regarded as a lucrative business venture. Private businessmen continued to increase in number, but prices were low: 'These business people are very tricky. They come when farms have been prepared and offer inputs based on an agreement that a recipient farmer will sell crops only to them. Some come when cotton plants start flowering and negotiate with farmers for low prices before the actual harvest', one participant explained.

The reduction in the farming of traditional agricultural exports in the study areas has led to movement into other crops, including paddy in coastal Nkasi district and in Magu district, maize in inland Nkasi district (linked to grain reserves) and maize and cassava together with groundnuts and pulses in Newala district. The decline in income from cash-cropping and livestock has also been replaced by a rise in income from local off-farm employment and migration. Many of these jobs are in agricultural labour, charcoal production, timber and firewood collection and petty trade. These trends are reflected in aggregate data at the all-Tanzania level in Household Budget Survey data for 1991/92, 2001/02 and 2007.

Table 4.1: Distribution of main source of household income in rural areas in Tanzania

	1991/92	2001/02	2007
Sales of food crops	48.5%	48.9%	50.4%
Sales of cash crops	25.6%	20.5%	15.3%
Sales of livestock and products	5.3%	5.5%	4.2%
Business income	6.1%	8.1%	7.4%
Wages and salaries	5.8%	3.8%	8.9%
Remittances	1.0%	3.0%	2.5%
Fishing	1.9%	2.2%	2.6%
Selling of local brew	NA	NA	2.4%
Charcoal	NA	NA	1.6%
Timber sales	NA	NA	0.6%
Firewood	NA	NA	0.6%

Source: National Bureau of Statistics (2008c)

One result of this fall in support for local cash-cropping was a rise in men's migration in search of work, marking a reversion to the gender division of labour of colonial times. Men's migration can become permanent as they find new wives and fail to return home. Bintimusa Khalfani's father grew cashew nuts through the 1970s and early 1980s quite productively, marketing them through the local Nkangala cooperative in Mtwara, which functioned well back then. Her father could produce 7 to 10 bags of cashews per acre with no inputs, whereas today Bintinmusa, who is thirty-nine years old, can produce only 1 to 2 bags. In 1986, around the same time that the local cooperative was dissolving, her father's production levels began to decline. This prompted him to search for more productive cashew land in Massasi. He did not return and eventually abandoned his wife, having found a new one in the new place. His wife, Zulfa, was forced to move into her sister's derelict house and lived there with the help of her daughter Bintimusa.

The fall in male work in cash-cropping following liberalisation has been accompanied by a fall in male livelihoods in remote areas of Tanzania bordering commons (oceans, lakes, grazing lands, hunting grounds), including fishing, hunting and pastoralism.[12] The decline of the commons was always a feature of colonial modernisation, but liberalisation and deepened commercialisation in the 1990s and in the new millennium continued to drive the situation (commercial fishing, private clubs restricting hunting (particularly of Sandawe), overgrazing by pastoral communities such as Maasai and Sukuma which are pushed into farming and conflicts with farmers over land resources).

In our study sites, mostly those near water sources, we noted a decline in the traditionally male occupations of fishing and fishmonger work. In some regions, the fall in income from fishing is a result of commercial fishing reducing stocks; in other regions, climate change is warming inland waters; in others, regulations put in place to restore stocks penalise the fishing of 'small, young fish'. Octavian Sapi, forty nine years old from Kalesa, told us that fishermen who had used fishing nets that had been prohibited (those with holes up to 2 inches in diameter) had become impoverished since February 2009, when the government burned all such nets in the area.

Moreover, the structure of payments among casual fisherman is low. Octavian Sapi also said that employers on fishing boats divided the catch unfairly (all people get a share, then the fishing equipment—owned by the employer—also gets a share. For instance, the boat and each of the lamps gets a share.)

Local fish traders seem to be suffering too, with prices of fish (essentially a staple) becoming unaffordable. We saw this in Nkangala and Wazabanga. Peter Nyanza is seventy-five years old and lives in Wazabanga. His main livelihood is fish trading: he buys fish to sell in the village. Before, he had enough capital to go offshore and buy fish, but now prices have increased sharply and he cannot afford to buy a large amount. Fish that were sold at TZS 2,000 in the 2000s are now sold at TZS 5,000. The fish market is dominated by big traders to the extent that smaller traders are marginalised and pushed out. 'The arrival of fish traders with more capital increased prices and opened up the local market in the lake to other competitors such as traders from Magu and sometimes Mwanza when they have less fish there.' Peter also explained that, 'We see fewer and fewer local fish traders in the village because sometimes they make a trip to the lake and come back empty-handed because all the day's catch is purchased by big traders.' Peter felt he was getting too old to go to the lake to buy fish to bring to the village, especially as there was often no fish to buy. He said, 'How can you compete with someone whose pocket is deep?' If local traders are not protected, people may lose their business and villagers will be unable to buy fish in the local market.

Fisherman in our study region had tried to diversify into farming but in recent years had seen little support by way of extension. As such, men were losing traditional employment without a suitable replacement. In Magu district, the declining fish stock in Lake Victoria was cited as a reason for many people turning to paddy and sugarcane production. In Nkasi district, Fipa fisherman in Kalesa along Lake Tanganyika tried to farm paddy but needed support in this transition, as they struggled to learn new techniques, especially training oxen to drive ploughs. In Newala district, Mtwara, the fish trade from nearby River Ruvuma and imported from the coast had died in recent years, as no one could afford the high cost of fish, the one protein source in poor people's diet. Many of these men are now unemployed.

The rise of effectively female-headed households: male chronic illness, despair and semi-permanent migration

Over the past ten years, there has been a rise in the number of female-headed households and 'effectively female-headed households'—households headed by women who still live with men but where the men contribute little to family provisioning. As a result, more women are taking on responsibility for household provisioning: in the words of Platteau et al., women have become 'the managers of household poverty' and of any likely escapes that policy would like to promote.[13]

About a quarter of all households are fully female-headed.[14] However, female headedness is rather difficult to capture given its fluidity: women drift in and out of marriage through successive divorces and widowhood. Nevertheless, it seems their responsibility for provisioning is constant: for the most part, women are responsible for supplying food and clothing, primary school educational costs, health costs for themselves in pregnancy and for young children and water costs. Effective responsibility for family provisioning is even harder to capture through survey data without long interviews with both women and their husbands: in most of our interviews, men spoke of responsibility as if they were responsible and did the work (farm labouring); when we spoke to women it was clear that they were fully responsible.

Three key drivers are behind the rise of effectively female-headed households. These are male chronic illness, usually resulting from HIV and AIDS-related diseases; male despair resulting from chronic underemployment and from rising barriers to escape from poverty (the cost of productive assets and extension support). Such despair can promote refuge in alcohol and mistresses, which drains men's income; and semi-permanent migration when remittances are not sent home (preceding abandonment).

Chronic illness, often resulting from HIV and AIDS, deprives a woman both of an additional breadwinner and of her ability to work herself, as she needs to take days off from wage labour to care for the chronically ill. Maternal health failures, on which little progress has been made, also cuts severely into women's ability to manage a family income.[15]

According to a focus group discussion, inhabitants of Kalesa seem to be particularly prone to illness—notably typhoid and malaria—which may be related to HIV and AIDS or to Kalesa's port location and wet swamplands. We asked the female focus group to describe the destitute, which they did by speaking of this group as chronically ill, unable to earn and dependent on others for care. This includes those with an HIV or AIDS-related illness (malaria, typhoid, cholera or tuberculosis) or epilepsy, leprosy, asthma or diabetes.

Two key issues were highlighted in relation to linkages between ill-health, inability to work for a wage and extreme poverty (most women in the group worked as labourers or tenants on paddy farms): maternal health difficulties (miscarriages and problematic caesareans and dilation and curettage); and husbands or other members of the family being chronically ill, meaning women become the full-time carer, unable to go to work and thus keep the family going, ending up destitute themselves as they become dependent on relatives and neighbours for basic needs.

When chronic illness ends in widowhood, or semi-permanent migration results in permanent abandonment and divorce, this can lead to a women's loss of the family farm and dispossession of assets, including her children (see below).

A key feature of the rise in effectively female-headed households is men 'giving up' as a consequence of immobility, underemployment and exploitation when working as casual labourers. At a recent Chronic Poverty Research Centre workshop in Dar es Salaam, quantitative panel researchers at the National Bureau of Statistics identified a worrying trend of households remaining clustered at or below the poverty line over time (2007–09)—in other words, the majority of Tanzanians were stagnating in poverty, despite rapid growth. Qualitative research into a subsample of households reveals similar results, with very few households moving out of poverty over 1999—2009.[16] One major reason is that the cost of agricultural capital—land purchase or rental, oxen purchase or hiring in a plough driver and oxen—has become very high in the past ten years, erecting an increasingly robust barrier between the poor and the non-poor. Poor people find it very difficult to expand acreage owing to the rising cost of land, or to intensify production using new technologies. In Kalesa, Josephat Mpama, a retired school teacher, said emphatically that despair was one among the main factors in the persistence of poverty. Young people do not have capital and do not seem clear on how to acquire it, and most trading enterprises are owned by people from other places.

Some men fall into despair and alcoholism and take up mistresses as an adverse response to the de-masculinisation of their livelihoods and frustration at being unable to see a way out of poverty. In all districts there were descriptions and phrases for this—underemployed men who quite literally give up. Pankras Mndoa of Kalesa was given 6 acres of wetland when the agricultural officer distributed land. However, he did not have the capital to farm the land from year to year. One year, he found he had to work all season as a casual labourer merely to raise the funds to hire in an ox driver to plough his land rather than hoe it. This costs at least TZS 300,000—way beyond the means of most farmers of his level. Farmers such as him 'despair' and turn to alcohol—as TZS 1,000 for a drink *is* within their means.

In Wazabanga, a male focus group discussant said that the poor found it easy to give up since they had a sense of not making it in life. He used the word 'disheartened'. Another important attribute highlighted was that the poor are likely to be suicidal. Another participant said, 'they become thin as they always have deep thoughts about life which build stress and depression. When you take them to hospital for a thorough examination they develop hypertension.'

One way for men to attempt to regain their masculinity is through drinking clubs. Respondents noted that one out of three households contained an alcohol abuser and that drinking, which used to be reserved for Sundays and post-harvest, now occurred throughout the week and during all seasons. Homebrew has become neatly distilled and homemade spirits and alcohol clubs have risen in number.

In Kalesa, focus group participants described the poor as 'the alcohol club'. One female discussant reasoned that the very poor could not afford to drink but the poor could, and spend whatever they earn in drinking clubs. The group complained that this group tends to brag that they have more money than they really have, and that the women in these families have no voice. 'Women whose husbands are alcoholics often mobilise their children to farm. The husband after harvesting will sell it without telling the woman. [By contrast] We women look after our families—we buy charcoal and resell in small amounts, we sell rice in small amounts.'

Despair also encourages men to express their virility by spending meagre resources on gifts for mistresses (often single mothers). Sleeping with a girlfriend, whether already married or unmarried, entails the expectation of small gifts of food or clothing. This arises in most villages. More formalised prostitution occurs in towns.

The rise of fully female-headed households: permanent migration, widowhood and conflict

As men's traditional involvement in and control of cash-cropping declines, and with the rise in male migration, men are leaving women to farm and bring up dependants on their own in a context of rapidly rising costs. Platteau et al.'s argument for sub-Saharan Africa as a whole applies here:

> The management of agricultural households in sub-Saharan Africa has progressively become women's responsibility as men migrate to other regions for better economic opportunities, and as the HIV/AIDS pandemic takes its toll. Land becomes even more important for women to be able to provide a living to their families, especially when the husband and the other male members of the family die; and other opportunities for income are scarce.'[17]

Another key factor promoting the rise of female-headed households is widowhood. Focus group discussions held with women in Kalesa cluster and life histories of women whose husbands have died (in the same cluster) revealed that men often die prematurely, mostly from HIV or AIDS-related illnesses, particularly if through trading, fishing or migration they have come into contact with various diseases. Men also die early deaths from excessive or toxic alcohol consumption and they have less longevity relative to women's. As in the case of Bintimusa Khalfani (below), widowhood often leads to asset-stripping by the deceased man's family. As a consequence, women have to raise their family without the means to do so. Meanwhile, it is not uncommon for women to have to contend with abandonment and widowhood throughout their life.

Zulfa (eight-two years old from Nkangala) was abandoned twice. Her daughter, Bintimusa, one of her three children, on whom Zulfa depended after her husband left, was subsequently widowed and dispossessed. Bintimusa was a good farmer but when she was widowed her husband's family took the house, land and livestock—but left their children. Bintimusa needed more land to farm in order to survive and support her children and mother. However, she could not farm her brother's share of her father's land, despite the fact that it was uncultivated, because her brother had migrated. Neither could she rent it out. She was afraid that he might get angry if she destroyed its fertility.

Family conflict leading to divorce, particularly in the past decade, has also contributed to the rise of female-headed households. Rising costs and limited income have led to fierce battles over traditional gendered roles, rights and responsibilities and pushed women and children in poor families into casual and/or petty labour. Women have also increased their participation in market-oriented activities, which has in turn increased their control over economic resources, leading to a shift in the balance of power in many families and giving women more negotiating strength—but this has also increased gender conflict. Men often respond harshly, marrying second wives, spending more money and time outside the home, labelling women prostitutes, which destroys their reputations and leads to social exclusion, and exerting physical abuse. The ensuing conflicts can end in divorce or abandonment. Flora (now eighty years old and from Wazabanga) said that family conflict has become the rule of the day compared with other times when couples respected each other. Here Flora is referring to the breakdown of the conjugal contract where women are expected to obey husbands and adhere to certain gendered social norms regarding their responsibilities, behaviour and mobility. With their new found voice from breadwinning and extending their own mobility through trade, some women are challenging traditional norms of respect e.g. working and moving outside the village and this leads to conflicts, sometimes domestic abuse. Men's status vis-a-vis the community is also threatened leading to family conflicts.

Respondents in Nkangala village argued that roughly thirty years ago families were better-off and land abundant. If a man took on an additional wife, farm sizes were large enough or more land could be taken in freely—labour, not land, was scarce.[18] Land is now the scarce commodity, and resources are simply insufficient to maintain two families. Men and their new (second) wives or girlfriends may try to force the first wife out, partly because the farm and available resources can maintain only one family. Flora explained that a woman who is married to a man who still has a wife (i.e. a second wife) is likely to face downward mobility because it is rare that the first wife agrees to share what she has attained with her husband with the 'newcomer' despite the fact that in some cases husbands dictate/force first wives to surrender part of the assets to the new wife. Thus, the second wife 'will never have wealth until the first wife agrees to share some with her'. So, in a situation of scarce resources, a second wife will try to oust the first wife.

Flora also argued that alcoholism is an important factor in downward mobility in the area. Such people leave in the morning and come back in the afternoon completely drunk.

When has this person worked? If this is the tendency daily then after some time the person will become destitute and live like a beggar. Since this person does not work, it means he or she is an "exploiter" in the sense that he or she survives by expecting others to feed him or her.

Flora said that the majority of these people are men, spending most of their time in local clubs consuming *pombe*, with little or no time for household chores.

Some of them take loans for drinking and become bankrupt and bring about unnecessary tension and conflicts in the family, particularly when a woman queries his attitude. When the situation is out of control, a man will assume he has all the authority to sell the farm and house. At the same time, he assumes the authority to sell the food stock inside the house without telling his wife to pay for beer.

Conflicts also arise when men take on mistresses and give them gifts, while conflicts over money can also lead to domestic abuse. Melina, aged thirty-five and from Ndite, was separated from her second husband in 2006 because her life was threatened. After her husband used her income to pay for his own children's school fees, she felt angry, 'because I could not make any decision on the money obtained nor could I use it for my children'. She ignored her husband's commands and decided to abandon farming; this made her husband furious and he started to threaten to abuse her physically. When she decided to leave him he did not permit her to take anything.

Men may strongly disapprove of their wives working because of the potential shame it can bring for them. Erick Kateti (forty-two years old from Wazabanga) explained that, if a woman does not farm or care for cattle, people will think she is not fulfilling a woman's role. Women who rebel and work to set up businesses may end up as victims of domestic abuse. Successful women may be labelled prostitutes (meaning a woman who is unfaithful to her husband, perhaps through accepting small gifts from her lover, or one explicitly selling sex for money) and excluded from society. He said that women who perform non-farm activities are labelled *tes*. These are women who should never have been married in the first place because 'they are stubborn and always compete with men'. If the man is behind what the woman is doing, that is tolerated. Otherwise, 'even though you will never be told that you are a prostitute, deep down everyone will think so and a woman by herself also thinks that this is what the community thinks about her'. Erick said some women had coped with this community disapproval and others had felt forced to go back to traditional ways of living.

The rising costs of bride price can intensify the shame men feel about 'disobedient' wives and increase the pressures on new wives to be obedient, adhere to tradition and accept beating/exclusion if they dissent. According to Flora, a real Sukuma man will never tolerate three things in a woman. He will never tolerate a woman being a prostitute, laziness in work and or scandal mongering/gossiping. If he has married a woman with these three characteristics he can immediately marry a second, third and even fourth wife. This is also a punishment for a woman who has the characteristics that he does not like. A 'real man' does not like to argue or punish a woman physically but brings someone as a replacement who is more obedient and respectful.

Asna (thirty-two years old from Nkangala) begged her husband to let her work more outside the home—she was keen to send her eldest daughter to secondary school and to work in the village office to assist the village executive officer and as an agricultural labourer to pay for it. He refused, in an attempt to establish her respect. However, the local street chair said she and other women must send their children to school. This gave Asna the moral justification to leave her husband—which she said her mother would not have done in the same situation.

De-feminisation of assets and legal and clan entitlements

As occupations are de-masculinised, and work and responsibility for family maintenance is feminised, women need even greater rights over assets and to social protection in order to support their families. However, enforce-able rights over land and traditional entitlements seem to be undergoing pro-cesses of 'de-feminisation'. Customary/tribal rights concerning who gets what following divorce/abandonment or widowhood differs in each region in terms of assets or income from the husband; custody and responsibility for raising children; and access to social protective networks in the husband's or wife's family.

Women never received much after widowhood and divorce but now what little they are afforded seems to be contested, given limited resources. Many female respondents said that, compared with in their mother's time, on divorce or death of their husband they are faced with a more thorough dispossession of assets, income and networks and failures in male kin traditional social networks. Who gets the children and who gets the assets seems to be discretionary and won by the more powerful, negotiated by self-serving opportunists interpreting laws and norms according to what serves them best: tribal, religious. Where this fails, physical abuse of women may occur.

Disputes regarding widow's and divorce shares tend either to be settled out of court or to be adjudicated by elders from the ethnic group or religious clerics, which heavily favour men's ownership of productive assets, even though such advantage to men is anachronistic in terms of men's contribution to family maintenance. As a result, following divorce or widowhood, women are often stripped of ownership of and access to productive and other assets, despite several pieces of legislation designed to prevent this from happening. The National Land Policy (Land Act 4 of 1999 and Land Act 2 of 2002) gives women the right to acquire land through purchase or gift, but leaves inheritance of clan or family land to be governed by custom and tradition— although it states that customs and practices that contradict the principle of women's equality are nullified. The Land Act was further amended in 2004 to allow women to mortgage their land, and also strengthens women's rights in relation to marital property by stipulating that spousal consent is necessary in mortgaging the matrimonial home.

The Marriage Act, meanwhile, confirms women's right to acquire, hold, use and deal with land equally to men. The 1999 Village Act, which has been in force since 2001, invalidates customary laws that discriminate against women and recognises a wife's rights to land on the death of the spouse or on divorce. It also enables a woman to legally acquire and own land through registration and to have a title deed. Women can use this for residence and for production. In addition, it stipulates that both spouses be registered and mortgages be issued only with the consent of both spouses, who are both entitled to a copy of the mortgage agreement.

In practice, though, women are not afforded protection. The first key problem is that, in relation to divorce, the court is required to take into account the customs of the community to which the parties belong, even if such customs are discriminatory. It appears that the stipulation that customary law will be nullified in any case of discrimination is not being evoked. As a consequence, in primary courts and village offices of adjudication, discriminatory customary and religious laws are given primacy over statutory law.

The second problem is that, although adjudicators occasionally agree that women can keep whatever they brought into the marriage (e.g. gifts from parents or family, land purchased before marriage or items she purchased using her own money during marriage), they do not recognise women's indirect contribution to marital assets through unvalued work which may have helped men buy a house, land or business assets in their own name. Married women are responsible for producing food crops and selling the surplus to meet clothing and basic needs, and for supplementing those basic needs with casual labour and petty employment. Their money does not go directly towards purchasing permanent land or houses. A house might therefore be in the name of the husband and presumed to be his property unless the wife is able to prove she has contributed to its acquisition (despite what is stipulated in the law)—which she cannot do in the case of farm and domestic services because adjudicators do not give these activities value.[19] Moreover, in many societies, women inherit less than their brothers. For instance, Sharia clerics say that a son's inheritance share must be double that of a daughter because a grown son needs it in order to support his family and to pay bridewealth for male members of the family. Other reasons why statutory law is not enforced include men's hiding of assets or bribing judges; women's ignorance of their rights and women's feeling of powerlessness—men will beat them or society will exclude them.

The key consequences of this lack of justice are that women are sometimes fully disinherited or divested of assets, regardless of the number of years they have contributed to the building-up of the family wealth. Following widowhood, male kin seize widows' assets; following divorce, men walk away with the lion's share of the property, including land, livestock, home and household furniture, utensils and clothing. Women are deprived of the means of supporting themselves and their dependants, and may have no support from the husband's family unless, as widows, they are 'inherited' by the husband's male kin (as wives). In some areas, women have sole responsibility for the children (e.g. the matrilineal Makonde, see below). In other situations, they have to leave their children with the deceased husband's family, where they may be ill-treated.[20]

In Newala district, tribes such as the Makonde have a social structure based on a matrilineal system. In this, the inheritance of resources or assets passes to the female, although the uncle (the mother's brother) oversees such resources. Historically, women in these societies have had rights to land and economic autonomy over its proceeds.[21] However, over time, such matrilineal societies have been exposed to patriliny by Islam, Christianity, commoditisation/modernisation and 'villagisation'.

According to a key informant from Nchinga, in practice Makonde women today have little independent control of assets and lose out during marriage and divorce:

> This society is matrilineal but in practice men control and own resources; even chickens, a woman cannot decide to slaughter one without the permission of the husband. If women who are involved in a business secure credit and show it to their husbands, their husbands make them give them the money. The husbands use the money to start their own businesses and marry other wives. That is why most women who are involved in business do not grow […] A female widow will get

one-third of the value of all assets, with the remainder divided between her children and his family members. However, Islamic law is now prevailing, whereby women inherit a third of the property when their husbands die but if they have a child they get an eighth.

While the 'third and third rule' seems largely to be understood, our life histories revealed that men or male kin can take 100 per cent of the assets because women are not coming forward to village offices to seek customary (or statutory) rights after divorce or widowhood, despite the hard work they put into the farm and other assets. We were told that, in 2008 in Nchinga, a man divorced his wife by giving her a letter and ordering her to leave the house. He gave her no material things, just a few clothes. The injustice was clear. Neighbours advised the woman to take legal measures to claim a good share of the wealth she had generated with her husband. Instead of heeding the advice, she said that she would leave it to God to punish him. Afterall in most cases legal services are costly due to widespread corruption practices among members of the local authorities.

The Sukuma in Magu district and the Fipa in Nkasi district, in contrast, are governed by a patrilineal system. In such societies, which make up 80 per cent of Tanzania, all resources *including children* are controlled and owned by men, who make all the decisions in the household. A woman can provide her opinion but not make decisions. A widow in a patrilineal society has three choices: to be inherited as a wife by her husband's kin, whereby she retains some use of the marital land; to go back to her own people (losing rights over assets and her children); or, if she has adult children, to go to their residence. As Ellis et al. point out, each choice renders her dependent on networks.[22] Customary laws were designed to ensure that women do not transfer land outside the clan through marriage, and wife inheritance was originally designed as a form of social protection for older widowed women to secure their access to assets through their husband's brothers.

One reason men get a double share in both Makonde and Sharia law is based on men's perceived greater financial responsibilities. In Islam, a husband must use his inheritance to support his family and pay bridewealth; a wife has neither obligation. As an example, the brother of a deceased man may feel that, as he had to help pay bridewealth for his brother (and perhaps other members of the family), he has a right to claim his brother's widow's house and land, as his male kin would have had much more responsibility than the woman. However, this has become irrelevant in modern times, as women are responsible not only for feeding and clothing children from their farm work (in the context of rising prices) but also for funding primary school education costs (in the context of rising contributions) as well as secondary costs (it is up to family whether to help her or not).

On divorce, a women's family has to pay back the dowry, even if the husband is declared to have abused his wife (note that this is not the case for

Fipa women). Deductions are made for the number of children produced. A daughter stands for three cows and a son two.

Jestina, who is fifty one years old and from the lake zone of Ndite, had few assets during her marriage. She and her husband struggled together to raise their living standards. They cultivated cassava for consumption and sold the surplus at the market. After two years, they were able to start a business selling fish, and later to buy more assets and to eat three meals a day (rice, cassava and potatoes). In the tenth year of marriage, she caught her husband cheating on her and demanded a divorce. This was settled using traditional customs, whereby her parents had to pay back one cow and she received utensils. She lost her house, savings, land and the businesses she was running with her husband and had to depend on her poor parents for survival. 'The divorce made me poor because I lost everything I worked for over ten years. Since then I have not been able to reach the level that I was at before. I have accepted my fate as this is how our customs are.'

Asna Burhan knew of one woman who was the wife of a very rich man who owned 'many cars, trucks, lorries (even pistols!) and nice houses and livestock'. Her husband took the decision to divorce her: he 'overpowered her', forced her out of the house and took their children. The women took it to the primary district-level court which decided in her favour, awarding her a house, a car, 10 cows, 5 goats and the chickens. Even though this was far less than half his wealth, the man decided to appeal anyway, and it was taken to the referral court, which also decided in favour of the woman. The man appealed again, taking it to a regional-level court, where court officials told the women, 'if you give us TZS 300,000 we can push this decision faster'. It was at this point that the courts failed her; she found that, because her husband held the wealth, she could not pay the bribe (men will succeed in a legal system based on bribes, as men often have better ability to pay bribes and women do not). As a consequence, the man kept all his wealth and their children.

Asna's story is hearsay, of course, but it does reveal a poor woman's perception of how lower-level courts work for women, that is, even if you succeed at lower levels, higher-level courts are also corrupt and that even a rich women cannot win in a world where men hold the power/wealth. These ideas further inhibit poor women from taking their disputes to court, even relatively powerful, outspoken and capable women like Asna.

The law does not protect women's rights to assets, but there are early signs that it is beginning to protect the rights of children to stay with their mother. Ordinarily, rights to children after separation or widowhood follow tribal law: in matrilineal societies, they stay with the wife, in patrilineal societies a woman has to leave the children with her husband's clan and returns home to her native place, or she stays with the in-laws with the children. However, these rules are contested today.

In Makonde matrilineal tradition in Nkangala and Nchinga, on widowhood or divorce children are supposed to stay with their mothers.

However, we found cases of slightly better-off men attempting to retain or recover children.

In patrilineal Rukwa, on the other hand, we found men leaving their children when they divorced. In Mwanza, one woman sought help from the village office to retain her children. Dafrosa, fifty-two years old from Wazabanga in Mwanza, ran away from her first husband because he was addicted to alcohol and other women and hence wasted resources. Moreover, he was not available at home and was not contributing to the well-being of the family. She left the three children because the man forced her to do so. But he could not take care of them properly, so she went to the Social Welfare Department to claim them. She was given the children and she stayed with them with her new husband. This could not be done in her mother's era because she is from a patrilineal society where the children belong to their father. In both these cases, the state seems to be intervening successfully in child rights, but not women's rights to the assets or paternal maintenance necessary to provide for children.

It is assumed that women will seek support from their own parents or siblings on divorce or widowhood. However, women are often not welcome at home once their husbands have died or abandoned them—despite the customary right to social protection in the natal family—particularly in situations of scarce resources and when women are named as prostitutes. We found that, whereas many fathers help their daughters after abandonment/ divorce, brothers (those of this generation) are failing in their responsibilities to provide social protection.

A son might inherit more assets than his sister and receive preferential access to education, to capital to set up a business and to family (clan) power. The rationale is that men require these resources in order to support their extended families and to pay the bridewealth for male members of the family. The implicit 'sibling contract' expects that he will take care of his siblings, particularly female ones: if his sisters (or nieces) are divorced or become widowed, they are entitled to return home and receive support from her male kin—father, brothers and uncles. In recent times, women have received less support from brothers/uncles than in their mother's generation: 'tradition' is being contested. Meanwhile, women—particularly unmarried women—are naming their children after their brothers to win their support.

Erick, forty-two years old from Wazabanga, explained that a woman who has a child born out of wedlock tends to name the child after a brother whom she trusts and who keeps an eye on her if things go astray. She will do this in order to establish a very close bond with that brother so that he can look after her and, more importantly, the child. Although this is not directly related to the brideprice, it shows the importance of brothers for those women who have no chance of getting married officially. Importantly, when these children are married, the uncle they are named after will be in charge. He will decide on girls' brideprice but also be responsible when boys are married.

However, with life becoming increasingly hard, brotherly support is becoming more difficult to come by. Brothers might give assistance only if their mother is still alive and puts pressure on them. When Jamal, thirty-seven years old, from Wazabanga, was in primary school, his parents divorced. His father abandoned them. When his mother remarried, he went to stay with his grandmother, and later used his grandmother's farm to maintain himself and his wife. He also received support from his uncle, whom he stayed with for some time before he moved to his grandmother's house. After his grandmother's death, his uncles chased him out of her farm. He tried to put up a battle for the land but he lost. He was sad and his life deteriorated because he had depended a great deal on the farm to sustain his family.

How do female-headed families manage poverty and how can policy expand on this?

While women are increasingly becoming managers of household poverty, as a consequence of the rise in female-headed households, they are without rights to assets or the power to enable an escape from it (and an intergenerational escape through investments in children's education). This is because of their deteriorating access to land; a decline in men's rural livelihoods and income; a rise in separation, abandonment and widowhood followed by asset-stripping by men or male kin; and a demise in traditional male kin support networks. Moreover, within marriages, women suffer continued assaults from their husbands on their freedom to work, including their taking-on of additional wives to quell 'disobedience'; slander of working women as prostitutes and threats of social exclusion; physical abuse; and finally threats of divorce and penury for their parents' through repaying the bridewealth.

Within this space, how have some women managed to survive and support their dependants? Some women have been able to maintain control over their own labour power, their body, their female networks (family and organised) and, in some cases, capital they have earned or borrowed officially. Women have used such assets in various ways.

Assets and livelihood activities available to female-headed families

The variety and amount of work that women undertake has expanded over the past fifteen years, with women now earning money through activities which were previously in the realm of 'men's work.'

There is fast growth of larger-scale, heavily capitalised female trading among those lucky few women who have access to larger amounts of capital. This is monetarily rewarding and socially empowering and has a powerful ideological effect on a much larger group of poorer women. The latter are learning financial discipline and feel empowered to demand from their husbands the ability to seek employment and control the proceeds. Larger female traders in all three districts tend to be textile merchants, followed by fish merchants in Kalesa in Nkasi district (near Lake Tanganyika) and Wazabanga in Magu district (near Lake Victoria). These female traders seem to be travelling outside the village more than men, despite the social stigma attached to this. However, big rice traders in Magu and Nkasi districts still tend to be men. Two groups prosper: those doing large-scale trade (mostly unmarried or divorced women) and those doing small-scale business but in a functional household/partnership where the small business is part of a diversified strategy (farming, labouring, another business, etc.).

Eric Kateti, forty-two from Wazabanga village, believes that acceptance of these women's activities is growing in the community. He was also keen to highlight that women are more successful in business than men in Wazabanga because they are involved mainly in businesses operating on small margins men would refuse to consider. He explained,

> The fact that women are more involved in small business, it means also the profit they are looking at is very minor. Women are willing to sell and get a profit of even TZS 50 while men would hardly see this as a business that pays. Many restaurants and shops and even stalls at the local market are dominated by women. They have won people's trust and we usually don't negotiate much with them because they are our mothers and sisters and they will never exploit the community.

Certainly, there are large differences among women involved in trade. The vast majority of female traders are involved in petty trade, selling small quantities of crops, especially those considered to be female crops (vegetables such as tomatoes and onions), fish and grains. Some of these products involve processing (homebrew, tea, doughnuts, dried fish, processed cassava, mats, etc.). Most of these activities are small scale and service oriented, with small-scale traders facing flooding markets. Only so many women can sell snacks to eat or tomatoes to farmers whose income is limited. Margins and profits are small partly because women have little choice in oversupplied markets. Aziza Mabina, fifty years old and from Nkangala, had a doughnut business which was heavily dependent on the fortunes of farmers, which rose in 1995–99 and fell thereafter. After cashew farmers' incomes fell in 2005, wives of cashew farmers and older women who could not farm also became doughnut sellers and the market was flooded. She decided it would be more lucrative to try to increase the productivity of her cassava land and to sell the surplus to traders from Kenya.

A number of women said that they would like to focus on farming rather than trade to get their families out of poverty. Sirila, a twenty-seven-year-old single mother of four living in Wazabanga, believes that if there is anything the government can do to support the exit from poverty it has to be providing loans to buy farms. As with others in the community, Sirila think that rice production is the quickest way someone can get money and exit poverty.

> If I have 1 acre of rice and if I utilise it effectively, then I am assured of harvesting at least 15 sacks of paddy, which is equivalent to 8–9 sacks

of rice. I can sell each sack of rice at TZS 50,000 and get at least TZS 400,000. After deducting what I have invested, I still have a profit.

Sirila continued that there was no such a business in Wazabanga that pays like this. She explained that many of the people lack basic skills and knowledge on how to produce rice, but markets are everywhere, starting from the village, to Magu, all the way to Kenya. Policymakers should be careful about promoting petty trade in the context of flooded markets and rather support female farming and agricultural extension in production and marketing.

In addition, women seem to be in greater demand than men as agricultural workers and in other types of labour, given their availability and their willingness to do hard work for low wages. In particular women are working more days as agricultural labourers (especially in paddy, cotton and cashews) and also have a larger share than before in tasks traditionally considered male (the more arduous male agricultural labour work). They are also engaged in off-farm labour to a greater extent, including construction and cashew processing, an exclusively female occupation. Erick, forty-two years old, of Wazabanga, explained that even when it comes to the construction industry, people trust and recruit more women than men, except in jobs that demand extra energy. Women do not ask for that much, are more honest and trustworthy and will do the job according to instructions.

However, this willingness to work on a low wage must be seen in perspective: it is a reflection of the fact that most women are thrust into flooded labour markets, are not well remunerated and thus work to survive rather than being able to move out of poverty. Agricultural labouring work in particular is often at subsistence level or below, and is subject to exploitation (the destitute are paid less) and even non-payment. Sirila, mentioned above, has four children to feed and lives at her mother's house. She complains that she must be permanently available for work, and it is clear from her wage levels for cotton- and rice-weeding that she is paid less than the going rate. Her destitution is reflected in her low bargaining power with employers. Through desperation, women are also forced to scavenge (such as for firewood, poles and grass for thatching) as well as to work in prostitution, both locally for gifts and in more formalised contracts in urban areas.

Policymakers should consider legislation to support women's wages and conditions of employment. Employment guarantee schemes are one way of encouraging fair labour standards and fair wages for women. They can also re-skill men for new jobs and work towards ending the despair cycle and the single income maintenance of children.

Women's additional engagement in income-generating opportunities in this decade has further intensified their working day. They also remain responsible for domestic work (cooking, water and fuel collection, care of young children, the old and the sick), tilling food and cash crops and off-farm employment. Men work far less than women on farms. Ellis et al. cite national sample census data that reveal just how prominent women's role in agriculture is compared with men's.[23] We think this is likely to underestimate the growth in women's work this decade.

Table 4.2: Division of labour in agriculture in Tanzania

Task	Female	Male
General crop production	56%	44%
Food crop production	75%	25%
Land tilling	56%	44%
Sowing	74%	26%
Weeding	70%	30%
Harvesting	71%	29%
Marketing	73%	27%

Source: National Sample Census of Agriculture (1996), in Ellis et al. (2007)

The burden of women's domestic work has also increased, given water scarcities and the need to care for the chronically ill, which is rising with the HIV pandemic. A female focus group in Kalesa believed that women foregoing income was a key to destitution. Policymakers should be aware of women's work burden when designing policies: putting additional responsibility on women (e.g. financing children's education) would add to their overwork.

Feminisation of networks of support

Women forge and rely on female networks throughout their lives. They report that the only support they can depend on comes from male (father) and female (mothers, sisters, daughters and friends) kin. While fathers often help out, they die younger than mothers and may well have divorced them. Brothers do help out sometimes, mostly under pressure from mothers, but this is not secure. However, in most life histories, we found that women provided land, a home, food and, crucially, day-to-day labour to support other women. Quite often, older women in their fifties and sixties were shouldering the responsibility for feeding their daughter's children. That female networks work so well for women might be one reason for the success of rotating savings and credit associations (ROSCAs) and burial societies in the past ten years (see below).

A second network of support is when women organise themselves into all-female economic groupings (for credit, production and marketing), which affords them a greater chance of controlling income earned and forging a new, socially empowered identity. For instance, in Mtwara region, groups of women process and sell packaged cashew nuts to the airports. However, in the three districts we visited it is credit, however small, that is the most capable of hav-

ing a transformative effect on gender relations, particularly if processes of individualisation of control of income can accompany the individualisation of
livelihoods (see below).

The rise of women's groups in Mwanza has enabled women to contest
unfair gendered relations safe in the knowledge that they have the support
of both unorganised and highly organised female networks (production and
credit groupings). Flora Malando, eighty years old of Wazabanga, believed that
the relationship between women and men today was much better than when
she was young because women are now freer and can form a new identity, such
as belonging to a group whose members help each other socially, morally and
economically. This includes groups making traditional pots and selling them
in the open market in Magu.

The success of burial societies has been a reflection of the strength of female networks in the context of the HIV crisis. Poor female residents of Kalesa
suffer a particularly tough life: men contribute little, suffer despair, drink heavily and have mistresses; single women depend on prostitution, agricultural labouring and scavenging. Yet, despite this, burial societies have flourished and
supported women. Restituta Kasoto, secretary of one such society, explains
that it is designed to enable members to cope with costs associated with hospital treatment, funerals and other ceremonies, and has grown to accommo-
date any small borrowing needs of members. Most women fund their monthly
deposits of TZS 1,000 through agricultural labour, and the society empowers
them through the capital they amass and through the social support they receive.

Burial societies have clear advantages for very poor women over more
official credit, including that they offer a low interest rate of 2 per cent on small
loans (TZS 10–50,000). These loans must be paid back in three months, when
another loan can be taken (this works out at 8 per cent annually). In addition,
these loans are flexible and can be used for any purpose. People do not need to
draw up a business plan. Moreover, burial societies do not discriminate against
women who have difficult home circumstances (e.g. an alcoholic husband).
The only condition is prompt repayment with interest.

The social benefits of burial societies include that they generate a sense
of empowerment. Each member has capital in the society which grows yearly
from the interest on loans. For instance, in one group, each member has TZS
76,000 amassed over the past two and a half years. Members also provide a
network of social support, with advice available to women on the crises they
confront, such as maternal health issues, funerals and ceremonies, as well as
donations of food, clothing and other gifts (from each member).

The disadvantages of burial societies include occasional expulsions for
activities the group of women find unseemly (such as abortion or abusive language) as well as the very small size of the loan women can take, which means
that societies can prevent downward mobility but not yet enable many women
to invest in the types of livelihoods that might enable them to escape poverty. It

makes sense that such burial societies be linked to larger financial institutions (rather than relying on members' contributions), such as savings and credit co-operative societies (SACCOS), which would treble the size of the loans available. In some burial societies, the treasurer is a member of a SACCOS, saves funds there and is entitled to loans equivalent to three times the amount saved. According to the chair of the Mwandima ward SACCOS in Kalesa village, although the local SACCOS has few poor people, there are many treasurers from ROSCAs (including burial societies), who represent up to twenty-five members in their respective ROSCAs.

The third way women have coped in recent years is by borrowing from SACCOS. It is often argued that credit is scarce in Tanzania, particularly for women in rural areas, where banks and microfinance institutions have made little progress by way of finding cost-effective ways of lending.[24] This is compounded for the poor by administrative barriers (e.g. having to write up a business plan) and security barriers (need for collateral in the form of titled assets or a full-time salaried job). Moreover, private banks do not like giving unsecured loans, so are less likely to lend to microfinance non-governmental organisations or SACCOS whose clients are poor.

However, in the past few years, SACCOS have followed the Building Resources Across Communities (BRAC) model of group lending. This has worked for burial societies and other ROSCAs which have already been in operation for about ten years, that is, which are organically grown with no outside support except friends in groups in more metropolitan areas. Such networks are also an important way to share business methods, and policymakers might do well to make use of them in extending further support.

SACCOs are the only potential source of credit for most rural Tanzanians. A 2006 FinScope survey found that women constitute 41 per cent of SACCOS lending.[25] Being part of a credit network means women do not need to find collateral for loans—they may own very little land and depend on wage labour but their involvement in a network is a source of security which seems to be recognised officially.

Key informants in Magu and Nkasi districts argued that women were outnumbering men in terms of borrowers, and that a key reason for this was that women were much more disciplined and much more likely to repay, whereas men were more likely to default.

Not all burial societies and ROSCAs are registered with a SACCOS (for example Restituta Kasoto's), and it is clear there is great scope for increasing the number of groups linked up to SACCOS in this way. This would both increase the capital available to women by three times and improve the existing framework of financial discipline.

According to Wiliam Semiono, chair of Mwandima ward SACCOS in Kalesa village, women are better at repaying loans in a timely fashion because they are more cautious and know they will want another loan in the future. This caution might stem from their family responsibility and the fact that they do not want to damage support relationships. Erick Kateti, of Wazabanga village, said it was easier for women to get credit than men because they are considered trustworthy and will invest the money and repay the loan on time. He also thinks credit schemes believe 'women are more careful than men' and abide by the agreed contract terms. If they ask for a loan to sell tomatoes, they do not change the nature of the business without prior agreement, in this way winning the interest and goodwill of credit schemes. This also means they are given easier terms than men, who have to prepare detailed business plans, offer assets as collateral and bring guarantors who will be responsible in the case of default

The view that all women are always more careful and trustworthy than men is of course highly gendered, but it works in women's favour when so much else does not. Because official financial capital is fairly new, there are no traditional gendered implications regarding control or who gets what after divorce/widowhood as with other assets (land, cattle, houses and children). Men and male kin cannot command control of this capital on divorce or widowhood if it is in the women's name, although a few try during marriage.

In rural Tanzania since 1994, following liberalisation and de-agrarianisation, the 'scramble for cash has caused an upheaval in age-old gender and generational divisions of labour. Types of work ascribed strictly to men, or alternatively women, have broken down. Since women were hitherto the most circumscribed, the nature of their cash-earning activities that they currently pursue are striking.'[26]

The way in which women have begun to take over paddy-farming on leased-in land, driven by credit networks and the influence of Congolese (women) traders, is an important case in point. In Kalesa, women lease in land for paddy and invest in assets such as houses separately from their husbands, in an effort to control their own income.

Wilium Semiono, chair of Mwandima ward SACCOS in Kalesa village, explained there are twenty-eight SACCOS groups for women taking out loans for farming. This is sending a signal to men that paddy-farming is women's work. The other 172 individual female SACCOS members are taking farming loans too. Men and women are cultivating their paddy fields individually. The SACCOS needs to supervise men carefully in order to ensure their harvest goes into SACCOS warehouses in the warehouse receipt scheme.

Meanwhile, taking SACCOS loans has empowered women. Women cultivate their own paddy separately, save money and build houses. Men watch them do this on their own and do the same thing, so some families have two houses. However, there are quarrels because there are no leaders now like in the old days. This change is in part a result of the presence of Congolese businesswomen who have taught local women how to take business risks.

The gendered individualisation of livelihoods and income which began with de-agrarianisation fifteen years ago has been compounded in the 2000s by land shortages and a further rise in the costs of essentials and of services.

However, the rise of female credit networks and the example of female traders have encouraged women to trade and farm on their own account—in some cases leading the way for others. In Kalesa village, poor men saw only barriers to paddy-farming: the high cost of renting oxen and a lack of sufficient knowledge. However, women through networks have been able to turn a negative situation around for themselves.

Conclusion

Since 1999, despite ten years of poverty reduction strategies and legislation designed to protect women's economic rights, liberalisation polices have deepened poverty for many and also fostered a sea change in the gendering of livelihoods, rights and responsibilities.

Poverty dynamics

Findings from nearly 180 interviews conducted in Tanzania in late 2009 demonstrate that policies have not reduced poverty significantly and in some areas have intensified it. Processes of impoverishment identified by Deborah Bryceson and others—the decline in institutional support for agriculture and exposure to world markets as a result of liberalising policies—have continued in the new millennium.

Initially, cashew and cotton farmers were hit particularly hard by poor sales, with a trend towards switching to paddy and HYV cashew pulses and oilseeds (more lucrative crops). Into the vacuum left by the state came large farmers with capital from non-farm sources, such as the Sukuma and traders, and the gap between them and smallholders in relation to technologies and marketing knowledge widened. Smallholders began to sell their land and became increasingly dependent on off-farm income. The land shortage was made worse by population growth and dwindling land inheritances, as well as rising costs of land and other productive assets (e.g. renting oxen for tillage) and inputs. Small farmers' reliance on off-farm work was made difficult because markets flooded and disposable incomes fell. The creation of new agrarian institutions (such as the warehouse receipt scheme and SACCOs) in the attempt to address inefficiencies (oligopolies) in crop trading and usurious money lending to smallholders is a step in the right direction, but as yet has not been able to address chronic problems in extension, land, land rental and labour markets for poor people. Such institutions need to be accompanied additional legislation.

Poverty has also deepened since 2005 as a result of rapid rises in the cost of food and other essentials and in local contributions (user costs) in education, water and health—which MKUKUTA was designed to reduce.

Gender dynamics

These poverty dynamics underpinned changes in gender dynamics, which we fear may have deepened the prospects of intergenerational poverty. De-agrarianisation has resulted in a long-term trend of de-masculinisation of rural livelihoods, notably in cash crops but also in male trades reliant on farmers' incomes (e.g. carpentry, tailoring) and traditional work such as hunting, fishing and pastoralism, as a result of privatisation of the commons. As a consequence, many women have been thrust into the position of primary breadwinner, either indirectly within marriage through male underemployment, despair and alcoholism or directly through a significant rise in female-headed households through divorce, widowhood or single parenthood. (Among poor women over thirty years old in our study, roughly two-thirds had been an unmarried mother, widowed or divorced at least once in their lifetime.)

Another key reason for the rise in the number of female-headed households is the rise in the intensity of battles being waged between husbands and wives over what is acceptable in conjugal contracts. Women seek freedom to work to pay for necessities, to move outside the village and to control their income. Men are found to be attempting to reinstitute traditional respect by marrying second wives, perpetrating domestic abuse and labelling women as prostitutes, which can result in social exclusion. Other factors are widowhood (as a result of HIV and AIDs-related diseases and men dying younger) and the rise in female abandonment when male migration becomes permanent. One set of researchers claims that women are 'the managers of household poverty' in sub-Saharan Africa.[27]

Female headedness and intergenerational poverty

Our key argument is that this major rise in women's responsibility for maintaining the family is located within a context where women are finding it increasingly hard to provide for their dependants, which therefore may promote intergenerational poverty:

- Following divorce and widowhood, women are dispossessed of productive capital (by husbands or their male kin) and other property (farms, homes, livestock, etc.). This situation has been more ruthless in the 2000s because of the high value of land and because of poverty in general. A significant number of women are serially dispossessed (divorced then widowed).
- Enforcement of women's statutory rights to marital property is wholly inadequate given provisos on the dominance of customary law.
- Women's own traditional male sources of support are less dependable: fathers and brothers do not always welcome widows and divorcees back and women are forced to rely heavily on their female networks. Traditional responsibilities to provide social protection are being actively contested.

- With little land, many women juggle incomes from small farms, an increasing reliance on agricultural labour, petty trade and prostitution—all in flooded markets.
- For the newly single mother, land is expensive and essentials and services (especially education and water) are becoming unaffordable.
- As a consequence, the very agents responsible for managing household poverty—women—are suffering the most in terms of their ability to do so.

With these forces rallying against women's ability to provide for their families, what is working? A lucky few have become involved in trade, although we find that for most poor women their income is based on a rise in casual farm labour and petty production and trade. Women have also increasingly been organising themselves into organically grown, highly disciplined and largely female networks based on social support, credit, petty production and sale. In two regions, SACCOS have more female than male members—through their linkages with ROSCAs—thus money capital is becoming an un-gendered terrain.

Policy recommendations

Employment guarantee schemes

The decline of village work opportunities for men since liberalisation has created a vacuum that women have been forced to fill. While wealthy and powerful men have always had a place (if they want it) in local villages, we are concerned with the lack of space for the majority of *poor* men who choose or are forced to stay local. Men abandon the mothers of their children because they are stressed—when they have no work and may have fallen into alcohol or depression.

Policy to promote women's rights, knowledge, power and assets must be linked to a solution for poor men. There are those who have been loath to afford men any more rights, power and assets in a situation which has remained so unequal for so long, but we urge them and policymakers to explore ways to enable poor men to recover a space for responsibility in family provisioning in order to help them to engineer a future for their children. Such ideas may be preferable to those which make support, such as cash transfers, conditional on children's uptake of services, which exacerbates women's time poverty and can hamper their ability to earn an income.[28]

Local employment must be stimulated through land redistribution; credit to enable access to productive assets like land, oxen or power tiller rentals; farming and marketing extension, especially to improve productivity, given land shortages; and reforms to the land law to enable more land rental. Employment can also be stimulated through employment guarantee schemes which can simultaneously teach men new skills, such as in construction, mechanical work or even farming (e.g. plots which can be used to supplement school lunches). Such employment will enable dry season work, preventing sales of land in that period; encourage men to stay local; push employers to adhere to basic levels of facilities (drinking water, shade, medical services, crèches for under sixes); and help with the accumulation of the necessary savings to invest in new technology which might serve to release men from underemployment or scavenging activities that are harmful to the environment, such as charcoal production.

Research has showed that the opportunity to be involved in school construction is uplifting for men.[29] For example, Ottaba invested in cashews at a time when prices were plummeting (the early 2000s).[30] He survived on charcoal production, despite being aware of the environmental damage it was causing. He then obtained work constructing a local school, which enabled him to pay for his children's schooling and other family needs. He also learned new construction techniques and terminology, something he is proud of.

A key feature of such schemes is that they tend to bolster local wage levels and labour standards.[31] They can also be used as a forum to discuss gender relations. Holmes and Jones argue that moves toward gender equality should be seen as critical to the success of gender-sensitive social protection policies, giving the example of Ghana's Livelihood Empowerment Against Poverty programme, which enables women to buy uniforms and books and pay fees and for improved health care but has not affected family relations.[32] In other words, for an employment guarantee scheme to be effective in achieving the Millennium Development Goals, it must work not only to achieve a technical goal (such as enabling families to earn a wage during the slack season) but also to transform gender relations by empowering women (financially, educationally, through rights training, etc.). This will improve their power *vis-à-vis* male kin, by making women's wages equal to men's, by making them aware of their legal labour rights and by improving their time availability through finding collective (male–female) solutions in relation to care/domestic work responsibilities.

Holmes and Jones also suggest that projects initiate community dialogues on paydays to make men and women aware of women's rights not to suffer domestic abuse, not to be married early, etc., as well as to underline the costs of child labour for long-term mobility, among other issues. We suggest that such dialogues also make men aware of their collective maintenance responsibilities, perhaps suggesting deductions from their wages to pay for the education of their children. We hope too that public works and other schemes can re-skill men to meet any transition to new crops and new employment demand.

Enforcement and expansion of women's legal rights to land

Approximately 98 per cent of economically active rural women in Tanzania are engaged in agriculture. Despite this contribution, women are estimated to own only about a fifth, or 19 per cent, of titled land in the country, and their plots are less than half the size of those of their male counterparts.[33] Insecure land rights discourage women from making the necessary investments in their land to increase its productivity and economic value. Ellis et al. recommend reforms, which include the following:[34]

(1) Reviewing laws on inheritance to create one uniform law on this issue:
  a. In relation to property rights on divorce, the Marriage Act could stipulate that a court should follow the customs of the community to which the parties belong as long as these are not inconsistent with the Constitution. In order to be able to recognise unvalued work, the court could be required to assess the extent of contributions made by each party to the marriage and to the care of the family.
  b. Property laws related to the death of the spouse should be brought in line with the Constitution.
(2) Amending the Marriage Act to stipulate that property acquired during marriage belongs to both spouses.
(3) Simplify and disseminate knowledge on existing land laws and enforce them:
  a. Simplify the land law to aid dissemination.
  b. Educate magistrates, customary leaders and communities on case law which establishes women's entitlement to property and support.

Meanwhile, as many villages, especially in coastal Tanzania, have become feminised, and yet also remain the site of education and care, it would seem appropriate to ensure women's access to uncultivated family land left fallow by brothers when they migrate, as a store of wealth for their own children. One way around this is to encourage user rights to unused family and clan land and to focus extension, input and marketing support on female farmers. Extension can build on existing female credit and marketing networks to aid dissemination and organisation.

Policy might also include linking more female ROSCAs to SACCOS lending. Moreover, the government should build competence in SACCOS by extending presidential funds to subsidise interest and capacity development in technical and managerial skills. The government should also consider ways to abolish supplementary user fees for example on health, education, and water through improved services.

1   D. Bryceson (1999), pp. 20–1
2   United Republic of Tanzania (1998; 1999a; 1999b)
3   United Republic of Tanzania (2005)
4   National Bureau of Statistics (2008c); United Republic of Tanzania (2009a)
5   D. Bryceson and M. McCall (1994) citing Richards (1939) and Boserup (1965)
6   Ibid., pp. 3–4

7   D. Bryceson (2002)
8   Baregu and Hoogeveen (2009)
9   See, for instance, D. Bryceson (1999) and P. Kessy et al. (2008)
10 National Bureau of Statistics (2008c)
11 See, for instance, D. Bryceson (2002) and Ellis (2006)
12 See L. da Corta and L. Price (2009)
13 J. Platteau et al. (2005)
14 Tanzania Gender Networking Programme (2007)
15 Department for International Development (2009)
16 See K. Higgins (2010)
17 J. Platteau et al. (2005), p. 1
18 See Sender and Smith (1990)
19 A. Ellis et al. (2007)
20 Tanzania Gender Networking Programme (2007)
21 R. Mwaipopo (1994)
22 A. Ellis et al. (2007)
23 Ibid.
24 F. Ellis (2006)
25 Finscope (2006)
26 D. Bryceson and M. McCall (1994), p. 17
27 J. Platteau et al. (2005), p. 1
28 M. Molyneux (2006)
29 L. da Corta and L. Price (2009)
30 Ibid
31 See, for instance, D. Campbell (2010)
32 R. Holmes and N. Jones (2010), p. 2
33 A. Ellis et al. (2007)
34 Ibid., pp. 59–60

Chapter 5

Escaping Poverty in Tanzania—What Can We Learn From Cases of Success?
Kate Higgins

Introduction

Alleviating poverty has been at the heart of much of Tanzanian policy for decades. Between 2001 and 2004, Tanzania's poverty reduction strategy guided poverty reduction efforts, focusing on the priority sectors of primary education, basic health, water and sanitation, agriculture, rural roads, the judiciary and land.[1] There was broad consensus, however, that this strategy paid inadequate attention to economic growth. The subsequent strategy, the National Strategy for Growth and Reduction of Poverty, widely known by its Kiswahili acronym MKUKUTA, sought to rectify this and guided Tanzania's poverty reduction efforts between 2005 and 2010.[2] During this period, a central concern among government and the policy community in Tanzania was bolstering the rate of gross domestic product (GDP), as well as ensuring that this growth was translated into welfare improvements at the household level.[3]

Despite a concern that the initial poverty reduction strategy paper had paid inadequate policy attention to growth, Tanzania did experience GDP growth throughout the 2000s, peaking at 7.8 per cent in 2004.[4] All key sectors of the economy—agriculture, hunting and forestry, mining and quarrying, construction, fishing, manufacturing and services—grew in GDP terms, albeit to differing degrees. Critically, GDP growth in the agriculture sector did not match overall GDP growth. In addition, the contribution of agriculture to GDP declined from 29.6 per cent in 1998 to 24.0 percent in 2008.[5] This compares rather awkwardly with how the employment of the population is distributed: according to the 2006 Integrated Labour Force Survey, approximately three-quarters of Tanzanians are currently employed in agriculture.[6] This means that the largest share of the population is getting significantly less than their proportionate share of GDP.

This is one of key reasons cited for growth without commensurate levels of poverty reduction in Tanzania. Despite sustained GDP growth, with the exception of Dar es Salaam, there was a limited decline in both food and basic needs poverty levels in mainland Tanzania between 1991/92 and 2007. Tanzania has experienced substantial growth over the past decade but this has not been accompanied by a significant reduction in poverty: between 2000/01 and 2007, the percentage of people in mainland Tanzania living below the basic needs poverty line fell only slightly, from 35.7 per cent to 33.6 per cent. Given population growth, this translated into an *increase* in the absolute number of people in poverty, from 11.4 million in 2000/01 to 12.9 million in 2007.[7]

In a context where movement out of poverty has been limited, this chapter examines how and why some people have experienced upward socioeconomic mobility. Specifically, it seeks to identify, based on qualitative data collected in six research sites, how and why people have experienced upward mobility and, in some cases, moved out of poverty. What can we learn from cases of success? Through systematic analysis of the qualitative dataset, this chapter argues that agriculture is a key factor in supporting upward mobility. But, critically, it is non-farm businesses, the accumulation of physical assets (such as land and housing), salaried employment and favourable marriage—some of which agriculture plays a role in supporting—which are most effective at moving people out of poverty. When it comes to moving beyond vulnerability, these findings hold.

There have been some attempts to understand and elicit lessons from the relatively small proportion of households that have managed to escape poverty in Tanzania in the past decade. Most prominently, analysis of the Kagera Health and Development ten-year panel survey (1991/94–2004) compared people who escaped poverty with those stuck in poverty.[8] The key finding was that movements out of poverty were enabled by the diversification of income-generating activities, both on and off the farm. More specifically, on-farm diversification was critical to income growth, and lack of it was associated with stagnation and/or declines in well-being. Diversification into non-farm activities (e.g. trading crops, having a nearby shop and owning plots of timber (tresses) was found to have strong explanatory power when it came to understanding movements out of poverty.[9] Importantly, with the exception of those in remote villages, this route out of poverty was not found to be dependent on physical capital but rather on good health, the trust of benefactors and exposure to different, innovative ways of doing things. Education was also a key part of the story: each additional year of education was associated with significant additional assets. Degrees of connectedness were also critical: people in better-connected villages had more opportunities.

Analysis of the 2007 Tanzania Household Budget Survey yields somewhat similar results.[10] Owning multiple assets and being involved in monetised economic activities (e.g. involvement in markets, credit society membership and access to bank loans) are found to be correlates of avoiding poverty. Level of education of the household head, number of dependants and being on the electricity grid are also important. When it comes to agriculture, the story is more complex: farming is generally associated with poverty, though the quantity of land owned could mitigate this association (only in rural areas), and farm households engaged in commercial crops have done better. Large agricultural households with high dependency ratios, and older household heads with lower education levels, are especially prone to falling into poverty.

These analyses highlight the importance of on- and off-farm livelihood diversification in the poverty escape story in Tanzania. Hoogeveen has suggested a path for enabling this diversification: investment in human capital and enabling poor households to build physical capital, so as to enhance on- and off-farm income-generating activities.[11] His analysis highlights the instrumentality of education—and higher levels of education (e.g. post-primary education)—in moving out of poverty. Mkenda et al. conclude similarly: they find that the difference in poverty indices between primary education and higher education is considerable.[12]

This chapter outlines the conceptual framework for analysing upward socioeconomic mobility and poverty escape. It then presents results, drawing predominantly on two data sources: well-being ranking focus group discussions conducted in each research site and life history interviews conducted with selected individuals in each research site. Finally, it concludes and identifies broad policy implications.

Conceptualising and identifying upward mobility and poverty exits

The aim of this chapter is to understand socioeconomic mobility and, more specifically, the resources, capabilities and events that influenced people's *upward mobility* or *exit out of poverty*. In line with Peter Davis,[13] socioeconomic mobility can be conceptualised as: 'an outcome of a person's set of resources and capabilities interacting with events that occur through a person's life trajectory. 'These events exert either downward pressures, coped with, or upward opportunities, exploited, to determine a person's trajectory of well-being.'

Relevant capabilities and resources are those that are either *constitutive* of well-being—for example having a house or being of good health—or *instrumental* in supporting well-being—for example skills used in employment (instrumental *capability*) or arable land (instrumental *resource*).

In this study, upward socioeconomic mobility is defined as an improvement, by one well-being classification or more, in well-being. Poverty exit is defined as the movement from well-being classifications 1, 2 or 3 to well-being classifications 4, 5 or 6. Figure 5.1 shows a life history trajectory. It illustrates how socioeconomic mobility is a product of people's resources and capabilities, as they cope with downward pressures or exploit upward opportunities, which will result from resources, capabilities and events, over time.[14]

Figure 5.1: Life history trajectory to illustrate socioeconomic mobility

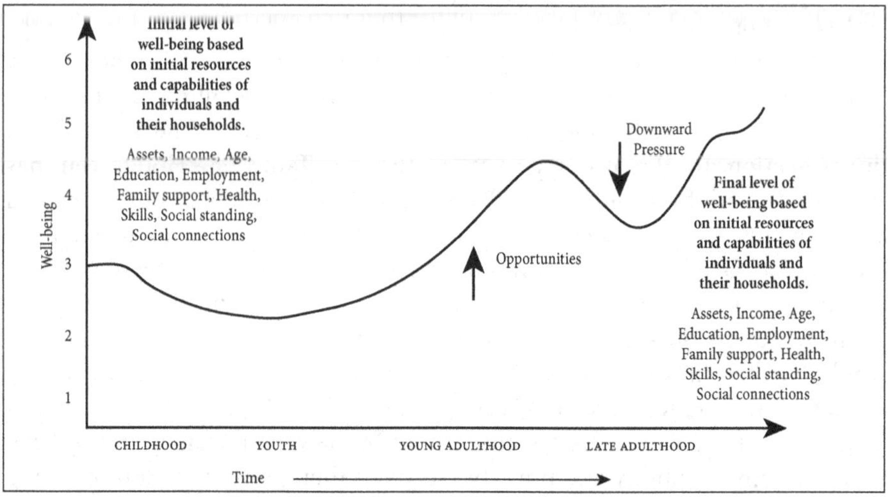

Source: Adapted from Davis (2010)

Findings: exploring poverty escape trends

Poverty status

Focus group discussions ranked the well-being of the twenty-four Household Budget Survey households in 1999 and 2009. As Table 5.1 shows, we found that, in 1999, of the six well-being classifications, 'poor' was the most cited in six out of the eight well-being rankings. In one of these rankings (Wazabanga men), 'very poor' was equally cited; in another (Kayumbe men), 'vulnerable but not poor' was equally cited. In the ranking by men in Nchinga, 'very poor' was the most cited classification; in the ranking by women in Wazabanga, 'very poor' and 'resilient' were equally cited. In 2009, 'poor' was again the most cited classification, in seven of the eight well-being rankings. 'Vulnerable but not poor' was the most cited classification in the ranking by women in Kayumbe.

Table 5.1: Well-being rankings in the study areas in Tanzania, 1999 and 2009

Well-Being Classification	Mtwara								Mwanza								Rukwa							
	Nchinga				Nkangala				Ndite				Wazabanga				Kayumbe				Kalesa			
	W	W	M	M	W	W	M	M	W	W	M	M	W	W	M	M	W	W	M	M	W	W	M	M
	99	09	99	09	99	09	99	09	99	09	99	09	99	09	99	09	99	09	99	09	99	9	99	9
1	-	-	1	1	0	0	-	-	0	0	-	-	0	0	0	0	1	2	1	2	-	-	0	0
2	-	-	11	7	4	7	-	-	3	2	-	-	5	5	5	3	1	2	1	1	-	-	4	3
3	-	-	6	9	13	8	-	-	5	8	-	-	4	8	5	10	9	6	11	13	-	-	13	15
4	-	-	1	2	2	4	-	-	2	0	-	-	3	3	3	2	9	8	6	3	-	-	3	2
5	-	-	0	0	0	0	-	-	0	0	-	-	5	1	2	0	2	5	1	2	-	-	1	1
6	-	-	0	0	0	0	-	-	0	0	-	-	0	0	0	0	0	0	0	1	-	-	0	0
0*	-	-	5	5	5	5	-	-	14	14	-	-	7	7	9	9	2	1	4	2	-	-	3	3
Total			24	24	24	24			24	24			24	24	24	24	24	24	24	24			24	24

Note: * unfamiliar to group or no longer living in cluster

It is obvious, then, that when collapsing the six well-being classifications into 'poor' (classifications 1, 2 and 3) and 'non poor' (classifications 4, 5 and 6) groups, the 'poor' classifications are overwhelmingly the most cited. The only exception was in the well-being ranking by women in Kayumbe, where 'poor' and 'non-poor' classifications were cited equally in 1999, and 'non-poor' classifications were most cited in 2009.

This indicates that the overwhelming majority of households ranked in this study—derived from a representative sample from the 2007 Household Budget Survey—were identified by representatives from their community as being poor.

Poverty dynamics

By asking focus groups to rank Household Budget Survey households in 1999 and 2009 according to the well-being classification system, we were able to analyse socioeconomic mobility and identify:

- *Poverty exiters:* households that moved out of poverty (from well-being classifications 1, 2 or 3 to 4, 5, or 6);
- *Poverty fallers:* households that moved into poverty (from well-being classifications 4, 5 or 6 to 1, 2 or 3);
- *Upward movers:* households that experienced improvement, by one well-being classification or more, in well-being;
- *Downward movers:* households that experienced decline, by one well-being classification or more, in well-being, and downward mobility; and
- *Non-movers:* households that did not experience any change in well-being according to our well-being classification system.

Table 5.2 outlines the findings.

Table 5.2: Socio-economic mobility between 1999 and 2009 in the study areas in Tanzania

	Nchinga		Nkangala		Ndite		Wazabanga		Kayumbe		Kalesa	
	W	M	W	M	W	M	W	M	W	M	W	M
Poverty exiters	-	2	3	-	0	-	2	2	3	3	-	2
Upward movers*	-	8	3	-	1	-	5	7	8	7	-	4
Poverty fallers	-	1	1	-	2	-	6	5	1	4	-	3
Downward movers**	-	3	4	-	2	-	10	7	4	6	-	4
Non-movers	-	8	13	-	7	-	2	1	10	7	-	13
No mobility data	-	5	4	-	14	-	7	9	2	4	-	3

Note: * includes the 'poverty exiters' category, ** includes the 'poverty fallers' category

As Table 5.2 shows, 'non-movers' were the most prominent group identified in the poverty dynamics analysis, most common in six of the eight well-being rankings. Upward movement was the next most common trend, equally prominent as 'non-movers' in the rankings by men in Nchinga and Kayumbe. Upward movement was the most prominent trend in the ranking by men in Wazabanga, alongside downward movement. Downward movement was the most prominent trend in the ranking by women in Wazabanga. The prominence of 'non-movers' reflects that, between 1999 and 2009, there was little socioeconomic mobility across the research sites. These findings are in line with other documented poverty trends in mainland Tanzania, which highlight the stubbornness of poverty despite sustained economic growth nationally.

Upward mobility

While in the minority, there were cases of households experiencing upward mobility and poverty escape. A total of 43 'upward mover' cases were identified through the well-being ranking process (see Table 5.2). In each community, however, the same households were ranked twice – once by the women and once by the men. So while 43 'upward mover' cases were identified in total, this constituted just 32 households (in 11 cases households were identified as 'upward movers' by both women and men focus groups discussion; in the remaining 21 cases only one of the two focus groups identified the household as an 'upward mover'. A total of 17 'poverty exiter' cases were identified. In the case of three households, both the focus group discussions identified the households as 'poverty exiters'. In the remaining 11 cases, only one of the focus groups identified the household as a 'poverty exiter'.

Focus groups were asked to cite reasons for the well-being classifications attached to households, and for upward, downward or no mobility between classifications. Table 5.3 outlines the reasons cited during focus groups discussions for the improved well-being of households that experienced upward mobility between 1999 and 2009. Note that in all focus groups, more than one reason was given for upward mobility.

Table 5.3: Reasons for upward mobility between 1999 and 2009 in the study areas in Tanzania— findings from focus groups discussions

Reason	Frequency in upwardly mobile but still poor households	Frequency in poverty exiting and upwardly mobile non-poor households
Agriculture/fish farming	6	10
Non-farm business	3	4
Farm-related trading/business	3	2
Salaried employment	2	2
Remittances from children	1	0
Renting land for farming	1	1
Stopped drinking alcohol	1	1
Death of ill family member	1	0
Bridewealth	1	0
Accumulation of livestock	0	1
Preserving produce for higher prices	0	1

This analysis highlights the importance of agriculture/fish farming for upward mobility. It also highlights the importance of non-farm business, as well as (albeit to a slightly lesser extent) farm-related trading/business and salaried employment.

Looking at what *combination* of factors contributed to upward mobility uncovers interesting trends. In eight cases where agriculture/fish farming was cited as a reason for improved well-being, it is the sole reason given for upward mobility. But in the remaining eight cases (one from upwardly mobile but still poor households and, critically, seven from poverty exiting and upwardly mobile and non-poor households), it is a combination of agriculture/fish farming *with* another activity—most prominently a non-farm business but also farm-related trading/business and salaried employment—that was cited as the cause of upward mobility between 1999 and 2009.

Life history interviews, and the well-being trajectories that were mapped, offer another source of data for understanding the causes of upward socioeconomic mobility over the life course. The life history interview sample was not representative, so speculating on proportions of upward and downward movers is not valid. What it useful is to seek to understand *why*, in a context where poverty is the overwhelming trend, people experienced upward mobility. What resources, capabilities and events were responsible for improvements in well-being?

Analysis of all life histories in the sample document the reasons cited for each case of upward mobility over the life course.

Table 5.4 tabulates these reasons.

Table 5.4: Reasons for upward mobility in the study areas in Tanzania—findings from life history interviews

Reasons	Total
Agriculture/fish farming	35
Non-farm business	33
Purchase/construction of house	25
Favourable marriage	23
Salaried employment	22
Purchase of land	19
Selling labour	16
Farm-related business/trade	15
Inheritance of land	13
Secondary/post-secondary education/vocational training	9
Accumulation or inheritance of livestock	8
Inheritance of capital	6
Labour migration—domestic	5
Loan (institutional)	5
Remittances from children/children working for household	4
Government project/initiative	4
Loan (family and friends)	3
Borrowed/rented land	2
Improved health of individual or family member	2
Political position	2
Labour migration—international	1
Division of land/assets in family	1
Rental income	1
Support from family	1
Improved roads and access to larger markets	1
Acquisition of a milling machine	1

Agriculture/fish farming again features most prominently. Non-farm business is also important. Physical assets—particularly land and housing—are key (and if 'purchase of land' and 'inheritance of land' were collapsed into one category, acquisition of land would rank higher than it currently does). Salaried employment and favourable marriage (defined as 'marrying up', or marrying someone with a better level of well-being) are also factors that feature in upward mobility stories.

Escaping poverty

In the sample of 106 life history interviews, there were 19 cases where the individual escaped poverty at one or more points in their life. By analysing the life history interviews, we can identify 'tipping' factors, or reasons why the individual managed to move from being 'poor' (classifications 1, 2 or 3) to 'non-poor' (classifications 4, 5 or 6). Table 5.5 outlines the tipping factors articulated in the nineteen cases of poverty exit.

Table 5.5: Factors which enabled people to escape from poverty in the study areas in Tanzania—findings from life history interviews

Tipping factor	Frequency
Purchase of house and/or land	4
Non-farm business success	4
Salaried employment	3
Favourable marriage	3
Loan + non-farm business expansion	1
Salaried employment + non-farm business success	1
Agriculture + non-farm business success	1
Agriculture + farm-related business	1
Agriculture	1
Total	19

This analysis highlights the criticality of physical assets (land and/or house), non-farm business, salaried employment and favourable marriage to poverty exit. It also indicates that agriculture features only when it is *linked with* something. This offers a contrast to the upward mobility analysis contained in Table 5.4, which looks at *all* cases of upward mobility (even if a person remained poor) and suggests that agriculture on its own is not the factor that moves an individual, or a household, out of poverty in these research sites. The accumulation of physical assets and the rural non-farm economy were the factors critical to moving people out of poverty.

Escaping vulnerability

Households in the 'vulnerable but not poor' classification were considered vulnerable to moving back into poverty as a result of idiosyncratic and covariant shocks. So what did the life histories reveal about what was needed to move not only beyond poverty but also *beyond vulnerability?* Looking across the life histories, there were fifteen cases where an individual was 'resilient' or 'rich' at one or more points in their life. Commonalities, in terms of the capabilities and resources these individuals had at these points in their life, can be identified. We see there is much *value in being born non-*

poor. Ten of the fifteen individuals that were 'resilient' or 'rich' at one point in their life were born into non-poor households. In three cases, the only time they were 'resilient' or 'rich' was during childhood. A shock during childhood or youth led to a significant well-being decline and they did not recover to previous levels of well-being at any point in their life. *Multiple sources of income* were also critical to movement beyond vulnerability (commonly combining agriculture with salaried employment and/or non-farm business), and these individuals *owned a number of valuable physical assets* (e.g. multiple houses, large landholdings, furniture, electronics, bicycles and livestock).

Rural and urban trends

In the 2007 Household Budget Survey, Nchinga, Ndite and Kayumbe were classified as rural clusters and Nkangala, Wazabanga and Kalesa as urban clusters. As we have seen, poverty in both rural and urban areas (excluding Dar es Salaam) had been stubborn over the past decade—neither rural nor urban areas had experienced a significant change in poverty levels since 1991/92. Our research concludes relatively similarly in terms of socioeconomic mobility. When aggregating well-being ranking results from the rural and urban clusters, we found 'non-movers' to be the most common trend. Comparing the poverty status results of rural and urban areas yields interesting results, however. In both rural and urban clusters, in 1999 and 2009 'poor' was the most common classification for households. For rural clusters, however, in both 1999 and 2009 'vulnerable but not poor' was the next most common classification. For urban clusters, 'very poor' was the next most common classification. This challenges Household Budget Survey findings which highlight higher levels of poverty in rural areas.

Upward mobility trends identified in the life history interviews do indicate some differences between the rural and urban sites, however. In rural areas, agriculture and fish farming is the most common cause of upward mobility, followed by non-farm business, land purchase, house purchase or construction and favourable marriage. Perhaps unsurprisingly, in urban areas, non-farm business was the most commonly cited reason for upward mobility. This was followed by salaried employment; agriculture and fish farming; and the purchase or construction of a house.

Intergenerational and age trends

We know that wealth and assets (or lack thereof) are often transferred from one generation to the next.[15] On the whole, evidence from this study supports this claim: individuals born into poor households tended to remain poor, and individuals born into non-poor households tended to remain non-poor. In the case of 'poverty exiters', however, no significant intergenerational trends can be identified by looking at the well-being of the individual at birth and in early childhood (as a proxy for the well-being of his or her parents at that point in time). In some cases, individuals who moved out of poverty at one or more points in their life were born into poor households. In others, they were born into non-poor households. This does not mean that more in-depth analysis would not uncover trends among this group (e.g. when it comes to asset transfer at critical points in the life course, such as marriage). Quite simply (and probably because of the small sample size), it just means that, in our sample, 'poverty exiters' were born into households with differing levels of well-being.

A trend can be identified when it comes to age, however: in the vast majority of cases, individuals escaped poverty in their twenties or thirties. This was most often the point in the life course when events, resources and capabilities supported upward mobility. This suggests it is in this age bracket where it is most likely that people will move out of poverty and, potentially, where policy interventions could be most effective. It also suggests that moving out of poverty in late adulthood or old age may be more difficult.

Findings: exploring poverty escape narratives

Exploring the life history narratives of those who experienced improved well-being or moved out of poverty illuminates this aggregated analysis and illustrates the combinations of factors that drove upward mobility and poverty escape.

Agriculture and asset accumulation

Analysis of life history interviews revealed that agriculture on its own was not cited as a factor that supported movement out of poverty. It was physical assets, non-farm business, salaried employment and favourable marriage that typically 'tipped' people out of poverty. But closer analysis of life history interviews shows that agriculture is a key part of the upward mobility story—in some cases, *because of agriculture*, households were able to accumulate the assets, businesses and employment that moved them out of poverty and, in some instances, gave them the security to withstand shocks.

The life history of Alex Nanzala, a forty-six-year-old farmer from Kayumbe, illustrates how he improved the well-being of his household through the gradual acquisition of physical assets: he moved from owning very little, to now owning 100 acres, 8 cattle, 2 ox-ploughs, a bike and 2 radios. He accumulated these assets not through inheritance, loans or even dowry, but through sustained agricultural success.

After marriage, Alex started farming on 0.5 acres of land. He cultivated onions, tomatoes, maize and beans and through savings he bought a cow and a donkey. He moved to Kayumbe in 1992 to 'experience his own life', where he sold the cow and donkey and bought 10 acres of land. Land was cheap then—he noted it is much more expensive now because of population growth, as well as the migration of Sukuma pastoralists to the area. He was farming maize and groundnuts and every season after harvesting he bought a cow. He was getting around 50 bags using the hand hoe, but in 1996 started farming with an ox-plough and was able to double his yield to 100 bags of maize per harvest. Now, in a good season, he can get 150–200 bags of maize, using two ox-ploughs. He sells maize as he needs to—mainly when he needs money to pay costs associated with sending two of his children to secondary school—but he tries to keep stock to sell when he will fetch good prices. A key factor in his agricultural success is that he has not had to buy fertilizer. He considers it too expensive, at around TZS 35,000 or TZS 50,000 per bag, and instead uses manure from cows (note that few other farmers in Kayumbe do this). While he acknowledged it was hard work to transport the manure, he was convinced it was worth it, and his hard work had made him the best farmer in the village. Figure 5.2 shows his life history trajectory.

Figure 5.2: Life history trajectory of Alex Nanzala, Kayumbe

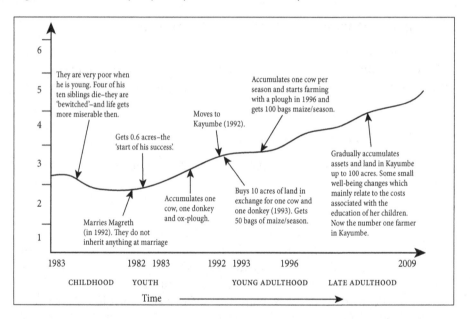

The life history of Fatuma Ntanda, aged forty-five from Nchinga, also sheds light on how agriculture can support the accumulation of physical assets, which in turn helps people move out of poverty. It also highlights how women's access to land can support upward mobility and economic empowerment. Fatuma was born into a 'vulnerable but not poor' household in 1964. She was married when she was around sixteen years old, and gave birth to her first child. In 1990, her husband divorced her because she had not conceived a second child. Her well-being fell drastically. Following the divorce, her grandmother gave her 2 acres of land, and she started farming cashew nuts. She worked hard and in 2001 was able to build a house of her own. She continued to farm—maize and rice as well as cashew nuts—and in 2007 was able to buy another house. At this point she moved out of poverty and back into the 'vulnerable but not poor category'. She felt her life was better since the divorce—she was able to work hard and buy things she needed, unlike when she was married and had to seek consent from her husband. She had benefited from a credit scheme called the Credit Scheme for Income Generating Activities. She used credit to buy sulphur to spray her cashew nut trees.

Combining agriculture and non-farm activities

Analysis of both the well-being rankings and the life history interviews reveals that non-farm livelihoods and opportunities are key drivers of poverty escape. In many cases, these activities were found to be not an exception but a complement to agriculture. As Kessy notes, in rural contexts in Tanzania, households use non-farm enterprises as a way of tapping the complementarities between the agricultural cycle and household (including non-farm) enterprises.[16] There is an interdependence between capital sources from the sales of agricultural produce and capital that comes from non-farm enterprises (and vice versa).

The story of Hilari Ndasi, a forty-one-year-old man from Wazabanga, demonstrates how the combination of agriculture and non-farm business supports poverty escape. Hilari's well-being started to improve after he left the family home as a young man. He was producing cotton, and with the profits he built a house, bought a bicycle and paid bride price to marry his wife. Once married, he continued with cotton production, and in 2005, with capital he had saved (TSZ 1,200,000), he started a shop in Wazabanga village, where he sold petrol, diesel and engine oil. This business really helped improve their well-being, and they moved into the 'vulnerable but not poor' category within the community. He had good relationships with richer households and was able to borrow cash at no interest. He now found himself in a position where he could lend cash to friends and other traders at no interest. He collaborated with friends and other traders to hire lorries to transport goods from Magu to the larger market at Wazabanga. He offered casual labour work on his farms to poor people and could afford to pay for pesticides and fertiliser in cash. He noted that the costs of producing cotton were going up while its price was declining. He was able to cope with these price changes because of his petroleum business, which remained successful and profitable.

The life history of Zaituni Kawale, a thirty-eight-year-old woman from Nkangala, also illustrates how diversified livelihoods support upward mobility. At marriage, Zaituni and her husband Hussein owned nothing but a goat. However, they had strong social networks, which gave them access to productive activities: Zaituni had access to her mother's farm, and Hussein had access to income-generating activities such as casual labour and selling clothes through his stepfather. Over the past twenty years, they have managed to move from being 'poor' to being 'resilient'. One reason for this is that Hussein encouraged his wife to keep working: while she is now 'resilient', she continues to sell samosas and textiles, work on their farm and even do some casual labouring (which many women poorer than her would be too proud to do). In addition, her husband has good entrepreneurial skills and has been able to move between different livelihoods: as markets fail in one, he has moved to another.

For example, from one goat he bred a herd, which they sold to get capital to open a second-hand clothing business. The profits from the business were used to buy a house and a large plot. He took a loan from his stepfather, repaid in instalments over five years, which enabled him to buy a cashew farm and later to get a loan from a private company, which enabled him to buy a shop and motorbike. When profits failed in his clothing business (as the price of cashews fell, destroying the disposable income of local farmers), Hussein decided to invest in their hitherto unproductive cashew farm. They spent three solid months making it productive and were rewarded with a bumper harvest, which he sold and used to repay a private loan and purchase a small cassava/maize farm. More recently, Hussein began trading textiles and electronics in Mozambique, where he has relatives. He uses a tractor or a trailer to transport his exports. He also imports low-priced goods from Mozambique that are very expensive in Newala, such as sugar, soap, oil and clothing. He also buys US dollars in Mozambique and sells them in Newala town. The experience and decisions of Zaituni and Hussein demonstrate how agriculture and non-farm business can be used in a complementary way to maintain and improve well-being.

Jonas Wamyenda, a thirty-eight-year-old man from Kayumbe, believes non-farm business has been central to the improved well-being of his family. When Jonas was a child, his father was an assistant supervisor for the construction of the Catholic mission church in Makazi (near Kayumbe). He went to school but finished in Standard 7, as he failed the secondary school entrance examination. When he left school, he started gardening sugar cane, carrots and onions with a hand hoe, using skills he had learnt from agricultural education at school. His business was profitable. After a while, he started learning how to fix radios, and slowed down his farming business to do more in electronics. He was earning enough to dress and eat well and travel to bigger towns when he needed to, and the work was easier than gardening with a hand hoe. After getting some money, in 1989 he moved to Sumbawanga, a larger town in Rukwa, and started working in an auto workshop. He was not paid—he actually paid the mechanic to train him, using savings to pay for the apprenticeship. If he needed more money, his father would sell one of his pigs. After two years he left. He married in 1990. He did some work as a casual labourer on the construction of the health clinic in Kayumbe, and was farming 2 acres of land that his father had given to him. He was also dealing in bicycles and trading sugar. He did this up to 1998. During this time, things were difficult: he had started a family and they were not able to save. In 1998, the family migrated to Mbala, Zambia. In Mbala, he continued trading sugar. He also worked in a garage, using the mechanic skills that he had acquired. Life was good there—he was working hard and the pay was enough to ensure the family was eating three meals a day. He was saving money and also exchanging money at the border to make a profit. They returned to Makazi in 2005, as his father retired and called for him. In Makazi, he established a motorcycle shop. He is renting a place for the shop and the business is profitable. He does not have to pay any taxes because he is not selling goods—he is just selling his labour to fix motorcycles. He is optimistic about what the future holds for his business because in Makazi more people, such as agricultural extension officers and policemen, are acquiring motorbikes. His business brings in between TZS 5,000 and 10,000 per day—he takes home TZS 5,000, and if he makes more he pays his helper and buys some spare parts.

Salaried employment and education

Salaried employment was identified as a key contributor to upward mobility and poverty escape. In many cases, post-primary education was a prerequisite for the salaried employment people attained. The life history interviews indicated that post-primary education was highly valued, primarily because this level of education may lead to a salaried job.

Khali Makumburi is forty-eight years old and lives in Nkangala. His life history shows how formal education can help improve well-being and help a person move out of poverty. It also highlights a trend observed across a number of life histories—education attainment is in many cases an intergenerational phenomenon. During Khali's childhood, his father was a primary school teacher and a farmer, and his mother sometimes sold local brew for additional income. They were a 'poor' household. He finished his primary education in 1977 and became independent. These times were hard. His first business was buying and reselling second-hand clothes from missioners in the village; while the income was enough to survive, it was not enough to acquire assets. He started agricultural college and in 1985, after graduation, was employed in Ruvuma region. Three years later, he went to study for a diploma and was posted to Newala district in Mtwara region as the agricultural extension officer. At this time, his salary was low and he had to send funds home to his father, who was getting old and depended on him. He married in 1992 and his life gradually improved. He was able to buy some assets—a mattress, a radio and a bicycle. He continued with his salaried work and in 2004 he was promoted. He was also selected as the secretary for the food security committee in the district. In 2009, he was selected to be a coordinator for the WISE organisation project and appointed coordinator of a new cassava value chains initiative in the district. These opportunities led to a gradual improvement in his well-being, and the activities that were 'additional' to his job helped him acquire assets such as a television, a music system and a satellite dish, as well as care for a number of dependants (e.g. his sister died and he had to cover the schooling and upkeep expenses for his three nephews). Overall, his education was critical to the upward mobility of his family.

The life history of Dafrosa Liku, a fifty-two-year-old woman from Wazabanga, also highlights how formal education and salaried employment can support poverty exit. Dafrosa was born into a 'poor' family and married when she was eighteen years old. Around this time, she was elected a Tanzanian African National Union branch secretary and started applying for other employment and professional training opportunities. Eventually, in 1977, she was employed as a trainee assistant nurse at a government referral hospital in Mwanza. In 1983 and 1984, she pursued other formal training and became a qualified nurse. This employment proved to be critical in helping her maintain her level of well-being when she left her husband in 1980—he was drinking too much alcohol and having affairs with other women. She remarried in 1982 and experienced an improvement in well-being because her new husband was better-off. Her salaried employment enabled her to access loans, which helped her acquire assets. For example, in 2007, she took a loan of TZS 900,000 from the National Microfinance Bank and used it to start building a fourth house. She felt this access to credit had enabled her to improve her life, and one of the reasons she was successfully awarded loans was because her employer endorsed her loan applications.

The life histories of Faraji Namande and Ashura Mzee, a thirty-five-year-old married couple from Nchinga, illustrate how salaried employment—as well as agriculture and non-farm business—can help move people out of poverty. Faraji and Ashura only recently moved into the 'vulnerable but not poor' category. The tipping point for them was that Ashura was employed as a volunteer (but salaried) teacher at Nchinga Primary School.

Faraji had previously moved out of poverty—from 1996 to 2000 he was a clerk at Nchinga Primary Cooperative Society, where he bought cashews on behalf of the society. With his income, he bought a bicycle, started a kiosk and paid bride price. This moved him into the 'vulnerable but not poor' category. But in 2002, after a poor season, his kiosk business collapsed and his well-being declined. In 2004, he married Ashura (his first marriage had ended) and they worked together improving their crops and, as a result, their well-being. In 2005, they built a bigger house with three rooms. A little later, he bought a bicycle. In 2007, Ashura started her job at Nchinga Primary School. She qualified for this job because she completed Form 4 at secondary school. As a volunteer teacher, her wages were variable and much less than those of the qualified teacher. However, they were more than they were earning through agriculture. She has been applying to go to teachers' college, so she can attain a certificate in education, as this would result in her being employed on permanent and pensionable terms, but she not yet had any success.

The life histories also highlight how much people value post-primary education for their children—even if they have not been given educational opportunities themselves. Many people expressed their feelings that the world was changing, and that non-agricultural employment would lead to a better life for their children. For example, Hilari Ndasi left school when he was eleven years old. His parents did not go to school at all. Yet he had prioritised education for his children: all of his seven school-age children were in school, and the eldest had moved on to secondary school, where he was in Form 4. In his words, 'What young people should do to improve their life is educate themselves, so that they can use the education for self-employment or salaried employment.'

Alex Nanzala and Magreth Machikira (a married couple from Kayumbe) felt similarly. They both left school once finishing primary level and, as discussed above, had moved out of poverty through hard work in agriculture and asset accumulation. They had decided to prioritise the education of their children: one child had been to teachers' college and was now a primary school teacher, one child was in Form 4 at secondary school and one child was in Form 3 at secondary school. Magreth noted that the annual cost per student for secondary school was TZS 100 000 but she felt it was a worthwhile investment: 'I hope by sending my children to secondary school they will not have to be farmers and have the same life we had … they may be able to have a better type of employment.'

Favourable marriage

Favourable marriage was identified as a tipping point in some cases of poverty escape. Typically, it involves a woman 'marrying up'–marrying a man with a better level of well-being. For example, Joyce Magembe from Wazabanga considered her marriage the reason she had moved out of poverty. Joyce had enjoyed a happy childhood, but when she was fourteen years old her mother passed away. After this, her father remarried and she had a harder life. After she finished primary school, she married. Her husband—who was much better-off than her—paid a brideprice of 10 cows and 5 goats, plus TZS 200,000 and he was given 2 acres of land by his parents at marriage. They worked hard at farming cotton and food crops, and were eventually able to establish a shop.

Mwanaidi Halidi, aged fifty two from Nchinga, also considered a favourable marriage a key factor in her move out of poverty. She was first married when she was thirteen years old, and during this marriage she was 'poor'. In 1980, her and her husband divorced—he was drinking and he did not buy her new clothes when she bore a third child. She recounted, 'I was so angry that I left him because that was a sign that he was tired of me.' She married again in 1982, and experienced a vast improvement in her well-being. Her new husband was much better-off, and they worked together growing cashew nuts, enjoying great agricultural success and food security to a point where she was 'resilient'.

Conclusion and policy implications

This chapter has examined qualitative data from six research sites in mainland Tanzania to understand why and how people experience upward mobility and move out of poverty. While our evidence—and the evidence of others—suggest that many people are stuck in poverty in Tanzania, there are cases of households experiencing upward socioeconomic mobility in recent decades. There are also cases (though fewer) of households which have managed to escape poverty.

What can we learn from these cases of success? We learn that agriculture is a key factor in supporting upward mobility in mainland Tanzania. This is unsurprising, given that agriculture is the primary livelihood for most Tanzanians. But, critically, we find it is non-farm businesses, the accumulation of physical assets (such as land and housing), salaried employment and favourable marriage—some of which agriculture plays a role in supporting—which are most effective at moving people out of poverty. When it comes to moving beyond vulnerability, these findings hold. Those who manage to move beyond vulnerability often have multiple sources of income and own a number of valuable physical assets.

What are the broad policy implications of this? What could be done to support more households to escape poverty?

Agricultural development should remain a priority: The majority of poor people in Tanzania are farmers, and supporting agricultural growth—as articulated in Tanzania's Kilimo Kwanza strategy—should remain a priority. As Mashindano et al. suggest, there is an urgent need to develop and implement effective agriculture programmes, which support and transform smallholder agriculture and increase agricultural growth.[17] But, as Shepherd highlights, output markets are critical and improvements here could potentially have a bigger impact.[18] Local purchase and storage schemes, for example, would help moderate seasonable fluctuations, as well as support local food security by reducing food price inflation.

Rural industrialisation requires greater attention: Rural industrialisation would support business and employment growth through local, domestic and foreign investment. This requires infrastructure investment, particularly in roads, transport and energy (low levels of electrification are a significant constraint for businesses in rural Tanzania). This is in line with the recommendations of Ellis, who has argued that promoting non-farm employment and sustainable urban growth is a sounder option than promoting a 'green revolution' in the liberalised agricultural market context of sub-Saharan Africa.[19]

Promote asset accumulation: Asset accumulation—particularly the accumulation of land—is central to the poverty escape story in rural Tanzania. Policy needs to support this accumulation processes, by ensuring people can access land as well as enabling equitable distribution. The interests of the poor need to be protected. The interests of women also need high consideration: life histories featured in this volume chapter highlight how land access and ownership can support women's upward mobility. As da Corta and Magongo highlight, women remain significantly disadvantaged when it comes to land access and ownership, as a result of entrenched customary law practices and cultural norms around asset ownership.[20] While women have rights under the 1999 Land Policy, awareness among women, the judiciary and local leaders remains low.

Support business development: Policies need to facilitate and support, rather than impede, entrepreneurship and business development needs. Programmes that enhance the marketing and business skills of micro-entrepreneurs should be encouraged.

Promote access to credit: Loans—from family or social networks or through institutions such as credit societies and banks—play a role in enabling people to enhance productivity, both in agriculture and non-farm business. But taking a loan was viewed by many as a source of significant risk, and as a result they were reluctant to borrow. Improving financial literacy and reducing the risk associated with loans may increase demand for credit and support agricultural and business expansion. Shepherd suggests that adding a small premium to insure against defaulting may be one way to address this, if the costs can be spread widely enough.[21]

Support secondary and vocational education: Post-primary education is considered by many as the key to a salaried job – which as our evidence suggests can be a route out of poverty. As life histories featured in this chapter show, upwardly mobile families are prioritizing the post-primary education of their children – and hope that their children won't have to struggle as farmers. But this is an unattainable option for most poor households. Finding ways to increase access to secondary and vocational education – through bursaries, lowered fees and more schools (which would lower transport and accommodation costs) would in the short term increase access to post-primary education.

Protect assets against shocks: Central to upward mobility is *acquiring assets*. But, as Kessy and Tarmo note, *protecting assets* against shocks is also critical—and failure to do so can result in fast and detrimental downward mobility.[22] Shepherd flags social transfers as a policy option to help people to smooth consumption during shocks, as well as to promote livelihood development by enabling people to preserve assets and take investment risks.[23] Some pilot programmes are in operation, and a draft National Social Protection Framework was established in 2010.

Resources to respond to these broad recommendations are of course limited, and institutional constraints hamper the effectiveness of existing policies in these areas. But our research does—through systematic analysis of our qualitative dataset—point to factors that support upward mobility and poverty escape. Corresponding policy areas can and should continue to be identified, explored and acted on.

---

1   United Republic of Tanzania (2000)

2   United Republic of Tanzania (2005)

3   K. Kayunze et al. (2010)

4   Ministry of Finance and Economic Affairs (2009), p. 4. GDP growth was 4.9 per cent in
    2000, 6.0 per cent in 2001, 7.2 per cent in 2002, 6.9 per cent in 2003, 7.8 per cent in 2004,
    7.4 per cent in 2005, 6.7 per cent in 2006, 7.1 per cent in 2007 and 7.4 per cent in 2008

5   Ministry of Finance and Economic Affairs (2009), p. 8

6   A.F. Mkenda et al. (2010), p. 12

7   National Bureau of Statistics (2008a)

8   J. de Weerdt (2010)

9   Research by K. Beegle et al. (2008) supports this: they find that moving out of agriculture is
    associated with higher levels of consumption

10 Luvanda (2011)

11 J. Hoogeveen (2008)

12 A.F. Mkenda et al. (2010), p. 47

13 P. Davis (2010), p. 9

14 P. Davis (2010), p. 10

15 K. Bird (2007)

16 F. Kessy (2010), p. 47

17 O. Mashindano et al. (2010)

18 A. Shepherd (2011b)

19 F. Ellis (2010)

20 L. da Corta and J. Magongo (2010)

21 A. Shepherd et al (2011a)

22 F. Kessy and S.V. Tarmo (2010)

23 A. Shepherd et al (2011a)

Chapter 6

Hidden Hunger in Rural Tanzania—What Can Qualitative Research Tell Us About What To Do About Chronic Food Insecurity?

Andrew Shepherd, Kim Kayunze, Simon Vendelin Tarmo, Emily Darko, Alice Evans and Lucia da Corta

Introduction

Using a qualitative dataset comprising focus group discussions, more than a hundred life histories and key informant interviews from six widely dispersed rural communities in Tanzania, this chapter investigates the nature of hunger, its causes and its consequences, along with people's preventative strategies, before drawing policy implications for the Tanzanian government.

The interviewees were a diverse group, from three regions, with an average age of forty-six years in a range between thirteen and eighty-two. Sixty-nine were women and seventy-eight were men. Farming was the primary occupation for most people, but many were also or exclusively labourers, some had migrated and others had gone into trade or other non-farm occupations. A few had salaried jobs.

A qualitative analysis provides a useful counterpoint to recent more statistically based publications on food security and malnutrition. Quantitative research, including the government report on 'Trends in Food Security in Mainland Tanzania'[1] and the analysis in 'Childhood Poverty in Tanzania: Deprivations and Disparities in Child Well-being'[2] show broad trends in hunger. Average food security (measured by dietary energy consumption) is demonstrated to have improved between 2001 and 2007, but this change largely reflects improvements on the part of urban, not rural, populations. Improved averages also mask worsening household consumption and hunger in the lowest quintile. A quarter of the population remains food deprived.

There are major persistent food security and malnutrition problems in Tanzania, especially for rural households. Two in five rural children and more than one in five urban children were stunted mid-decade (stunting indicates long-term malnutrition) and one in five overall was underweight (a composite indicator of long- and short-term malnutrition).[3] Child malnutrition depends partly on food security, but also on maternal education, child health and caring practices, which vary regionally. This means that child malnutrition is more prevalent across the income/consumption distribution than food insecurity, especially across quintiles 1–4 in rural areas. Here it is probably a strong deficit in maternal education which remains low by comparison with urban areas, where increasing incomes are correlated with increasing maternal education.[4]

The three regions studied as part of our qualitative research have made different progress overall in reducing chronic hunger. The situation in Rukwa worsened between 1996 and 2004, whereas Mwanza and Mtwara showed no or little improvement. Only five of the fourteen regions in Tanzania showed strong progress. Areas of cereal surplus in the south and west are also high malnutrition regions and have shown little improvement.

Experiencing hunger: trying to achieve two meals a day

Qualitative findings from focus group discussions in the six research sites produced a varied picture of experiences of hunger. In all cases, individuals and households in the poorest two categories ('destitute' and 'very poor') were likely to have difficulty ensuring sufficient food intake from day to day. Destitute people[5] might have one meal a day—boiled, with no salt or oil. Even the very poor and sometimes poor households only boil their food. A participant of the women's focus group in Nkangala said 'food doesn't taste good'.

Sometimes, workers have to do with only one meal a day. Jonas Wamyenda from Kayumbe village[6] worked in Sumbawanga until 1990. When he felt he had acquired enough skills he returned to Kayumbe. His father was still working in Kayumbe at the district office. He secured a job as a labourer for the district and helped to build the health clinic. While doing this work, he met his future wife, who was working fetching water for the construction workers. While he was doing this work, he had only one meal per day. They were working hard and so there was less time to eat, and he was trying to save money.

The more normal pattern, though, is to have two meals a day, and richer people often manage three. Two meals a day does not necessarily mean hunger, if the meals are nutritious. There is a big difference between meals which include proteins and vegetables as well as staples, and those which consist of staples only. In this sense, the number of meals a day (the question asked in the Household Budget Survey) may be less important than the quality of the meal.[7] In our interviews, two meals a day seemed to be the norm, although three would be preferred. These two meals come in many different forms, and clearly social practices mix with availability and affordability in deciding what people eat:

'This is a typical village life that breakfast is either not important or it comes after farm work' (Joyce Magembe, Wazabanga)

'*Ugali* and vegetables or *dagaa* for lunch and the same for dinner during hunger season. It is only when we have harvested that we enjoy the morning porridge' (Violet Limbu, Wazabanga)

'We take two meals as before, the meals consist of lunch (*ugali* with greens) and dinner (cassava with fish). We could have three meals but during that time we did not know about breakfast' (Abdul Mnali, Nchinga)

Cooking a meal with minimal food and cooking utensils can be very time and energy consuming (all ingredients prepared from scratch, fires to build up, water collected) and, given the heat at midday, there is drudgery involved in preparing several meals a day. What is remarkable in many accounts is the absence of protein, especially fish, despite the proximity of all communities studied to lakes. Either people cannot afford fish or it is not available, or a combination of the two. Only sardines are mentioned. This means that people have to eat more staples to make up for a lack of protein.

Hunger has a seasonal pattern, following the rhythms of harvest, seasonal availability and food price rises, as more and more partly self-provisioning people come on to the market. Lugodagula, aged thirty seven from Wazabanga village, remembers that, during childhood, he at only two meals a day rather than the normal three. He described how it is very painful, especially when you are hungry and you know there is no way you can get food: 'It is better that you are assured of eating and for your own reasons you don't than not having it at all and even when you are hungry there is nothing to put in the mouth.' He explained further that, soon after harvest, they enjoyed three meals a day, but some months later they had to reduce this and usually they would skip the morning porridge.

When food is short, the number of meals eaten a day is reduced, as is the quality of the meals consumed, until 'you just pass a day without eating', as Kurthumu Mbonde (fifty-four-year-old female from Nkangala village) said of her childhood, when she was reliant on her grandmother. Farmers either do well or badly out of the highs and lows of seasonal prices. Those who can store food till prices are high do well; those who have to buy when prices are high do badly. Being able to produce food for the year and sell some, or to market cash crops, remains a very important indicator of household well-being, as recognised in the well-being rankings. Poverty is defined largely in terms of food security. Meanwhile, it is noteworthy that people who are doing better—categories 4–6 (the 'vulnerable but not poor', 'resilient' and 'rich')—are doing so partly off the misery of the 'food poor' categories 1 and 2 ('destitute' and 'very poor'). Table 6.1 presents more information about food intake among people in the six well-being categories.

Table 6.1: Meals/nutrition by poverty well-being level in the study areas in Tanzania—findings from focus group discussions

	Nkangala women	Nchinga women	Nchinga men	Kayumbe women	Kayumbe men	Wazabanga women	Wazabanga men	Kalesa women	Kalesa men	Ndite women
Destitute	Depend on others for basic needs	1 meal/day Not sure of next meal Depend on others for food Casual labour paid in kind	Never produce enough food Harvest in April, nothing to eat by August No regular eating habit 1 meal/day or less	Sometimes 2/3 meals/ day sometimes none Get food from other people offering free food or by begging	1 meal/day but through begging	Get at most 1 meal/day Most are chronically ill			Beg for food Normally eat 1 meal/ day of poor quality Sometimes go to bed hungry	Live by begging Not sure of having a meal
Very poor	1 meal/day Other meals not assured Reliance on casual labour	1 meal/day Not enough food for whole year	1 meal/day Sometimes don't eat at all Many feed from small harvest	1/2 meals/day	1 meal/day During hardship eat maize stem or local brew	1 meal/day	Suffer during hunger and when there is less or no demand for their labour		Don't beg for food Normally eat 1 meal/ day	Dependent on casual wage labour
Poor	Have to sell assets in a crisis Production low owing to low levels of input	1 meal/day Not enough food to sustain them throughout year Get support from relatives to get food	Assured of meals – 2/day (porridge; ugali with green vegetables or sardines) Sometimes have late breakfast which acts as lunch	1/2 meals/day (ugali with salt or mlenda) May harvest green maize (before maturity)	1 meal/day which they are assured of	2 meals/day Husbands drink May not cultivate whole farm Casual labour			2 meals/day Don't own cups since never take tea at home	2 meals/day Limited productive assets: have to sell them in a crisis

	Nkangala women	Nchinga women	Nchinga men	Kayumbe women	Kayumbe men	Wazabanga women	Wazabanga men	Kalesa women	Kalesa men	Ndite women
Vulnerable	Usually 3 meals/day (morning: tea with remains of rice or cookies; lunch: ugali with fish/ beef; dinner: rice with fish or beef)	2/3 meals/day	Eat meat 2 times a week during agricultural season, chickens not eaten—kept for income generation Can afford 2/3 meals/day Harvested food generally lasts whole year	2 meals/day (ugali or potatoes)	2/3 meals/day	3 meals/day	3 full meals a day Drink either porridge or tea in morning and have a full lunch that includes ugali or mahindi Can alternate in the evening by eating rice with meat or fish		Normally 3 meals/ day: breakfast, lunch, dinner	Have productive assets to generate food and income to last the year
Resilient	3 + meals/day	3 meals/day throughout the year Rice twice a week	Assured of 3 meals/day Also eat industrially made foods, milk, fruits, meat	3/4 meals/day (tea/soup in morning, lunch, supper)	Assured of eating today and tomorrow	At least 3 meals/day			More than 3 meals/ day of good quality and quantity Drink various types of drinks, beer, milk, soft drinks Sometimes don't eat even if they are given food	Many assets, not vulnerable to shocks
Rich	Eat very well	3 meals/day throughout the year Rice twice a week	Nothing mentioned	Can 'have as they want, even 5–10 meals per day' (someone who has breakfast is a rich person or has good knowledge about diet)		Eat delicious food, soft drinks and alcoholic drinks at any time			Eat more or less like the resilient	

Causes of hunger

There is no one, or dominant, cause of episodes and experience of hunger. Focus group participants identified four sets of factors leading to food insecurity: (1) covariant shocks (weather, disease); (2) effects of policies (villagisation and food security policies, including on maize and exports); (3) structural economic imbalances (e.g. wage/price relationships); and (4) more idiosyncratic but still widespread factors. The area-specific factors are detailed in Table 6.2.

Table 6.2: Food insecurity histories in the study areas in Tanzania—findings from focus group discussions

Region	Cluster	Event/factor(s)	Consequences/notes
Mwanza	Ndite	Villagisation (1974)	Impoverishment, hunger
		Livestock disease	(1983/4)
		Crop export bans	Mass loss of livestock
	Wazabanga	Drought 1948–50	Famine
		Heavy rain 1961/2	Impoverishment
		Villagisation (1974)	Unpredictable farming seasons
		Climate change since 2000	
Mtwara	Nkangala	Recent inflation	Impoverishment
		Cashew prices and wages not keeping up	Transfer of land to rich
		Land price inflation	
	Nchinga	Youth disconnected from farming	Unwilling/unable to feed themselves/contribute to household food supplies
Rukwa	Kayumbe	Maize market monopolised by government and not functioning well	No easy sale of main crop—hard to get cash when needed
	Kalesa	Low wages	Prevents work
		Caring for chronically ill	Loss of general security
		Gender conflicts leading to family disruption	

Together with covariant shocks which may trigger a descent into food insecurity, many smallholders despaired about perennial limitations to their agricultural productivity, which impede their escape from food insecurity. These include poor land quality; the unaffordable nature of improved agricultural inputs such as fertiliser, pesticides, herbicides, improved seeds and mechanisation; endemic livestock and human diseases; and adverse agro-climatic conditions. Price and market uncertainty also mean that the prices producers receive for commodities may be less than the costs incurred in production.

The shocks are both idiosyncratic and covariate, the latter often on a small scale—floods knocking out a small irrigation scheme, for example. We tend to think of covariate shocks as being big droughts or floods which affect large areas. But smaller-scale events like the above can also have devastating effects, particularly as very few smallholders have access to insurance against such shocks. Crop failure means a loss of time and capital spent on agricultural production. Robert Kashinje (thirty four years old from Wazabanga village) invested TZS 50,000 in agriculture using the capital gained from trade. He intended to multiply this investment so that he could obtain even more capital for trading. He used all the money to grow rice on 1 acre and hoped to harvest 20 bags. However, he managed to harvest only 3 bags.

Lack of access to improved agricultural inputs

Agriculture is clearly a risky business, with many and varied sources of risk. A major problem widely identified by our informants was the unaffordability of important agricultural inputs, such as fertiliser. These are key to resilience and upward mobility, but focus group participants in Kayumbe revealed that few people were using them owing to their high cost. In this particular, government-subsidised fertilisers usually come late and are not sufficient for everyone.

Life histories reflect a broad trend that only those able to invest in improved inputs have been able to participate in modest agricultural growth. 'The problem is getting capital' explained Mwanaidi, a fifty-two-year-old woman living in Nchinga village. 'If I got it I could trade cashew nuts, increase the capital and start another business. Otherwise I may die poor.' Mwanaidi's livelihood hinged on being able to afford sulphur to spray on her cashew nut trees so that they could produce more cashew nuts. She wished the government would make sulphur more affordable. Bintimusa (a thirty-nine-year-old single mother living in Nkangala village) similarly identified access to sulphur spray as the only way in which she could move her family out of poverty. Profits from high cashew yields might then be saved and used as a retirement fund, as planned by Haruna (a sixty-five-year-old farmer living in Nchinga, who eats two meals a day).

Rashidi (a fifty-two-year-old living in Nchinga village) similarly attributes his poor harvest, financial constraints and continued downward mobility to his inability to afford fertiliser. Because they do not produce enough maize to last the whole year, Rashidi and his wife have to work as labourers on other people's farms. This threatens not only their food security but also harmonious conjugal relations. Rashidi's wife, in accordance with Makonde tradition, is pushing him to construct his own house so that she can feel that she is married to a 'real man'. But Rashidi cannot, given his poverty of resources.

In contrast with these tales of apparent poverty traps, Hossam (sixty-seven years old from Nchinga) was able to invest in farming with financial support from his brother. Use of fertiliser soon enabled him to increase production. He sold part of the harvest and used the profits to climb out of poverty. Hossam's family was able to afford three meals a day, finance the education of their children, buy additional farm land for cultivation and build two houses and a well. Hossam explained that his well-being was dependent on fertilisers, which he used in order to secure high yields.

Land markets

Without the resources to make their smallholdings productive, many have turned to casual wage labour (see below), sometimes following the sale of land after a crisis. However, having sold land, it is difficult to re-enter the land market owing to its high prices—which result from population growth, income inequality and high demand for land on the part of those with the money to invest. Land prices were not always so high: ten years ago, a casual labourer in Nkangala could save up to buy some, but this is now impossible (see Table 6.3).

Table 6.3: Estimates of the cost of fertile land and land rental in the study areas in Tanzania—findings from focus group discussions

	Cost of fertile land 1999	Cost of fertile land 2009	Cost of rental in 2009
Cashew (with trees on it)	TSh 100,000	TSh 300,000	TSh 170,000 (more than half the price of buying land)
Maize	TSh 20–30,000	TSh 80–120,000	TSh 15–20,000 per acre (a fifth the price of buying it)

Rising population pressure has also reduced the size of farmland inheritances. For instance, young people in Kalesa speak of their parents inheriting 5–10 acres of land, but this young men and women in their twenties now are inheriting fractions of acres. Two respondents in Kalesa in Nkasi district had inherited 0.25 and 0.50 acres of land, respectively, to share with their husbands. In Mwanza region, many respondents spoke of grandfathers owning hundreds of acres; in Nkangala, grandparents had owned large tracts of land (downward intergenerational mobility was a key theme in all districts). Population pressure also reduces the fertility of land (through over-farming without fallow periods), so there is less fertile land available on the market. One focus group discussion respondent in Nkangala revealed that maize land is three times less fertile than it was in the past, so he needs to treble the acreage for the same production levels.

Land holding further reduces access, with a large amount of land held uncultivated as a store of wealth. Wealthier parents hold on to land, or acquire further land, so they can give it to their children. Out-of-town siblings—often migrating males—hold on to uncultivated land because doing this rather than lending to local siblings—often female sisters—will enable the land to become more fertile. Local siblings—often female kin—are afraid to sell or rent land

and damage its fertility, which could lead to family conflicts or, worse, loss of the potential support of a brother. Local kin renting land out to outsiders who would not care for it is commonly understood as destroying its fertility (apparently outsiders do not replenish with fertilisers).

Conflict over land is particularly prevalent in Kalesa and Magu. In Kalesa, the conflict began when Sukuma people (pastoralists) migrated to the area with a large number of cattle from northern Tanzania. They occupied land and started buying more from natives (the Fipa people). Ezekiel Bigabo, a newcomer, was reported to have tricked many smallholder farmers to sell land to him at below market prices. In doing this, he managed to hoard about 100 acres of land: he had oxen to till this large area and could then use the remaining land for grazing. Land is currently scarce and expensive, with a gulf between smallholder farmers and large landowners engaged in big business. It cost TZS 100,000 to hire 1 acre of land for one season. The situation is becoming worse, as hatred and tension are building up between the indigenous people and the newcomers.

If buying land is expensive, renting could be an affordable alternative. However, again, the supply is low. People are reluctant to rent out their land because they are concerned not just about renters damaging soil fertility but also about renters subsequently claiming the land as their own on the basis of customary land law. Such fears reduce the supply of land available for rent. As eighty-one-year-old Novath Nanzalaila, who had cause to regret renting out his land in Kalesa village, explained, 'I no longer lend land to anybody. If I am unable to cultivate it in a certain year, I just leave it fallow.' This may even lead to arguments within families, when fathers will not lease to daughters or when men who migrate do not let their sisters farm their share. Insecure land rights are an important problem encountered in all three regions, preventing the land rental market from working efficiently for poor people.

There are a few indications of exceptions, however. Angelina (twenty-five, living in Kalesa) thought she might be able to rent 0.5 acre of paddy by entering into a tenancy contract with the owner, whereby she would pay rent at harvest by giving half the harvest over to the landowners, since she cannot afford to prepay rent. Generally, though, there was little renting going on among the small sample of households.

Casual labour

Together, these dynamics ensure that those who have sold their assets and turned to casual wage labour are often trapped there. In addition, some casual workers who have smallholdings turn to wage labour when short of cash. Many smallholders do not produce enough food to feed themselves for the whole year, so this exchange of labour (between smallholders who at other times are labourers), usually against payment, is very common. Frequently, such employment occurs in the context of a long-established relationship which can be called on in various ways—to request seed at planting time or food when food is short. In Kalesa, households loan seed and other inputs against payment after harvest.

Working for others can also be an important way of building social capital. Loans are often requested from employers: having several employers to turn to for cash or food can be advantageous. It is common even for public sector workers to work on the farms of second employers. These ways of working can develop into trusting and reliable relationships, which can be called on in times of food shortage. In Wazabanga, some people have formed an association through which they work collectively on each other's farms on a rotational basis. This facilitates the quick completion of large tasks, even where tractors are lacking.

However, not all employment relationships are quite so egalitarian or mutually beneficial. With the supply of casual workers outstripping demand, they are adversely incorporated into the rural economy. Without an alternative economic option, labourers have little bargaining power with landlords, such as if the latter refuse to pay. Vulnerability may also result from the lack of legally recognised contracts. In this regard, it may be beneficial to educate labourers about their rights and how to enter into legally credible arrangements.

Working hours are long (twelve-hour days) and pay is often on credit: labourers have to accept payment when it suits the farmer rather than when the work is done. Wages are low, varying from TZS 1,000 to TZS 3,000 per day depending on the negotiating power of the labourer, their performance and also the nature of the work. This includes ploughing, weeding, planting, harvesting and transporting produce to the owner's house. Fetching or selling firewood, water and charcoal are other common jobs. Notwithstanding the hardness of the work, the high supply of labourers, together with relatively minimal demand (particularly during the dry season), pushes down remuneration. Sometimes, workers are paid not in money but in food.

Life histories show that, having turned to casual labour, many people remain trapped in food insecurity, as low wages are insufficient for daily food, let alone asset accumulation. In Nkangala, one women lamented during a focus group discussion that, 'if we work as a casual labour or make doughnuts for twenty days we are paid TZS 20,000, but if we go to the market with that TZS 20,000 we cannot get enough food to cover twenty days!'

Sabrina's husband, Hassan (in Nkangala), gets some money by working as a labourer on other people's farms. However, this is only a seasonal job: during the dry season, there is less agricultural work. Hassan is also working on a construction site but again this is not a regular job. He is also supporting his family by making and selling charcoal. Juma (thirty-six years old, living in Nchinga) works on farms on credit and gets paid after the harvest. If yields are poor, he is not paid all he is owed—a common complaint in Nchinga. Only able to afford two meals a day for himself, he currently considers himself too poor to marry.

With good health, two people working hard can sometimes manage to save and make small investments. In Nchinga, for example, Zulfa and her husband accumulated sufficient money to buy a 0.5 acre plot and build a home. Mwanaidi (Nchinga) purchased a 0.75 acre plot through casual wage labour, although she remains unable to feed her children and has not yet accumulated the assets to act as buffers against potential future crises.

Given the proportion of farms which are not self-sufficient, the functioning of the rural wage labour market is very important to minimum food security. However, low-paid, insecure casual labour is scarcely sufficient to provide for any more than two meals a day.

Food price inflation and the rising price of essentials

Food insecurity is also related to food price inflation and rising costs of basic essentials, both of which have eaten into household budgets (see Chapter 7). As the local councillor of Nkangala explained,

> Before 2005, money was not so available and our incomes (especially after 1999) were low, but the cost of living was not that high. But since 2005 money is still not available, our incomes are low and the prices of goods have risen steeply ... This is why poverty is so visible, especially in past five years. We can't afford fish or meat because the prices are too high—even businessmen find it hard and government employees too. Soap has doubled in price. The fish business is dead now because no one can afford to buy fish!

Wages offered for casual labour have not kept pace with the rising costs of food. Poor people spoke of being priced out of the market entirely for certain basic needs (such as beef, chicken, milk and fish, i.e. the protein content of meals). Asna (thirty-two years old from Nkangala village), who relies heavily on casual labouring to supplement her farm income, complains that her income is no longer sufficient to purchase beef, sugar, cooking oil, chicken, eggs and milk. When she was first married fourteen years ago, she could afford all of these items to accompany maize/cassava *ugali*. Now she can afford only vegetables, occasionally with some nuts from her farm. Figure 6.1 and Figure 6.2 indicate the extent of this, even before the subsequent food price shocks.

For the poorest, this has led to lower nutritional levels.[8] In a recent opinion poll, 52 per cent of respondents identified high food and other commodity prices as a major economic problem.[9] The United States Agency for International Development Famine Early Warning Systems Network outlook for Tanzania for October 2009 to March 2010, meanwhile, suggests that prevailing above-average prices for food have increased the numbers of food-insecure people across Tanzania. This price rise has also forced a reduction in food quality (protein and vitamins) for poor people.

Figure 6.1: Expenditure on food 2000/01–2006/07 (constant 2007 prices)

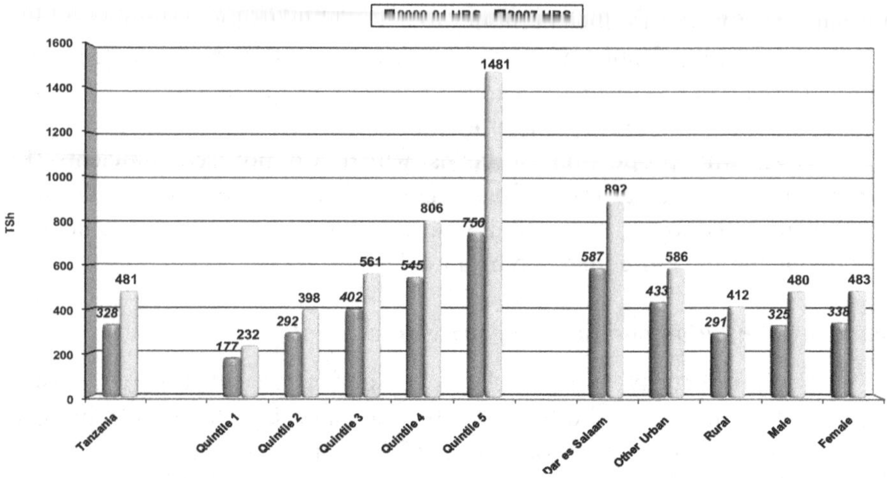

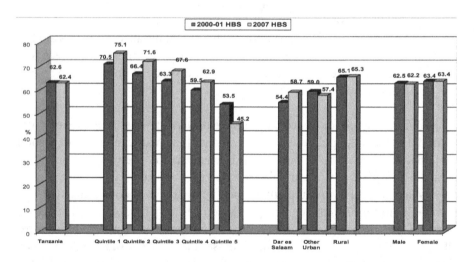

Source: National Bureau of Statistics (2010)

Figure 6.2: Share of budget on food (2007 constant prices)

Source: National Bureau of Statistics (2010)

Life-cycle risks

The reasons for hunger are not being able to access (produce or buy) food of the right amount and quality; such food not being available from own production or to buy or both; and constraints posed by the social norms dictating how food is distributed within a household. There are two stages of the life-cycle where people who may not be poor or hungry at other times of their lives are especially prone to hunger: childhood and old age.

Children rely on parents to feed them, so child nutrition is dependent on getting a good level of care from parents or other relatives. While most families prioritise the needs of children and older people when there is not enough to eat, sometimes children can lose out from a poor level of care. Children are particularly vulnerable to hunger on the loss of a parent or care-giver.

When Prisca (seventeen, from Wazabanga) lost her mother at the age of five, the family lost their main provider. She explained that when her mother started to become ill, they sometimes stayed the whole day without food. When her mother died, the family disintegrated, with their father marrying another wife and walking out of the village. Prisca and her siblings went to stay with uncles who also had their own family to support. Prisca and her siblings were not prioritised, although they did at least receive food until they were old enough to go to the farm and start working.

In some cases, food insecurity is caused by old age and exacerbated by a lack of support from spouses, children or other relatives. Mathias Wambuka is seventy-one years old and lives alone in Kamwanda. He is very food insecure and attributes this to his old age, which constrains his ability to produce food, and the lack of a wife to help him produce food. His wife passed away in 2008 and his efforts to remarry have not succeeded: women decline his proposals since he is not farming. With his former wife, he used to produce cassava on a 0.5 acre farm and get their own food. Since they were not producing maize or rice, their food status was not very good, but the situation worsened after her death. He is now almost entirely dependent for food on his daughter, Catherine, who is married and lives nearby.

Having many dependants also threatens well-being. Violet (aged thirty-four, living in Wazabanga) identified having too many children as a factor dragging a person into poverty. She explained that giving birth to many children is demanding on both time and resources. It means you never have time to concentrate on activities or help your partner. Furthermore, because children eat up your few resources, you never make a step forward. They demand health services, school fees, uniforms, clothes and food. She said that, for her, meeting the children's requirements has become a nightmare. Violet's husband also finds the demands unbearable. Violet regrettably foresees that their children will stop school and end up like themselves.

Disinvestment and disinheritance on divorce and bereavement

There are also gender-specific risks (see Chapter 4). Women interviewees commonly identified divorce as the cause of their impoverishment.[10] James' (aged nineteen of Kalesa village) father deserted his mother in 1993. They lost income and fish from his fishing activities after he stopped supporting them materially and financially. Food became scarce; they ate one or two meals daily, unlike previously, when they ate two or three times daily. Bereavement is likewise disadvantageous.

In both cases, women and their dependants are particularly vulnerable to food insecurity in the event of the dispossession of assets, including livestock, house, furniture, utensils and clothing.[11] Kened (aged twenty nine from Wazabanga) and his siblings suffered from the loss not only of their father but also of some of their assets, particularly the 2 acres of farm they relied on. He lamented that 'my uncles took away the farm that we used to grow rice. They simply sold the farm and shared the money among themselves. We had to look for another *shamba* and we are now hiring it.' When Alice (fifty-three years old, living in Ndite) instigated divorce, in fury at her husband's infidelity, she lost all the assets they had accumulated together: house, savings, land and fishing businesses. She recounted, 'the divorce made me poor because I lost everything I worked for for ten years. Since then, I have not been able to reach the level that I was.'

The consequences of hunger and malnutrition

Those suffering from food insecurity and consequent malnutrition are at acute risk of detrimental short- and long-term consequences: missing out on school or becoming less productive, unwell or depressed. In addition there are also wider social consequences, described in more detail in other chapters, including marital breakup (Chapter 4), witchcraft and theft (Chapter 3). Here a variety of consequences are explored – for the inter-generational transmission of poverty, for ill-health, physical strength and psychological state.

Inter-generational transmission of poverty

Malnutrition in children impedes their physical and cognitive development.[12] According to Hassan (aged thirty-seven, from Nkangala), hunger pushes some children to miss school and scavenge instead or to start employment to support their family. These responses to food insecurity undermine their prospects of escape. Some who missed out on school, such as twenty-seven-year-old Hamida (Nkangala) recounted the haunting pain and frustration of seeing friends go to school daily while labouring on the farm, suffering from hunger. The family remains trapped in poverty, still often eating just one meal a day. Hamida seems to have lost hope in life and simply prays to God that some miracle may happen. Alice (fifty-three years old, Ndite) likewise explained that, because her parents could not produce enough for them to eat, she spent more time farming than studying. Without an education, all she could rely on later in life were her physical assets, but she lost these on divorce and her daughter's ill-health.

Others do go to school but with an empty stomach are unable to concentrate. For this reason, Sirila (twenty-seven, living in Wazabanga) failed her primary school exams and was unable to continue with secondary education. She now does casual labour. Rafaeli Kurwa (sixteen years old, Wazabanga) similarly cannot afford to progress to secondary school and has already taken a long time to finish primary school—he has had to repeat grades which he studied for while also doing casual labour.

By contrast, many of Sirila and Rafaeli's educated peers now have government jobs that finance income diversification, investment and asset accumulation, As Violet (aged thirty-four, Wazabanga) observed, 'I know that there are a lot of opportunities for those who have gone to school. I have seen those who continued with secondary education have made it while those of us who did not proceed are roaming around in the villages.' She may be talking about people like Selemani (a fifty-year-old agricultural extension officer from Nkangala) and his wife, an assistant nurse. Their salaried government jobs facilitate their upward mobility through income diversification and investments, including in their own children's education, which ensures the intergenerational transmission of resilience.

Lack of strength

Those unable to afford food often lack the strength to work themselves out of poverty. Malnutrition impedes labour productivity and thereby reinforces food insecurity—since payment for casual waged labour is often at a piece rate. In Kalesa village, for example, slower workers earn TZS 1,000 per day while their faster, more energised counterparts earn double this. The importance of malnutrition to productivity is also recognised in the Tanzanian Agricultural Sectoral Development Programme.[13]

Emaciated Paula (sixty five, Kalesa) grows maize and cassava on her 1 acre of farmland, in addition to brewing beer and carrying out casual labour, in an effort to have more than one meal a day. But sometimes she is unable to work owing to ill health. She despaired, 'I will be declining in terms of well-being until I die since I am becoming weaker and weaker physically hence unable to produce, and I do not have well-off children who could support me materially.' Hawa, meanwhile (forty-seven, living in Newala), has a small paddy farm in the wetlands but she cannot farm it because of her health. This kind of farm, inherited from her parents, needs a lot of energy to till. She asked her siblings to give her a farm with cashew nut trees instead of the farm in the wetlands but they refused, telling her to sell it if she cannot till it. Nevertheless, she does not intend to sell it because she already has two grandchildren who will inherit the farm in the future. Currently, one of her aunts is tilling the farm.

Kurthumu (a fifty-four-year-old woman living in Nkangala) is in a similar situation. When asked when the family last had a meal, she replied 'yesterday at around 5.00p.m.' She was clearly exhausted and said she was suffering from a persistent stomach pain. She explained that for the past three months she had have not been able to work, yet 'if I could have money I could use it to maintain the farm and my family. I would then be able to pay the school fees of my children and cultivate enough land in the hope of better harvest.' Kurthumu dreams of getting capital from the government, so she can trade rice. Such work would enable her to support her family without being so physically demanding and injurious to her health.

Ill-health

Exhausting toil drains hungry bodies, making them vulnerable to ill-health. Violet (thirty-four years old, Wazabanga), for example, sometimes fetches water for those who make and sell local brew. For this she is paid about TZS 200 per 20 litres. Violet said that she could carry only 100 litres a day and sometimes the next day she felt fatigued.

Many families referred to child deaths, in which malnutrition may be a contributory factor. Ill-health death is not only distressing but also immensely costly. Although in some areas health facilities work well (e.g. Kalesa village), in many more sites people have to pay for consultations, medicines and supplementary procedures. The elderly and children are not supposed to pay for health services, but in practice women pay for under-fives because drugs are usually not available.[14] The elderly also pay for consultations and medicines, while village dispensaries have very erratic availability of drugs in general, and so poor people are found to pay for them.[15] Nkangala has a hospital, but it is too expensive for poor people. Assets often have to be sold to pay for health expenses, and income-generating work is disrupted to make time to care for sick family members. The death of a breadwinner further compounds household food insecurity, both through the loss of their future earnings and also if they are dispossessed of assets.

Despair

Feeling unable to work oneself out of food insecurity sometimes leads to feelings of hopelessness and depression, according to focus groups and individual life histories. Lugodagula (a thirty-five-year-old cotton farmer and casual labourer in Wazabanga) despaired, 'I have given up … as I don't see a bright future anymore.' He feels that there is little return for his efforts. Similarly, Rahman (a sixty-eight-year-old man living in Nkangala village) said bitterly that, although he had had great hopes of cashew production as a way out of poverty, he had been let down: 'it does not pay.' Rahman thinks it is waste of time and resources to continue investing in his cashew farm. Unable to see alternative pathways to well-being, many find respite in alcohol abuse, such as Samweli (thirty-five, Kalesa village), who was pulled out of school to chop charcoal to provide food for his family. As an unfocused youth, he drank away meagre earnings, but his character changed on the inheritance of livestock and land, as he increasingly thought like a commercial farmer: renting in paddy land and seeking to store crops so as to avoid forced sales at harvest and rather sell at a higher price. However, without fortunate social connections or equivalent support from government, the poorest may be tempted to give up hope, which may adversely affect agricultural production. In the Kalesa village focus group, despair was identified as a hindrance to production: weary people were said to be less inclined to work hard for little reward.

Buffers and strategies against hunger

Families that are unable to accumulate assets and appear to be stuck in poverty traps are extremely vulnerable to negative shocks. Arguably, it is not the shocks themselves which cause poverty or hunger, but the absence of 'buffers', or strategies, institutions and safety nets, which will prevent the shock from having an impoverishing effect.

There is much variety in how people respond to crisis and hunger, or the threat of hunger. The buffers respondents identified included growing 'famine crops', diversification, accumulating savings, undertaking wage labour and urban migration. Common strategies are eating fewer meals and a lower quality of food and working more; some children stop going to school. However, no common patterns or sequences emerged from the interviews.

One classic buffer is a famine crop, planted because its success is nearly guaranteed—cassava is a prime example and is very widely grown, contributing 17 per cent of Tanzania's consumed calories. It is likely that the research and extension going into cassava is minimal compared with that going into maize (26 per cent of calories). Efforts to protect people against hunger would involve much more work on cassava.

Diversification is also important. There are cases where agriculture supplies the capital for meaningful diversification into the non-farm economy. James (nineteen, living in Kalesa) has three main livelihoods: crop production, casual labour work and selling consumer goods in his own kiosk. Having sold 19 bags of rice harvested from his 1 acre piece of land, James established a kiosk, trading rice, maize flour, biscuits, sweets, kerosene, soap, cooking oil and body lotion. There are also cases of the opposite: investing in agriculture using the proceeds from non-farm enterprises. Hossam's (Nchinga) main livelihood is now farming, and he cultivates the cash crops such as paddy, *simsim* and cashew. He also cultivates maize and cassava. He raised funds for his farming venture by working in his brother's hotel and slowly built up his capital through other agri-business ventures, including selling sardines and butchering halal meat.

Erick (Wazabanga) explained that women's diversification into non-farm work had enabled significant improvements in household well-being. While men are not interested in these small businesses with minimal daily profit, these women, although labelled negatively by society, are able to support their children's education, including the provision of books and uniforms. However, profits from small-scale trading are dependent on incomes from agriculture. Given limited village incomes and demand, the market for trading is saturated.

If investment is accepted as critical to household poverty mobility, it may then be argued that, rather than receiving subsidies or cash transfers, poor people should bank on microfinance as a means of accumulating assets. In Kalesa, for example, some women agricultural labourers make small monthly deposits into burial societies, which they later withdraw in order to finance the costs of ill-health and funerals.

However, this research suggests two limitations to microfinance. First, while the loans that rural women currently access through burial societies may prevent downward mobility by acting as buffers, they are not sufficiently large to finance investments that would enable them to exit poverty. Lenders are willing to provide bigger loans in the case of group borrowing, from savings and credit cooperative societies. Such capital is often used for paddy-farming or off-farm diversification.

The second limitation of microfinance is that, even if larger loans were more commonly available, they may not be desirable. Borrowing funds for agricultural production or for trading agricultural products is risky, since the borrower may suffer a loss and have their property confiscated. In this case, the borrower may become poorer. The reasons for the loss may be a high interest rate on the loan or calamities in the course of the agricultural cycle or while trading agricultural products.

For these reasons, many people see credit as an altogether too risky a strategy. Although Magreth Nachikira (a forty-five-year-old married woman from Kayumbe village) wishes she had the capital to start a shop, and her husband would like a tractor, they have never sought microcredit because they are afraid that they would not be able to repay the loan and therefore would be unable to send their children to school. The interest rate is very high and they cannot afford to lose their livestock. Many people in the village have had to sell their house, farm or cattle when they have not been able to repay their loans. This makes them fearful and they have decided to remain patient and work with what they have. Others, like Alice (a fifty-three-year-old living in Ndite), do not even have any assets to risk: 'I cannot take loans from financial institutions because I do not have assets for them to take when I will not be able to repay.'

Assets, particularly livestock, act as savings. People try to keep them even through hard times. They can be hard to hang onto, though, especially if income is not coming in to replenish them. Chickens are a source of income, and are rarely eaten. People without even a chicken are seen as quite desperate. Mohamed Halidi from Nchinga had had a good life, and had been able to accumulate assets. But, in old age, without many sons to protect him, he had had to resort to selling goats. He had had 20; there were 4 left. Cassava has acted as a fallback crop since his rice field was destroyed in 1993, so he does not have to worry about destitution.

Borrowing money in exchange for labour, or simply going out to find work, is a common response to hunger. The existence of a wage labour market is a buffer in itself. Peter (aged seventy-five, living in Wazabanga) relayed this by explaining his situation:

> At times you could see that the family had nothing to eat; my wife had nothing to put on the fire for the family. This forced me to opt for quick money that is doing the casual labour on other people's farms where I was paid TZS 1,500 depending on the nature of the work.

Jamal, thirty-seven, living in Wazabanga, explained that his family is in good health, although 'minor diseases such as coughing and malaria are inevitable, particularly for the young ones'. When a family member is sick, they have to pull the resources together, with him, his wife and the sister all trying to sort out the best way to proceed. In many cases, they ask a rich person for money that will later be paid in cash or in labour if it is during agricultural season.

Having relatives in town is useful for poorer families: children are sent to richer relatives in urban areas to work as house girls/boys. But this can be risky—urban livelihoods wax and wane. With food price inflation in recent years, making ends meet has become more difficult in town. Some continually struggle to find a way forward, with episodes of migrant labour which have varied outcomes.

Hamida's story illustrates some of the pitfalls. Hamida, from Nkangala, is a twenty-seven-year-old single woman with two children by different fathers. She currently collects and sells firewood and engages in casual labour during the growing season, seeing this as the only way for her to advance her well-being. Her story is one of several migrant episodes in search of economic security. She first migrated, when she left school, to live with an uncle in Mozambique, but he then died. She later became a housemaid, first in Morogoro, then in Dar es Salaam, where she became pregnant and returned to the village, leaving the child's father in town. She then migrated to Arusha as a housemaid, became pregnant again and came home. At home, she lives very modestly with her widowed mother and other family members, including her own children. Hamida aspires to work as a housemaid again—it gives three meals a day and a small salary from which some saving is possible. If she were able to save enough she would invest in a business.

Policy implications

The policy implications of this analysis need further investigation and analysis. However, one thing is clear: many poor people rely on wage labour, whether local and mostly casual and insecure, or migrant and sometimes more secure, to achieve food security. Food-secure rural households are no longer the rule.

Controlling food price inflation is therefore a top priority, since most poor and food-insecure people in Tanzania rely on purchased food. But the controversial question is how? Food stocks and market interventions are part of the story, as is the modernisation of smallholder farming. The latter implies measures to enable land markets, including rental markets, as well as a focus on mechanisation and agricultural input markets. One priority is the expansion and development of rural roads to link rural producers in remote areas with urban consumers and to reduce food prices linked to high transport costs.[16]

The removal and decline of cooperative societies since the late 1980s has meant that private traders now operate as middlemen in food crop marketing, maximising their profit by paying the lowest price at the farm gate and selling for the highest possible price to the final consumers.[17] Mobile phones can play an important role in providing both producers and consumers with information on market rates.[18]

There is also a need to build new farmer associations. This could be by means of integrated producer schemes which develop the capacities of smallholders through the provision of a wide range of extension services. Contracts under these would include price information, and so prices would be available to all farmers and serve as the basis of decision making.[19] Alternatively, a new generation of agricultural cooperatives could be developed, designed in such a way as to ensure that they can respond to the needs of members and with a trained and educated leadership.[20]

Government is seen as having important roles to play in agriculture: structuring markets (e.g. cashew, maize) and protecting livestock against disease, but not always with good consequences. It would appear that aspects of food security policies themselves (control of the maize market, export bans) may have negative consequences for some. Maize export bans remain a sensitive policy issue. The main maize surplus regions are the southern highlands. Government policy is to allow the export of maize only when all regions of the country are said to be food secure. In practice, however, there is almost always a problem of food security in some part of the country, particularly in the semi-arid central region, meaning that maize exports are banned on an almost continual basis. The effect of this policy is to make prices of maize in the southern highlands not just lower but also more volatile than they would otherwise be, so harming the livelihoods of maize farmers.[21] It also makes it more difficult for poor households to plan their expenditure. This needs a much more thorough investigation than was possible based on the limited data we have. Certainly, sorting out crop payment systems so that farmers know what they are going to get, and then get it, would be advantageous.

The survey analysis of number of meals taken a day may not be as important in determining food insecurity as analysis of the quality of those meals, when considering the difference between two and three meals a day. However, consuming only one meal a day is a clear indication of distress in almost all cases. According to the Kayumbe women's focus group, 'knowledge of food' was identified as significant to intake. Awareness of good child-feeding practices is known to have a positive impact—community feeding posts were a successful programme in the 1980s, which lost momentum in the 1990s.[22] In the very short term, one way to ensure that children obtain the necessary nutrients could be through school feeding programmes.[23] Finding new ways, perhaps using modern media, of spreading knowledge about nutrition would contribute significantly to better nutrition outcomes, especially for children and infants.

Buffers against hunger can reduce rapidly for the old or infirm or for separated, divorced or widowed women, especially those without sons. Protection of these categories of people from asset loss, from having to work at the lowest wages in insecure, physically demanding jobs, would make a significant contribution to food security. One safety net could be the operation of food for work programmes in food-deficit areas.[24] Poor households with large numbers of dependants are also very vulnerable and would also benefit from protection.

Reducing food insecurity would give people more time and energy to try new ideas (e.g. crops), save and invest in enterprises, houses and water supplies. There is great willingness to do so, but the time, energy and above all cash to hire labour or buy inputs are all scarce.

---

1   National Bureau of Statistics (2010)

2   Research on Poverty Alleviation et al. (2009)

3   V. Leach and B. Kilama (2009)

4   This is a hypothesis which needs testing out on Household Budget Survey/Demographic and Health Survey data

5   Interviewees were categorised into six well-being categories through focus group discussion well-being ranking exercises, which included a historical well-being ranking. These were destitute, very poor, poor, vulnerable, resilient and rich

6   All people's and village names used in the chapter have been made anonymous

7   Food quality is extensively reviewed on the basis of the 2007 HBS in United Republic of Tanzania (2010) Trends in Food Insecurity in Mainland Tanzania Dar es Salaam, Ministry of Finance and Economic Affairs, National Bureau of Statistics

8   National Bureau of Statistics (2010)

9   Synovate (2009)

10   K. Higgins (2010)

11   L. da Corta and J. Magongo (2010)

12   K. Bird (2007)

13   United Republic of Tanzania (2006), p. 45

14   See K. Kayunze et al. (2010)

15   Ibid.

16   R. Haug et al. (2009)

17   Ibid.

18   E.E. Isinika and A.C. Msuya (2011)

19   A.C. Msuya (2007), in ibid.
20   S.A. Chambo (2009)
21   N. Minot (2010)
22   V. Leach and B. Kilama (2009), p. 16
23   R. Haug et al. (2009)
24   Ibid.

Part 2

Economic Growth and Poverty Reduction

Chapter 7

Growth Without Poverty Reduction in Tanzania—Reasons for the Mismatch

Oswald Mashindano, Kim Kayunze, Lucia da Corta and Festo Maro

Introduction

Tanzania has a long history of devising policy frameworks to achieve higher economic growth and poverty reduction strategies to improve the quality of life of its people. However, the country remains characterised by low per capita income and widespread poverty and it faces great challenges to achieving the Millennium Development Goals by 2015.[1] A recent review of the Tanzania Development Vision 2025 which, among other goals, aims to eradicate poverty in the country by 2025 reveals that, while economic growth has been relatively high, it has been insufficient to meet poverty reduction targets.[2] Sources of growth have been limited and, in most cases, have not reached the poorest people in rural and peri-urban areas, failing to generate adequate and decent jobs. Poverty has been reduced only marginally in rural areas and among farming households. Poorly developed infrastructure means that limited economic transformation has occurred.

Findings from four Poverty and Human Development Reports and three Household Budget Surveys also show that, while economic growth has led to notable positive changes over time, the reduction in poverty has not been proportionally significant.[3] Despite sustained economic growth over the past decade, with substantial annual gross domestic product (GDP) growth between 2000 (4.9 per cent) and 2007 (7.1 per cent), there has been no substantial reduction in poverty. Between 2000/01 and 2007, the percentage of people in mainland Tanzania below the basic needs poverty line fell only marginally, from 35.7 to 33.6 per cent. Moreover, as a consequence of rapid population growth, the reduction in the proportion of people living below the poverty line actually translates to an increase of 1 million people living in poverty in mainland Tanzania between 2001 and 2007.[4]

This chapter examines the growth–poverty mismatch in Tanzania and investigates the reasons behind the limited trickle-down process since the early 1990s. It is based mainly on desk reviews, including of Poverty and Human Development Reports and reports from Household Budget Surveys; the Chronic Poverty Research Centre survey in Mwanza, Mtwara and Rukwa regions; Tanzania Development Vision 2025 interviews in Morogoro, Lindi, Kigoma, Tanga, Dar es Salaam and Tabora; and information from the Tanzania Knowledge Network discussion forum. It also incorporates information from poverty reduction strategy progress reports and National Strategy for Growth and Reduction of Poverty (MKUKUTA) Monitoring Master Plan reports. In addition, it includes some primary data collected in the survey regions and districts mentioned previously.

Trends in, and composition of, GDP

The annual GDP growth trend since the late 1990s has generally been rising, from 4.1 per cent in 1998 to a peak of 7.8 per cent in 2004. In 2009, growth slowed down to 6 per cent, largely because of the sharp deceleration of the global economy, although it bounced back to 7 per cent in 2010 (see Figure 7.1). This is nevertheless in line with the 6 to 8 per cent targets spelt out in MKUKUTA I. Annual GDP growth did not increase on the previous year when Tanzania was facing the impacts of shocks such as the global food crisis, the power crisis, the global economic and financial crisis and, more recently, the state of turmoil which has been escalating in some oil-producing nations. While the global food crisis led to higher food prices in the country, the chronic power crisis in Tanzania not only pushed domestic prices up but also cut down on the production of consumer goods, including merchandise. The impact of the global financial crisis, meanwhile, was multidimensional, negatively affecting Tanzania's volume and price of exports, flows of capital and investment and tourism. These effects worsened the balance of payments and exerted inflationary pressures on the economy, which averaged 7 per cent between 2002 and 2010,[5] and raised to 19 percent between November 2011 and January 2012, with some sectors suffering more than others.

Figure 7.1: Annual real GDP growth rates in Tanzania, 1998–2010

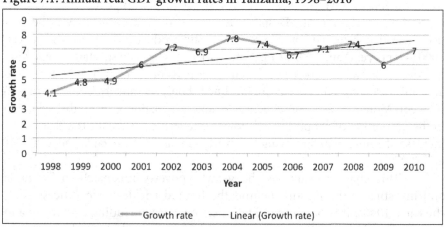

Source: Constructed using data from Bank of Tanzania (2010)

The relatively high growth rate enjoyed over the past ten years is the result of economic and financial reforms and prudent monetary and fiscal policies, all of which promoted domestic and foreign investment. However, this achievement is likely to be eroded with the ongoing power crisis, the current drought and the oil crisis, fuelled by political instability in the major oil-producing countries.

There are four important sectors in terms of GDP share and the growth rate in Tanzania: agriculture, services, industry and manufacturing. The services sector contributes the largest share of total GDP (Figure 7.2)—at an average of 46 per cent per annum between 1998 and 2009. Albeit marginally, the GDP share of the services sector, which includes trade and repairs; hotels and restaurants; transport; communications; financial intermediation; and real estate, has been rising, at least between 2001 and 2008. Other components of the sector include business services; public administration; education; and health care.

Figure 7.2: Sector contribution to real GDP in Tanzania, 1998–2009

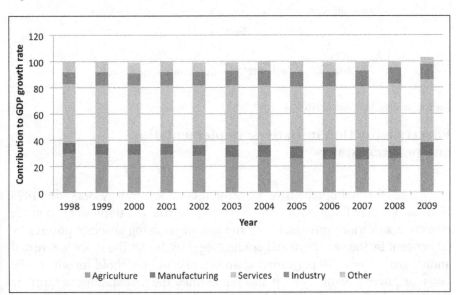

Source: Bank of Tanzania (2010)

Unlike services, the share of agriculture in total GDP has been declining gradually since 1999 (with the exception of 2008 and 2009, when its contribution increased marginally). Meanwhile, industry and manufacturing's shares in total GDP have been rising over time, although their respective total shares are lower than that of agriculture. Industry consists of mining and quarrying; water supply; electricity and gas; and construction. Agriculture is made up of crops; livestock; forestry; and fishery.

Several sub-sectors recorded growth rates of over 10 per cent in 2010, including communications (22.1 per cent), construction and electricity and gas (10.2 per cent) and financial intermediation (10.1 per cent).

Figure 7.3: Real GDP growth rate and contribution to growth rate of various sub-sectors in Tanzania, 2010

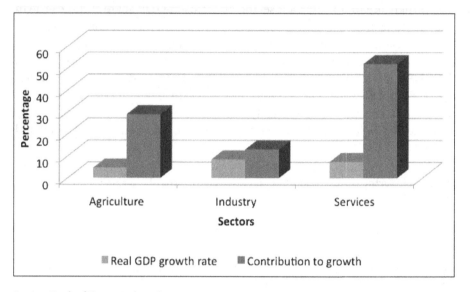

Source: Bank of Tanzania (2010)

Poverty reduction initiatives: implementation and progress status

The first comprehensive poverty reduction strategy was the 1998 National Poverty Eradication Strategy, which provided a framework to guide poverty eradication initiatives with the aim of reducing absolute poverty by 50 per cent by the year 2010 and eradicating it by 2025.[6] The strategy targeted annual growth of 8–10 per cent and an increase in household income as the basis for poverty eradication. It also represented the first attempt to translate the Tanzania Development Vision 2025, eventually finalised in 1999, into medium-term targets.

In 2000, the government crafted the Poverty Reduction Strategy Paper in the context of the Heavily Indebted Poor Countries initiative.[7] This three-year first generation poverty reduction strategy focused on the priority areas of basic education, primary health, water, rural roads, agricultural research and extension, the judiciary and HIV and AIDS (see Table 7.1 for major poverty reduction initiatives in Tanzania).

Table 7.1: Major Poverty Reduction Initiatives in Tanzania: 1998 – 2011

Sn	Name of the Initiatives	Duration	Objectives and Targets	Achievement
1	National Poverty Eradication Strategy	1998 - 2025	Reducing absolute poverty by 50 per cent by the year 2010 and eradicating it by 2025 Achieve annual growth of 8–10 per cent	Basic Needs Poverty is 34 percent Growth rate of 7 percent in 2010
2	Poverty Reduction Strategy Paper	1999 - 2000	Qualify for HIPC Initiatives	Tanzania qualified in 2000 and started to benefit from HIPC Initiatives in 2001
3	Poverty Reduction Strategy (Three-year first generation poverty reduction strategy)	2001 - 2004	Focused on the priority areas of basic education, primary health, water, rural roads, agricultural research and extension, the judiciary and HIV and AIDS	Basic Needs Poverty is 37 percent 2003
4	National Strategy for Growth and Reduction of Poverty (MKUKUTA I)	2005 - 2010	Reduce poverty (12.9 per cent in urban areas and 24 per cent in rural areas) To achieve high and sustained economic growth of 6–8 per cent per annum	Overall Basic Needs Poverty is 34 percent (24 per cent in urban areas and 37 per cent in rural areas) Growth rate of 7 percent in 2010
5	National Strategy for Growth and Reduction of Poverty (MKUKUTA II)	2010 - 2015	Reduce poverty and To achieve high and sustained economic growth of 6–8 per cent per annum	NA
6	Five-year Development Plan	2011/12 to 2015/16	To speed up realization of development goals as stipulated in the vision 2025 (The current socio-economic development performances though improved remain far below most time line targets of the Vision)	NA

The successor strategy was the National Strategy for Growth and Reduction of Poverty, also known by its Swahili name of MKUKUTA I. MKUKUTA I ran from 2005 to 2010 and aimed both to reduce poverty and to achieve high and sustained economic growth in a comprehensive outcome-based approach. The strategy was presented in three broad clusters: growth and reduction of income poverty; quality of life and social well-being; and governance and accountability. It targeted an economic growth rate of 6–8 per cent per annum from a base of 6.7 per cent in 2004. It also aimed to reduce basic needs poverty from 25.8 per cent (2000/01) to 12.9 per cent in urban areas and from 38.6 per cent (2000/01) to 24 per cent in rural areas by 2010. Adopting a five-year timeframe was considered to allow for a more sustained effort of resource mobilisation, implementation and evaluation of the poverty impact compared with the previous three-year strategy.

Consultations with the public on the lessons learnt during implementation of poverty reduction strategies and evidence from MKUKUTA I progress reports reveal little progress (if any) in the areas of income poverty, youth, gender, employment, rural electrification, agriculture and water.[8] Responses showed disparities across social groups, gender and geographical location, but the overall impression was that 'growth helped the poor but was much better for the rich'.[9] Among subsequent conclusions was that relying on growth alone to reduce poverty was neither equitable nor efficient. Table 7.2, using data from the three Household Budget Surveys (in 1991/92, 2000/01 and 2007), supports the view that, overall, growth has not translated into poverty reduction. While the economy recorded significant growth between surveys, poverty, measured using the basic needs or the food poverty line, reduced by only a small amount. Between 1991/92 and 2000/01, for instance, the economy grew by 59 per cent; basic needs and food poverty reduced by under 3 per cent.

Table 7.2: Population below the basic needs and food poverty lines in mainland Tanzania between 1991/92 and 2007

	1991/92	2000/01	2007	Change (1991/92–2000/01)	Change (2000/01–2007)
GDP				+59%	+19%
Basic needs poverty (headcount ratio)	38.6%	35.7%	33.3%	-2.9%	-2.4%
Food poverty (headcount ratio)	21.6%	18.7%	16.5%	-2.9%	-2.2%

Source: Constructed based on National Bureau of Statistics (1992; 2002; 2008a)

Following review of MKUKUTA I and the insignificant poverty reduction which occurred under it, the government developed a successor strategy. Known as MKUKUTA II, this five-year strategy (2010–2015 is now under implementation. To run alongside it, the government in June 2011 launched its Five-year Development Plan, spanning from 2011/12 to 2015/16. This is a formal implementation tool of the country's development agenda, articulated in the Tanzania Development Vision 2025.

Overall, then, so far, the growth process in Tanzania has not been pro-poor, which raises a critical question: why did this mismatch emerge and where did it originate?

The origin of the growth–poverty mismatch

Evidence suggests that economic growth is a significant determinant of poverty reduction as well as of improved livelihoods.[10] The impressive economic growth rate recorded during the past fifteen years in Tanzania should have meant significant reductions in poverty and improvements in the living standards of the population. However, these expectations have not translated into reality and this disparity has attracted debates about the causes of the mismatch between economic growth and poverty reduction.

These debates take place in the context of concerns about the accuracy of the data and methodologies used in Tanzania to estimate national income and growth as well as to estimate the magnitude of poverty and poverty reduction. Apparently, data precision and so their reliability has been doubtful for many years, despite the fact that notable improvements have been recorded over time. Limited resources and skills in data collection, processing and management are among the major barriers to improving data quality.

There is clear evidence that the national accounts in Tanzania contain a number of gaps in terms of both data sources and the methodologies used to estimate income.[11] For example, national income accounting has not been able to capture adequately the huge subsistence production in agriculture. Another challenge relates to standard measures of weights. The Household Budget Surveys use measures such as tins, bundles and heaps, but these tend to vary between sellers in terms of weight and size.

A huge part of the informal economy is also normally not captured in data used to estimate national income and growth, as these activities do not pass through the market and so market prices are not established. According to Chipeta, the informal sector consists of all economic activities that are neither monitored nor taxed by the government and are not included in government gross net product statistics.[12] Tax evasion is usually associated with transactions and incomes that are not reported, and these are mainly in the informal economy. The actual contribution of the informal economy to overall national income is therefore hard to establish, because calculations depend mainly on estimations and projections which employ weak methods.

Methodological challenges and gaps facing the national accounting system in Tanzania make it difficult to ascertain the extent to which economic growth has occurred in the country.

In the context of concerns about the methodologies used to estimate national income and the magnitude of poverty, explanations for the mismatch between economic growth and poverty reduction include demographic factors, underinvestment in education and agriculture, limited growth in agriculture and the rising cost of basic necessities. The following sections discuss these in more detail.

Demographic factors

Population dynamics are one possible explanation for the growth–poverty mismatch. The country's population increased from 23.2 million in 1988 to 34.4 million in 2002 to the 2009 estimated level of 41.9 million. It is estimated that the number will increase to about 50 million by 2015 and 65.3 million in 2025 (see Figure 7.4).[13] Based on an annual population growth rate of 2.9 per cent, by 2050 Tanzania will have a population of 88.8 million. Tanzania's population is very young and as a result its dependency ratio is relatively high, at about 0.85 (compared with 0.84 and 1.12 for Kenya and Uganda, respectively). This ratio reduces the real income and negatively affects the purchasing power and ability of households to save for future investments, thus making poverty levels persistent despite economic growth.

Figure 7.4: Population size in Tanzania 1948–2002 and projections to 2025

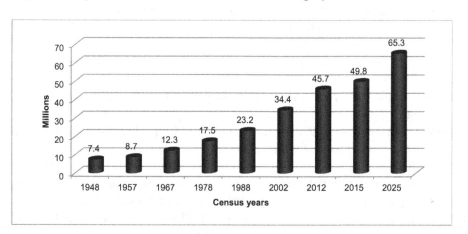

Source: Constructed using United Republic of Tanzania (2011b)

Given that most Tanzanians finish school at primary school level, girls are exposed to early marriage and child-bearing.[14] On average, each woman bears 5.7 children in her lifetime, which is among the highest fertility levels in the world, although it is declining. This means that Tanzania's population will grow further, despite the effects of AIDS. Over 1.3 million Tanzanians are born every year. Meanwhile, people below thirty years of age account for 73 per cent of the population (see Figure 7.5) and this large number of potential child-bearers provides an inbuilt momentum for accelerated population growth that has to be checked as a matter of urgency.

Figure 7.5: Population of Tanzania by age and sex, 1995–2010

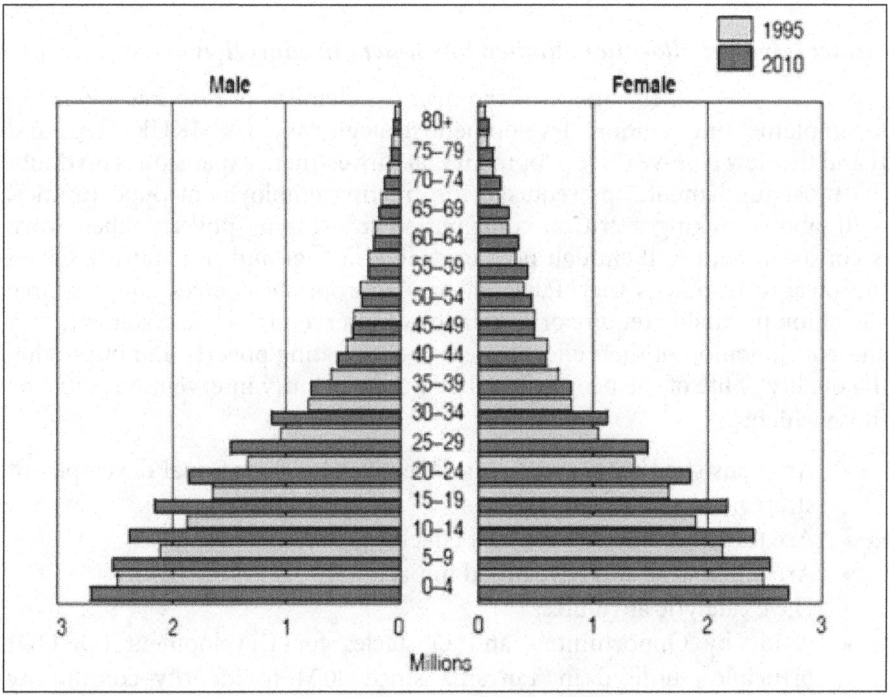

Source: US Censors Bureau: International Data Base (1995 – 2010)

Raising the minimum level of education of girls is one long-lasting solution to slowing down population growth in Tanzania, besides family planning education and other birth control measures. Increased schooling delays entry into family and reproductive life and also raises self-awareness and confidence to make reproductive health decisions. However, while primary education was enough to support the poverty escape of today's forty and fifty year olds, the strong emphasis placed on gaining post-primary education for today's young people suggests that primary education is widely perceived as not being enough for success in the future. Access to secondary education remains severely limited for poor households, though, and this should be addressed.

Another means of slowing down population growth in the long term is through increasing economic opportunities. Households which are engaged in farming, livestock keeping, fishing and forestry are the poorest. However, the change in rural per capita income is small owing to the fact that annual rural growth (as a proxy for growth of the agriculture sector) in early 2007 was about

4.5 per cent while the national population growth rate is 2.9 per cent. This situation further perpetuates the poverty problem in rural areas.

The growth of the population will have implications for many facets of planning and economic management besides food security. Chief among these is an increase in the numbers of people in poverty. Regional variations in the incidence of poverty exist and tend to mirror variations in the annual GDP growth rate. The highest economic growth rates are in Kigoma (7.4 per cent), Bukoba (7.3 per cent) and Shinyanga (7.3 per cent) and the lowest in Kilimanjaro (3.9 per cent) and Dar es Salaam (2.5 per cent).

Strategic budget allocation: limited investment in education and agriculture

The government budget is the main mechanism of resource allocation for implementing national development strategies such as MKUKUTA I and II and the new Five-year Development Plan. Investment expansion is no doubt the most fundamental prerequisite for creating employment opportunities, with labour making a critical contribution to escaping poverty when work is consistent and well enough paid to enable savings and remittances. Given the meagre resources that Tanzania has, appropriate choices and resource allocation inevitably require prioritisation of interventions in a systematic way and consideration of their effectiveness at eliminating poverty and improving the quality of life of the people. In other words, priority interventions must be those which;

- Are consistent with overriding objectives (as in national development strategies);
- Are the most efficient and cost effective;
- Are quick wins and have broad impact;
- Have catalytic attributes;
- Abide by Opportunities and Obstacles for Development (O&OD) principles, utilised in Tanzania since 2004 to identify community problems, prioritise solutions in terms of development projects and implement these.

The government of Tanzania should make careful and appropriate economic choices and decisions to ensure the efficient allocation and utilisation of available resources, based on existing rules and regulations as well as conditions spelt out earlier. However, as yet, Tanzania has not been able to ensure strategic allocation of resources and there is still huge room for improvements. Underinvestment in education and agriculture are two examples. Between 2008/09 and 2009/10 for example Education sector budget was scaled up in absolute terms despite the fact that the percentage share declined from 7.3 to 5.3 percent. The trends in agricultural financing nia from 2001/02 to 2014/15 show that, in nominal terms the total agricultural resource allocation has been increasing overtime. This is true in both absolute and relative terms. For example, from 2001/02 to 2004/05, the total agricultural budget increased from TZS 52,072 Million to TZS 3,347,539 Million, which is equivalent to 3 and 4.7 percent of total government expenditure, respectively. In 2008/09 and 2009/10, the corresponding figures were TZS 517,611 Million and TZS 722,000 Million, which is equivalent to 7.2 and 7.6 percent of total government expenditure, respectively.

Scaling up investment in education is inevitable given the high proportion of young people in the population. However, merely expanding the number of schools without ensuring their quality is probably not the optimal strategy. The low quality of education offered by the mushrooming numbers of primary and secondary schools and the crash training programmes offered to trainee teachers is likely to increase income disparity and inequality and intensify poverty in the country. The current education system allows only rich Tanzanians to educate their children better, enabling them eventually to dominate the decent employment positions available in the labour market.

Agriculture comprised nearly 26 per cent of GDP in 2009, yet the same year it received just over a 7 per cent share of the total budget (Figure 7.6). It has been demonstrated clearly that underinvestment in domestic agriculture is one of the root causes of Africa's growing dependence on imported food[15]. Thus, in 2003 the African Heads of State adopted the Maputo Declaration, whereby they committed to substantially raising public investment in agriculture to at least 10 per cent of government spending, in order to achieve their goal of a 6 per cent annual growth rate in agriculture.[16] However, in Tanzania, while there has been an upward trend in agricultural financing between 2001/02 and 2010/11, in nominal terms the total agricultural resource allocation has been persistently below 10 per cent (Figure 7.6). As 87 per cent of poor people live in rural areas and 75 per cent of rural income is derived from agricultural activities, investment in agriculture is central to poverty reduction.

Figure 7.6: Agricultural financing in Tanzania, 2001/02–10/11

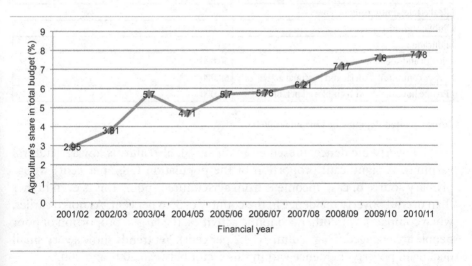

Source: Constructed based on Ministry of Agriculture, Food Security and Cooperatives (2010)

Limited agricultural growth

According to the Tanzania Development Vision 2025 review report,[17] although the share of agriculture in GDP has in recent years slowed down, agriculture remains the single highest ranking employer in the country.[18] For any growth to be inclusive and pro-poor, it must involve substantial growth in agricultural productivity and allow most of the rural population to benefit through selling to domestic and export markets. Growth in other sectors can then provide an opportunity for surplus labour to be employed in alternative economic activities without undermining agricultural productivity.

Table 7.3 presents monthly income by sector and clearly shows that average income generation in agriculture is the lowest when compared with other sectors such as fishing, manufacturing, construction and real estate.

Table 7.3: Median monthly income by sector in Tanzania, 2006

Sector	Median monthly income 2006 (TSh)
Agriculture and hunting	20,000
Fishing	40,000
Mining and quarrying	60,000
Manufacturing	35,000
Electricity, gas and water	190,000
Construction	85,000
Wholesale and retail trade	44,000
Hotels and restaurants	40,000
Transport, storage and communications	56,000
Financial intermediation	160,000
Real estate, renting and business	120,000
Public administration	55,000
Education	40,000
Health and social services	50,000
Other community, social and personal activities	60,000
Private households with employed persons	24,000

Source: United Republic of Tanzania (2007)

Poverty incidence, presented in Table 7.4, also affirms low agricultural earnings. A significant proportion of the population (38.7 per cent) whose primary source of cash income is from agriculture is poor. This is even higher than overall poverty incidence in the country of 33.6 per cent. As noted earlier, when compared with other economic activities, the largest proportion of poor people are engaged in agriculture (74.2 per cent). Yet trends show a very small decline in poverty incidence within this sector between 2001 and 2007.

Table 7.4: Distribution of poverty by main source of income in Tanzania, 2000/01 and 2007

Activity of head	2000/01		2007	
	Headcount ratio	% of the poor	Headcount ratio	% of the poor
Farming/livestock/fishing/forestry	39.9	80.8	38.7	74.2
Government employee	15.3	1.8	10.8	1.6
Parastatal employee/other	8.1	0.3	10.9	0.7
Employee/other	20.2	3.0	20.6	3.3
Self-employed/family helper	28.5	7.9	21.4	10.6
Student	-	-	17.9	0.0
Not active/home-maker	43.1	6.2	46.2	9.6
Total	35.7	100.0	33.4	100.0

Source: National Bureau of Statistics (2008a)

Despite a large proportion of poor people being dependent on agricultural income, between 2000 and 2008 the average annual growth of agriculture (4.6 per cent) was significantly below the GDP growth rate (7 per cent). As shown in Figure 7.7, to a large extent the GDP growth rate has been determined by that of the industry and services sectors, which have averaged at 8.6 per cent and 7.5 per cent, respectively. This pattern of growth is one of the main reasons why economic growth in Tanzania over the past decade has not been associated with poverty reduction—because that growth is taking place outside agriculture.

Figure 7.7: Annual growth in agriculture in Tanzania, 1998–2001

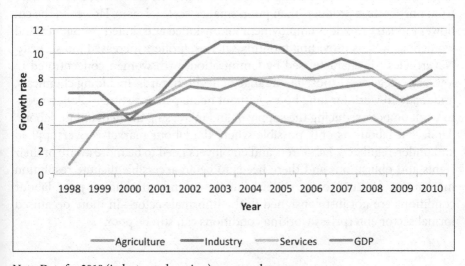

Note: Data for 2010 (industry and services) are annual averages
Source: Constructed based on United Republic of Tanzania (2011a; 2011b)

Pro-poor growth needs to target poor people and therefore respective interventions and investment must target agriculture, among other sectors. For example, in order for farmers to achieve maximum productivity, they need functional education because this is a productivity factor. Education can improve the innovation of farmers and increase their ability to adapt new methods of farming. However, only 20 per cent of the adult population in Tanzania obtain secondary education and above (secondary education 17 per cent, post-secondary education 2 per cent, university education 1 per cent).[19]

Meanwhile, interventions in agriculture do not necessarily imply just direct investments in the sector. Investment may also be directed towards transformation and modernisation of other sectors, including manufacturing, to which the agricultural workforce will gradually shift to engage itself in decent jobs, provided they have the necessary education and skills.

Investment in agricultural research and extension can also yield large and positive impacts on agricultural growth and household incomes. Findings from other studies suggest that, for every TZS 1 million investment in agricultural research (in 1999 prices), household incomes grow to TZS 12.5 million and moves forty people out of poverty[20]

Evidence from the survey and literature shows that small farmers' access to productive resources, assets and service is limited,[21] with these resources including land, agricultural financing, livestock and productive equipment. Without these assets, people have to incorporate themselves into the agricultural economy as labourers in oversupplied markets. One area of agricultural growth is flower production for export, with the quantity of exported flowers increasing from 5,862 tonnes in 2005/06 to 6,897 tonnes in 2006/07 from an estimated acreage of 137 ha. Empirical evidence indicates that large-scale farmers who are also connected to the export market benefit more from horticulture products than poor, smaller-scale farmers. However, the cut flower industry provides employment for unskilled and skilled young men and women; as well as providing monthly salaries, it offers increased job security. Nevertheless, is characterised by feminisation, with women concentrated in low-pay categories, exposed to a range of health hazards, including chemicals, and made to work for long hours without being paid overtime.[22] Policy needs to work on both reducing the supply of and increasing the demand for labour. 'Undecent labour' is only possible where the labour market is oversupplied and under-regulated. Labourers and employers need to be more aware of their rights and obligations and there needs to be an accessible dispute resolution mechanism for such cases. As the cut flower industry shows, poor labour conditions are not just consigned to the informal sector—in more organised formal sector enterprises working conditions can still be poor.

The rising cost of living

Rapidly increasing cost of basic necessities

While from 2000 to 2005 the population faced a slowly rising cost of living, between 2005 and 2009 people saw a very rapid rise. Poor people speak of being priced entirely out of the market for certain basic needs (such as beef, chicken, milk and fish—i.e. the protein content of meals). This rise in the cost of living is reflected in a range of consumer price indices for Tanzania. Figure 7.8 shows how consumer price indices for selected products have been rising gradually since 2002, and rapidly since 2005 in all areas, most notably food, followed by fuel.[23] Indeed, food inflation has been the most dominant component of inflation, particularly with the global food price crisis which began in 2006.

Figure 7.8: Yearly trend in consumer price indices from November 2002 to November 2009 by selected groups of indices

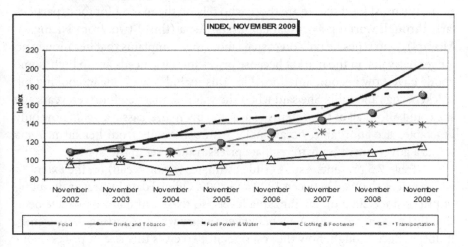

Source: National Bureau of Statistics (2010)

Figure 7.9 shows the purchasing power of the shilling in terms of consumption at different times. From November 2002, the value/purchasing power of TZS 100 fell to just TZS 59.28 in November 2009. Poverty resulting from inflation in terms of costs of basic needs is felt more acutely in urban regions like Mtwara, Mwanza and Rukwa, where people are more reliant on the market for employment and where price levels are higher than in rural areas. One respondent in Newala said that a cow in a nearby village cost roughly TZS 100,000 but in Newala it cost TZS 500,000. Moreover, people in peri-urban regions like Newala often have to pay rent, which also reduces the amount available for purchasing other necessities like power and foodstuffs.

Figure 7.9: Purchasing power of TZS 100 in November 2002 compared with November 2009

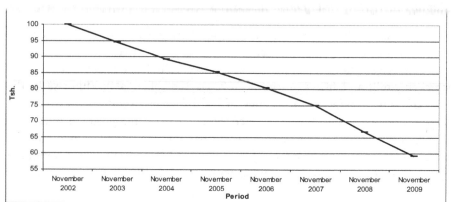

Source: National Bureau of Statistics (2010)

This rise in prices is particularly crippling for casual labourers. In Tanzania, the most food secure are those who rely on the market for food, particularly through working as casual labourers. Asna (thirty-two, from Nkangala, Mtwara), who relies heavily on casual labouring, complains that her money no longer has value in the market because prices for basic needs are so high; some goods have now become unaffordable. This includes beef, sugar, cooking oil, chicken, eggs and milk. She said when she was first married fourteen years ago she could afford all of these items to accompany maize/cassava *ugali*; now only vegetables are affordable, occasionally with some nuts from her farm. Asna wants a government body to regulate prices traders set in the market.

Table 7.5 presents Asna's crude estimates (using recall) on the extent to which prices changed between 1999 and 2009. Official data indicate a doubling of prices since 2002 on all Tanzania levels, so these estimates may have been slightly exaggerated, with Asna being very angry when reporting these trends. It does reflect, though, how the respondent perceives this rise in prices. Nonfood essentials such as soap and kerosene are also said to have doubled or even trebled over the past ten years (focus group discussion in Newala).

Table 7.5: Estimated changes in prices of foodstuffs in Tanzania between 1999 and 2009

Type of foodstuff	1999	2009	Multiplier
Maize	TSh 600–700	TSh 7,000	10
Cassava	TSh 2,000	TSh 18–20,000	10
Sugar	TSh 400	TSh 1,400	3.5
Beef	TSh 1–1,500	TSh 5,000	2.5
Whole cow	TSh 100,000	TSh 500,000	5
Cooking oil	TSh 6,000	TSh 23,000	4
Chicken	TSh 1–1,500	TSh 9,000	7.2

Source: L. da Corta and J. Magongo (2010)

It is feared that food insecurity may be on the increase in Tanzania despite fast economic growth rates, for three reasons: (1) a rise in the number of labourers as a consequence of rapid population growth and the dwindling size and fertility of farm land owned; (2) a sustained fall in agricultural production over time which reduces labour opportunities and leads to stagnating wages; and (3) a rise in the prices of food or non-food essentials.

One puzzle for economists is why costs have risen in the context of low incomes, as the lack of local effective demand for products should have depressed prices. A key reason for this is the fact that, since Tanzania is a net importer of intermediate and final goods, the depreciation of the shilling has served to exacerbate the diverse balance of payments position. This owes to the inelastic nature of imports (fertilisers, medicines, raw materials for manufacturing, clothing and oil), which has increased the cost of such imports relative to previous years. Consumers suffer the most because the added cost for imported goods and raw materials is passed on to them.[24]

The current market structure has also crowded out farmers. The wealth created in these localities does not benefit local producers but rather a few traders who deliberately suppress local prices and subsequently pay farmers marginally. This is enabled as local economies and respective local farmers are delinked from external (regional and export) markets which offer attractive producer prices. Private traders therefore make substantial margins from other markets outside the local farming communities where they sell products bought from local farmers at profitable prices.

Since market liberalisation, which started in the early 1980s, Tanzania has not been able to establish an alternative system to correct market distortions— but the market structure needs to change to reflect the interests of all market participants. It is important for the government to maintain a supportive policy environment and ensure that it plays an effective minimum regulatory role. The current structure has loopholes (owing to the passive participation of some key players, particularly the government) which encourage exploitation of farmers by crop-buyers and traders. It denies farmers direct access to attractive markets. There is therefore an urgent need to come up with effective agriculture-based strategic programmes which will transform smallholder agriculture and increase growth in the sector by way of stimulating agricultural activities and subsequently improving the livelihoods of people involved in agriculture.

Another reason for price inflation is the cost of transport. Across Tanzania, persistent rising fuel prices have increased the costs of transporting food to the market, contributing to increased prices of both food and non-food essentials.[25] Mtwara is high on a plateau and truckers face both high fuel prices and possibly injuring their tyres on exposed roads, so a premium is added onto the price of the goods imported. Likewise, the Kalesa–Kayumbe road is in a poor condition, particularly during the rainy season, thus pushing the cost of transportation up. This premium is also the outcome of additional costs (in form of corruption) met by private traders to overcome regulations imposed by authorities such as road barriers and export ban.

The persistent shortage of electricity in Tanzania has also tended to push consumer prices up because of increased production costs. Meanwhile, the government salaried sector, with their permanent incomes and superior access to credit based on their constant wages, are one of the few groups experiencing upward mobility. This salaried sector and the people who serve them (hairdressers, restaurant and hotel staff) may bid up the price of goods in local areas. Non-governmental organisation presence, particularly in Mtwara and Mwanza, further adds to this demand for goods together with steady stream of visitors (staff, visiting officials and crop-traders, for example). Other possibilities are that the rise in credit availability over the past few years has increased the amount of money in this economy.

Rapidly increasing cost of services: water, education and health care

Another very lumpy and growing cost for poor people is the cost of essential services. In many localities, the most pressing costs are for water, education and health. MKUKUTA I was designed to broaden access to basic social services, but service costs are making people poorer. The poor either pay or do without the service, resulting in undereducated youths and the hygienic and health consequences associated with minimal water usage.

People in Mtwara are angry at the shortage of water. In the 1960s, water was pumped from River Ruvuma into communal points and piped directly into buildings. This equipment is now twenty-four years old and requires both repair and a regular supply of electricity. There is a similar problem regarding piped water in Kalesa. Limited water availability contributes to poor people's downward mobility as they have to either spend increasing amounts of time fetching it (which can limit income-earning) or pay for it. Insufficient water fosters disease and malnutrition, and paying for water puts further pressure on consumption of better-quality protein- and vitamin-rich foods. Children tend to skip school because of unwashed uniforms. Asna, thirty-two years old from Nkangala in Mtwara region explained that it took up to six hours to collect water, and it is uphill coming back. The older children could help, but they come back exhausted and unwilling to go to school; if Asna goes, she may forfeit a casual labour wage. With four children, she needs to do the journey every two days. She could pay for trucked-in water, which costs TZS 500 per 20 litre bucket. She could also do without or scrimp, but then her children would not go to school because of the shame of having dirty faces or clothes.

School fees are supposed to have been abolished at primary level and set at TZS 20,000 for secondary education, but these and supplementary contributions represent another problem, and teachers tell children to go away if they cannot pay. Inability to pay for uniforms is also very common. In Kalesa, Samweli (thirty-five years old) complains that contributions for primary school are very high for his nine children. He pays TZS 2,500 a month for each child in order to pay salaries for some teachers not registered under the government system. Such teacher contributions are village policy. He also pays TZS 200 each week for stationery.

For the most part, it is only non-poor families whose children are in school, especially secondary school. Poor parents find the supplementary costs of education crippling and the poorest cannot afford to keep their children in school. Members of a focus group in Nchinga, Mtwara, conveyed this: 'We do everything possible to send our children to school! But the poor and destitute cannot meet the payments for fees, uniform and supplementary costs and so are turned away.' They further reported that, at the local government school, if a child does not either contribute TZS 30,000 for a desk and chair or supply one made at home, they can be told to go home.

Expenditure on education has declined somewhat for rural households following primary education becoming fee-free, but has increased significantly for urban households, except the poorest. Health expenditure has increased markedly for both rural and especially urban households, with the exception of the rural poorest, who were presumably unable to afford to spend more (Table 7.6).

Table 7.6: Trends in health and education expenditure by well-being category in Tanzania, 2000/01–2006/7

Poverty category	Change in rural health expenditure	Change in urban health expenditure	Change in rural education expenditure	Change in urban education expenditure
Very poor	5.3%	55.2%	-13.4%	4.7%
Poor	26.4%	29.0%	-18.1%	15.2%
Non-poor	28.9%	30.7%	-16.9%	35.9%
All Tanzania mainland	26.4%	32.3%	-13.8%	38.3%

Note: Very poor = households with expenditure below the food poverty line; poor = households with expenditure between food poverty line and basic needs poverty line; non-poor = households with expenditure above basic needs poverty line
Source: E. Luvanda (2011)

Despite the availability of dispensaries, health centres and sometimes hospitals, these services are too expensive for poor people. People often have to pay TZS 25,000 for each x-ray or visit, 'but few poor people can just come up with this when they are struck suddenly with a disease, so these people die' (focus group discussion in Newala, Mtwara). The elderly and children are not supposed to pay for health services, but in practice women pay for under fives because drugs are usually not available. The elderly also pay for consultations (TZS 15,000 in Nchinga in Mtwara district) and medicines while village dispensaries have very erratic availability of drugs in general and so poor people are found to pay for them. Also, when people are admitted at the hospital, they often find there is no medicine and that two or three patients are forced to share one bed.

MKUKUTA I attempted to increase service provision— health, education and water in particular– by taxing users. However, people are finding that their incomes from agriculture are simply not adequate to meet the rising costs of services

Conclusion and recommendations

The mismatch between economic growth and poverty reduction in Tanzania is evident in the three Household Budget Surveys, in the period covering 1991/92, 2000/01 and 2007. The ongoing debate and literature have associated this mismatch with a number of factors, including methodological challenges facing the national accounts in Tanzania, demographic factors, issues related to resource allocation and the distribution of wealth, the stagnation of agricultural growth and the rising cost of basic necessities.

The national accounts are affected mainly by limited resources and a lack of skills and expertise required for data collection, processing and management. To address these gaps and weaknesses, the budget for the national accounts must be scaled up and capacity building of the National Bureau of Statistics must occur. Meanwhile, to ensure strategic resource allocation, Tanzania needs to improve governance by way of adherence to national priorities and strengthen auditing and financial accountability.

Momentum for accelerated population growth in Tanzania must be checked as a matter of urgency. In addition, the government needs to raise the level of education of girls and increase economic opportunities for women. These are among the most sustainable ways to slow down population growth in Tanzania, besides family planning education and other birth control measures. Longer stays in schooling delay entries into family and reproductive life and also raise self-awareness and confidence to make reproductive health decisions.

Agriculture occupies more than 74 per cent of Tanzanians—and this is the most deprived population in Tanzania in terms of average household incomes and overall poverty levels. Thus, for any poverty reduction initiative to be effective, it must focus on agriculture. The sector has a higher income multiplication effect and higher income elasticity of total poverty than other sectors. It therefore has to be the priority sector for investment and it must grow by more than 6 per cent per annum if it is to contribute significantly to growth and poverty reduction.

More specifically, investment in productivity-enhancing factors (irrigation, mechanisation, research, development and extension, use of improved agricultural inputs, natural resources, environment, climate change mitigation and adaptation) is needed. Investment in rural roads/infrastructure, agro-processing and packaging will be needed to expand the market, especially for priority crops. Promotion of public–private partnership and investment in capacity-building at all levels are also prerequisites for agricultural growth.

In order to stimulate growth in the sector and reduce poverty in rural areas, public expenditure on agriculture should be increased. For example, making financial services accessible by the poor and very poor (for instance by effectively linking them to existing microcredit schemes) and effective is a priority. Some measures must be taken to enable access to land, livestock and productive equipment. Policies which make land easier to own or rent (in and out) would be especially helpful, and policies focused on helping poor people acquire or rent farm assets (e.g. irrigation and oxen) and non-farm business assets should complement these. The poor operate in labour, service and commodity markets which are oversupplied (e.g. petty trade, casual labour, brewing and subsistence foods). Returns are low as a result. Getting people from poor households into higher-return markets through skills upgrading and tightening oversupplied markets are two ways of facilitating escapes from poverty.

---

1   A.V.Y. Mbelle (2007)

2   United Republic of Tanzania (2011a)

3   See Ministry of Finance and Economic Affairs (2002; 2003; 2005; 2007) and National Bureau of Statistics (1992; 2002; 2008a)

4   National Bureau of Statistics (2008a)

5   United Republic of Tanzania (2011a)

6   United Republic of Tanzania (1998)

7   United Republic of Tanzania (2000)

8   A.V.Y. Mbelle (2007). See also the various Poverty and Human Development Reports (Ministry of Finance and Economic Affairs, 2002; 2003; 2005; 2007) and Household Budget Survey reports (National Bureau of Statistics, 1992; 2002; 2008a)

9   Ibid.

10   Economic and Social Research Foundation (2006); World Bank (2004)

11   See, for example, Z.E. Msokwa (2001)

12   C. Chipeta (2002)

13   United Republic of Tanzania (2011b)

14   Nationwide, about 66 per cent of girls will be married before their twentieth birthday and 7 per cent of young men will have sex before the age of fifteen.

15   See for Example Kilimo Trust (2009)

16   Ministry of Agriculture, Food Security and Cooperatives (2010)

17   United Republic of Tanzania (2011a)

18   See also United Republic of Tanzania (2011b)

19   L.A. Msambichaka (2011)

20   S. Fan et al. (2005) in K. Pauw and J. Thurlow (2010)

21   See L. da Corta and J. Magongo (2010); O. Mashindano et al. (2010)

22   F. Kessy (2010)

23   The National Consumer Price Index covers prices collected in twenty towns in mainland Tanzania. Prices are gathered for 207 items and are the prevailing market prices. The index is a statistical measure of goods and services bought by persons in urban areas, including all expenditure groups. It measures changes in price—not expenditure—which are the most important cause of changes in the cost of living

24   Tanzania Gender Networking Programme (2007)

25   Famine Early Warning Systems Network (2009)

Chapter 8

Agricultural Growth and Poverty Reduction in Tanzania—Emerging Issues and Major Recommendations

Oswald Mashindano, Kim Kayunze, Festo Maro, Lucia da Corta, and Andrew Shepherd

Introduction

The Tanzanian economy has recently registered impressive economic growth, averaging 7 per cent between 2000 and 2008. The highest growth has been recorded in sectors with a marginal contribution to gross domestic product (GDP), employment and poverty reduction, such as mining, with agriculture recording a persistently lower growth rate compared with industry and services over this period (see Chapter 7). Average growth in agriculture over the past ten years has been about 4 per cent, consistently lower than is required to reduce poverty significantly; that growth which has occurred has not 'trickled down' adequately to the poor. It is clear from recent field research, undertaken by a Chronic Poverty Research Centre team made up of researchers from the Economic and Social Research Foundation, Research on Poverty Alleviation and Sokoine University of Agriculture, Ifakara Health Institute in Tanzania and the Overseas Development Institute in the United Kingdom, that problems with marketing and production of agricultural crops are both holding back economic growth and reducing the impact of growth on poverty.

Agriculture remains the largest sector in Tanzania, contributing nearly 26 per cent of GDP and an average of nearly 24 per cent of the country's export earnings per annum.[1] In addition, about 87 per cent of poor people live in rural areas and 75 per cent of rural income is earned from agricultural activities. The sector's significance is amplified through its backward and forward linkages to all sectors of the economy.

Crops are the dominant contributor of agriculture to GDP, with an average share of 21 per cent of GDP, and are the focus of this chapter. Overall, agriculture grew by 4.8 per cent in 2008 compared with 4.0 per cent in 2007. In recent years, the share of export crops in total foreign exchange earnings has declined substantially, from 34 per cent in 2000 to slightly below 20 per cent in 2007. Agriculture's absolute contribution to exports has increased, but its relative share of total exports has declined because other sectors of the economy have expanded their share more rapidly.

Yet a 1 per cent increase in growth in the agriculture sector has been shown to have a bigger impact on poverty reduction than a 10 per cent growth in other sectors.[2] It is extremely important to support agriculture and fishing since income growth in these sectors will have the biggest effect on poverty, as Figure 8.1 shows. There are several channels through which this effect operates: reducing food prices, increasing farm household incomes and consumption and generating wage employment, as well as providing demand for non-farm goods and services, which in turn provides employment. A large majority (76.5 per cent, according to the 2001/02 Integrated Labour Force Survey)[3] of the employed labour force is engaged in smallholder agriculture, where underemployment is also high, partly as a result of dependence on seasonal rain-fed agriculture. Tanzania could have made use of this underutilised resource by adopting appropriate and strategic policy interventions aiming at skills development and human resource absorption. Transformation and improvement of agriculture is critical if rural poverty reduction and improved livelihoods are to be realised.

Figure 8.1: Elasticity of total poverty with respect to average income growth by occupation, calculated from the 2007 Household Budget Survey

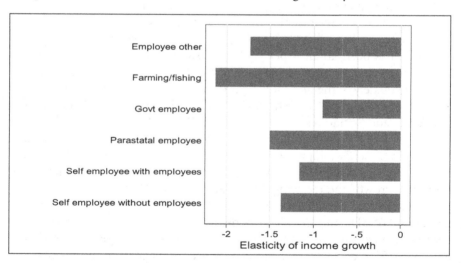

Source: Luvanda (2011)

Despite the notably positive contribution of agriculture to national economic development, a number of bottlenecks are hindering more rapid growth in the sector. The National Strategy for Growth and the Reduction of Poverty (MKUKUTA) and Agricultural Sector Development Programme target 10 per cent agricultural growth to successfully attain poverty reduction targets, but this has never been achieved. There are multiple manifestations of the various barriers facing agriculture in Tanzania. These include low income generation, low capital investment, low productivity, diminishing livelihood sources, food insecurity and therefore intensive poverty and poor quality of life. This chapter focuses on identifying critical barriers to agricultural growth and poverty reduction and the strategic interventions which can stimulate agricultural growth as well as enabling a significant reduction in poverty.

Emerging issues and recommendations for agricultural policy

The recommendations discussed in this section are based on findings from a study using a medium-sized qualitative dataset in Rukwa, Mtwara and Mwanza regions as well as national household survey data. A number of pertinent issues emerge from preliminary analysis of the information gathered from this research. Each of these is linked either to sluggish agricultural growth or to the slow pace of poverty reduction—or both. Although these findings and recommendations are grouped into different sections, they overlap. The prime focus is the organisation of markets: strategic interventions to improve the functioning of markets can boost agricultural growth and render it more pro-poor.

However, policymakers and the Tanzanian government interpret a liberalised economy (free market framework) as a system whereby the government machinery has no role to play in the economy, whatever happens. Farmers are therefore left entirely in the hands of private operators. This is a misconception of market liberalisation policy. For markets to work effectively and fairly there need to be 'rules of the game'; at the very least they must be embedded in a well-functioning legal framework.

A number of policy measures need to be considered to improve market efficiency and restore fair market competition. It is important for the government to maintain a supportive policy environment and to ensure that it plays an effective regulatory role. For example, it needs to revisit the current trend whereby top government and political executives own and operate buying firms: they are decision-makers and at the same time private buyers. This is particularly common in the cashew nut and sesame industries in Mtwara and Lindi regions. Tanzania may need to go back to the days when top government and political executives were not allowed to run high-scale businesses owing to potential conflicts of interest. This model may be working elsewhere eg in Developed World, but not necessarily in Least Developed Countries such as Tanzania, where capacity to monitor operations of the business enterprises is limited.

Improving market access

The research findings point to improvements in market access and the functioning of value chains as being more likely than taking a 'production first' approach to have sustainable impacts on production and poverty reduction.

Judging by changes in volumes of crop outputs and the acreage being cropped over time in Rukwa, Mtwara and Mwanza, it is evident that modest growth has taken place in the agriculture sector. However, this growth has not been associated with poverty reduction and changes in the livelihoods of people in the respective localities and/or markets. Access to external markets needs to be encouraged because these markets can stimulate significant demand for local agricultural production. At the same time, local farmers should be protected from traders seeking to maximize profits from high interest on farm credit and/or from suppressing farm gate prices at the time of sale.

As an example, in Kirando, a field site bordering Lake Tanganyika, paddy production was stimulated when demand from 'grain-hungry' interior countries across the lake grew rapidly. However, traders pocketed much of the profits of the small farmers by lending sacks of rice seeds before harvest and demanding three in return 'in kind' at harvest—that is, 200 per cent interest. In addition, before a warehouse scheme was introduced, smallholders sold off the remainder of this harvest in desperation at low, 'at harvest' prices and lost out on the benefits of storing and selling when prices rose. At the moment, local people consider the savings and credit cooperative organisation (SACCO) in the region to be only for the rich; small farmers continue to rely on moneylenders-cum-traders for their input needs.

Commodities traded between Newala district in Mtwara region and Mozambique include fabrics (*batiki* and *vitenge*) which are sold in Mtwara, cashew nuts and electronic appliances. Newala receives fabrics, iron sheeting, gin and sugar and sends second-hand clothes, mattresses, sardines and cashew apples, known locally as *kochoka* and used to make a local alcoholic spirit. However, not many urban farmers export crops to Mozambique. A key informant from Nchinga village in Mtwara pointed out that this was because there was no reliable bridge. Traders normally cross the river using small canoes without engines. Tanzanian producers are very limited in terms of what they have to trade and the Tanzania Revenue Authority is not present to streamline trade between the two destinations. It was estimated that only about 10 per cent of traders from Newala district in Mtwara are involved in cross-border trade. Meanwhile, in Magu and Silali (Mwanza) cross-border trade is booming.

Farmers need to be better linked to regional export markets through strengthened capacity to access these markets and to sell more at better prices. Better cross-border infrastructure (e.g. road networks), a cross-border market information-sharing network, better transportation and even contract farming arrangements would help. Farmers should be encouraged to unite and trade their product themselves; this should be enabled by supplying marketing information and exploring ways to offer SACCO membership to poorer farmers. Another response could be to extend the warehouse scheme to new crops. This is discussed in more detail later in the chapter.

In Magu district of Mwanza, for instance, urban respondents reported that, before 1982, when the main Mwanza–Tarime trunk road was constructed, markets for their farm produce were extremely limited. When road construction was completed, villagers had access to Kenyan markets through the border at Silali. Cross-border trade stimulated agri-business and moved people out of poverty, according to some key informants in Magu district. It also stimulated paddy production, with many farmers shifting from cotton to paddy production. This was furthered after the global economic crisis when cotton prices declined.

It is not just improvements in cross-border transport infrastructure that are necessary: road connections between villages and market and administrative centres are vital to increase access to local markets and services. The road network in the sampled districts is poorly developed. There are waterways (Lake Victoria in Magu and Lake Tanganyika in Kayumbe (Rukwa)) and very limited all-weather roads, but most areas in the districts have seasonal roads or none at all. High transport charges in remote rural areas make it difficult for farmers to sell their crops. For example, the fare for one person to travel from Kirando in Nkasi district of Rukwa to Kayumbe, the district headquarters (a distance of 59km), was TZS 5,000 in 2009. Transporting luggage, especially crop products, is also expensive. This is notwithstanding government efforts to improve rural roads under the 2000–4 Poverty Reduction Strategy and the 2005–10 MKUKUTA.

The story was different in Magu district, Mwanza, where transport costs and time to reach the district headquarters (25km) had reduced appreciably, as a result of road improvements in 2005. One interviewee said that it used to take two hours to make the journey, but now there were cars available for them from 7.00a.m. to 10.00p.m., and that they go to the district headquarters anytime they like, even three times a day. Likewise, the Kayumbe–Sumbawanga main road provides an important link between producers in Kanazi village and traders in commercial towns such as Sumbawanga and Tunduma town. Farmers are able to send their maize to strategic grain-buying points, where middlemen buy crops from farmers who cannot afford the cost of transporting them to the markets.

However, the lingering transport problem in most areas points to a recommendation that improving roads remain a priority, to facilitate the transportation of people and goods from and to rural areas in order to help increase agricultural growth that contributes to the reduction of poverty. However, improving roads is not enough to create a competitive transport industry: the factors determining this need to be investigated and addressed locally.

The access of the poorest to agricultural markets can also be improved through measures which enable greater access to land. Young farmers in particular suffer from inadequate access to farmland, as the size of their farm inheritance falls with each generation, particularly in peri-urban regions. This problem is made worse when the older generation, unable to till land, fear renting out unused land owing to concerns that the person leasing it in will subsequently claim it as their own. As a consequence, the older generation with uncultivated land is not renting to the younger generation, who face rapidly rising prices for farmland, making new land purchase unaffordable for many. For instance, in Mtwara, land prices have trebled over the past decade for cashew farm land and quadrupled for maize.

Another problem relating to land ownership and access is uncultivated family land held jointly among family members. In land-scarce regions like Mtwara, much land is uncultivated as it is owned jointly with siblings who are not resident; residents fear that, if they cultivate the land or lease it out, their siblings will get angry at them for reducing its fertility. This problem is on the rise as siblings migrate to urban regions for work, leaving land at home uncultivated. Indeed, sometimes, non-residents retain land simply to pass on to their own children when they grow up. With the rise in the prevalence of feminised villages (with women of all ages, children and only elderly men), it is increasingly important that women gain access to male kin's unused land, especially as they are often responsible for financing the maintenance of children and ill elderly relatives.

Researchers and policymakers should explore ways to enable residents to access unused clan land through secure leasing agreements. Recommendations may consider prioritising attention to female residents who have children to maintain. Further work could explore changes to customary rights which would enable more effective functioning of land and rental markets. This may include educating farmers so that they are not in any doubt about the safety of renting out land. This would put underutilised Tanzanian land resources to good use and at the same time solve some of the underemployment and poverty of young farmers currently heavily reliant on casual labour and petty trade.

Another priority area relating to land access concerns women's inheritance of land. It is well known that women lose access to assets—farm, livestock and house—to their husbands when they separate or to husbands' families when widowed (see Chapter 4). Both widowhood and separation are on the increase as a result of male illness and the decline of polygamy in land-scarce areas (farms are becoming so small that they are insufficient to maintain two families). Yet single women continue to be responsible for financing the costs of education, food and clothes for their children, with these costs rising in recent years. When women seek help in securing a widow's or divorcee's share of the land, customary law often prevails, as disputes are adjudicated by local elders and clerics which, under traditional ethnic group or Sharia law, will allocate a third, or less, of marital assets to women, or only what she brought in to the marriage from her parental inheritance. In Newala, Mtwara, only one woman had heard of legislation which entitles women to a fairer division of assets—on the radio. None of the local officials had heard of this legislation. This is also true in Magu (Mwanza region) and Kirando (Rukwa region). There is a need to raise awareness among women and local officials of the need to enforce the statutory land law (1999), enabling women titles to land inherited from parents and to receive a fairer share after separation, divorce and widowhood.

However, improving market access for, and reducing the poverty of, the poorest people is not just a matter of increasing access to land but also the associated employment opportunities. Education, skills development and information are all necessary to improve the terms on which people are able to engage with the market. The level of education of most farmers and pastoralists is generally too weak for them to meld indigenous skills with the uptake of improved practices from public and private extension agents. In the villages surveyed, life history interviews indicated that few farmers are aware of farmer field schools; some of those who are aware do not appreciate the knowledge delivered. They continue to practise indigenous skills in production, harvesting, storage and marketing. Farmers' field school is a chosen piece of land where a few representative farmers who are under training are practising. The intention is to encourage these farmers to disseminate the knowledge after graduating. One problem is that, as training courses come at the end of the farming season, it is difficult for farmers to recall knowledge gained in the subsequent season. Meanwhile, an agricultural extension officer in Nchinga village, Mtwara, blamed farmers and their 'poor mentality' for the non-adoption of improved agricultural practices;

> Most farmers have an attitude of poor attention to agricultural messages. I invited seventy farmers to attend demonstrations on farmer field schools but only five farmers attended. This poor attendance owed to the bad notion people in this area had that agriculture is politics and that the ruling party had sent the experts to mislead them. Almost all the respondents were members of the opposition party.

Agricultural skills development needs to be integrated into the education system, including teaching curricula for primary and secondary schools. The question of what sort of agriculture is appropriate to teach through schools or farmer field schools needs much more reflection: 'farmer first' approaches, involving farmer participation, would help to ensure relevance. This hands-on delivery of information can be supplemented, but not replaced, by reinforcement through, for instance, the satellite television cinemas that are rapidly increasing in number in rural Tanzania and cell phone YouTube-type video clips, to capitalise on the recent uptake of cell phones in many remote villages. Difficulties may arise with using cell phones to post market information (people may flock to markets where good prices are said to be), they can be very useful for posting the latest information from agricultural stations on region-specific inputs. It may be difficult for remote villagers to travel to get advice on yellowing cashew leaves, but they would be able to access information or advice using their cell phone. Recorded voice messages could be used for illiterate farmers.

Increasing agricultural productivity, particularly through input markets

The emphasis in agricultural policy remains on increasing productivity, especially by improving input markets. In particular, MKUKUTA II emphasises investing in physical and irrigation infrastructure and financial and extension services to promote investment in agriculture, livestock and fisheries.

Delays in the delivery of agricultural inputs have been one of the main constraints to agricultural growth. For example, in Newala district of Mtwara, sulphur, bought by primary cooperative societies in 2009 using money deducted from farmers' sales of cashew nuts in 2008, reached farmers only in August 2009. This was after their cashew nut trees had been affected by disease: the sulphur was supposed to be sprayed onto cashew trees in May. This delay meant lower yields. One ward agricultural officer reported that cashew nut producers who used sulphur would harvest about 8kg of cashew nut per tree, whereas other farmers harvest below 5kg per tree.

A key aspect in increasing agricultural productivity, then, is the timely supply of inputs to farmers so they can use them optimally. Clearly, correcting this issue requires knowledge and research on what the critical institutional and organisational constraints are. Supplying such inputs through primary cooperative societies or selected agents should be maintained to ensure competition between traders and agents who supply good quality materials at reasonable prices. Ensuring that cooperatives are accountable to members is another important condition for success.

Private companies involved in supplying the inputs should also be accountable, to prevent suppliers offering inferior inputs to the warehouse scheme (discussed in more detail later in this chapter). In Newala, Mtwara, larger farmers expressed a fear that subsidised inputs were of low quality. Community members explained that there was corruption in the tendering process: an unscrupulous businessman had won the tender from the government through a bribe and now provides low quality inputs. There has also been a failure to carry out proper research into the type of sulphur and inputs required in different locations. Newala has a milder climate Masasi district and thus needs different inputs. Indeed, two farms in the same region require different inputs, thus different types of sulphur should be available.

Even when suitable agricultural inputs are available, most farmers do not use the recommended ones, notably improved seeds, organic fertilisers and other post-harvest agro-chemicals. According to the National Sample Census of Agriculture (2002/03), conducted two years after the implementation of MKUKUTA I,[4] just 18 per cent of smallholder farmers use improved seeds, 17 per cent used fungicide and 12 per cent used inorganic fertilisers Life history interviews found little knowledge among farmers in relation to usage of farm inputs. Respondents often discussed only their use in cash crops; other responses discussed just fertilisers. The interviews put forward many reasons for the low application of inputs, including the high price of fertilisers, lack of awareness and long distances to input shops. Others believed that the land was fertile enough even though yield levels were very low.

In terms of the government's Input Voucher Programme, which discounts the costs of agricultural inputs for farmers, farmers were not well informed; in addition, distribution was discriminatory. Some farmers receive input vouchers but the majority do not, because of weak political capital, lack of information or a preference for using other approaches to fertilise crops. In all the research sites, many unused fertiliser vouchers remained in the district offices. In Nkasi district of Rukwa—one of the leading producers of maize— only 200 vouchers out of 12,000 were used (less than 2 per cent). Farmers who have received inputs complained that the subsidy package for 1 acre was not enough for their needs.

Policy responses to this could include developing a menu of options for increasing soil fertility, so that farmers have greater choice, as well as increasing farmers' awareness and understanding on the subsidy package and application procedures.

In addition, many farmers do not abide by recommended agricultural practices, including spacing and timely weeding. Meanwhile, all respondents use a hand hoe for farming in 0.5–5 ha plots. This wastes time and energy and contributes to production that is lower than the potential. Such practices, alongside poor input usage and rainfall fluctuations, mean that production differs from year to year. For example, one farmer in Magu district, Mwanza harvested 817kg of cotton per acre in 2008 but 610kg in 2009, when he did not apply pesticides. Similarly, only very rich farmers in Newala plant fast-maturing hybrid cashew trees, which mature in three years rather than the usual six, and maximise the number of trees per plot by using appropriate spacing.

The potential yields of major crops using optimum amounts of inputs in various geographical zones should be assessed, recorded and then publicised. Farmers producing crops in these zones can then access this information to help attain such yields and demand services which would assist them in doing so. Since cash availability determines what inputs can be purchased, information needs to be disaggregated into low and high cash options.

Most farmers do not practise irrigation. For example, in several valleys in Rukwa region where rice is grown, there are no appropriate irrigation canals. Farmers rely on rainfall and rice is produced only once per year. If irrigation were practised, rice could be grown in the valleys three times a year, with significant knock-on effects on incomes and employment. Water in rivers, ponds and lakes is an underutilised resource in Tanzania, and one which can provide an important dry season source of income and local food supply. Irrigation technicians and engineers should work towards increasing irrigation levels, including through the construction of canals and the skills training and supervision of farmers who practise irrigation techniques. This requires the creation of an adequate cadre of technicians.

Another area which requires the development of a fully trained cadre is agricultural extension. Currently, local extension staff are not trained adequately to implement programmes or projects. Interviews in Rukwa found that ward extension officers have certificate-level training, which is inadequate with regard to the responsibilities of the post. Ideally, their skills should be developed further and education upgraded to diploma level. Meanwhile, a shortage of extension staff at the village level has contributed to limited project coordination and a slow pace of implementation. In addition, in all the districts and villages in the research sites, nearly all extension officers, with some exceptions at the district level, do not have the necessary equipment and a means of transportation. One district agronomist said that the implementation of extension services was hampered by a lack of equipment and fuel to use in moving around the villages. In some instances, there are difficulties travelling during the rainy season.

Implementation of monitoring and evaluation activities has also been constrained by a lack of fuel to run vehicles. All ward extension officers are required to submit monthly monitoring and evaluation reports as a condition for receiving their monthly salaries, but this is not enough to ensure accountability—some agents simply do not travel to the villages. Not only do the numbers of extension staff need to be increased but also measures to improve their accountability need to be explored.

Livestock production is also constrained by a shortage of extension personnel and of inputs, including veterinary drugs and dip tanks. People owning cattle have a higher chance of moving out of poverty or not being poor, since they can use oxen to till larger land areas and are able to sell livestock products, by-products and live livestock for cash to buy food, assets or inputs for agricultural production. Smaller livestock, including goats and chickens, are also a critical source of income and investment, yet they were found to die easily from preventable diseases. The importance of livestock as a route out of poverty and the current underperformance of the sector points to the value of greater investment in veterinary and livestock extension services. A significant upgrading of the capabilities of extension agents would mean that they could work with farmers in improving farming systems rather than individual technologies. This would include the promotion of mixed farming—both crop and livestock production—where it is technically feasible.

Currently, mixed cropping and intercropping farming systems are used widely in all research sites. Farmers are mixing crops or intercropping crops which are not officially deemed suitable for this. For example, cotton, which is a mono-crop, is mixed with either maize or cassava or both. Inappropriate land use may contribute to low crop yields. The reasons for such practices need to be understood and appropriate responses developed. Certainly, there is a need to strengthen and disseminate on appropriate farming systems in order to improve crop husbandry as well as crop productivity.

The Association of Mango Growers in Tanzania (AMAGRO) was created in 2001 with the aim of collectively finding a way of obtaining sufficient knowledge and relevant expertise on how to grow fruits efficiently and profitably and reap the opportunities of the export market. Specifically, AMAGRO has three main purposes: to train and educate members on best practice in mango production; to facilitate the availability of farm inputs and other services such as extension; and to consolidate joint marketing to increase the bargaining voice of farmers. AMAGRO is a role model of an approach to improve farmers' productivity and reduce poverty. It directly helps eighty mango growers from various regions of Tanzania, as well as others who are not members but who enjoy some positive externalities.

Members of AMAGRO acknowledge great benefits. They have better knowledge on how to grow mangoes that meet international standards; can easily access farm inputs that are too costly to be imported by an individual grower;[5] have increased knowledge on how to preserve mangoes and produce mango-related by-products; and have better negotiation power for the products they sell and hence experience improved productivity and incomes. Using modern mango-growing techniques, a farmer can grow up to 64 mango trees on 1 acre, each tree producing a minimum of 300 matured mangoes. One mango fetches a market price of at least TZS 250, implying that a farmer obtains a total revenue equal to TZS 4.8 million per acre (TZS 75,000 per tree) per year. It costs a maximum of TZS 300,000 to farm 1 acre of mango trees, covering all costs, labour and other inputs, from initial to harvesting stage. An acre therefore yields a net profit of TZS 4.5 million at a minimum (i.e. TZS 375,000 per month). This is more than the monthly salary of most government officials, even those who have graduated with a Masters degree. The number of mango plants per acre (and hence the profit) has more than doubled compared with the period prior to the acquisition of knowledge and access to inputs through AMAGRO.

Another way to overcome the barriers poor farmers face to entry into high-value agricultural activities involves credit. Where small loans are available to farmers, this can relieve them from one of the major obstacles to agricultural development. For example, Mwandima ward SACCO in Kalesa requires members to save and subsequently borrow, and has also been encouraging members to buy shares. A single share has a value of TZS 5,000, and the entry fee is TZS 2,000. Members need to have shares amounting to at least TZS 50,000 per year and minimum savings of TZS 50,000 to be able to borrow.

Life histories in Rukwa, Mwanza and Mtwara make it clear that becoming an active member of a credit scheme is difficult for an ordinary person, but that once people have fulfilled the initial requirements the benefits are significant, particularly in terms of access to capital for agriculture. Another major challenge, though, is the low literacy rate among members and the public in general. Members do not know and acknowledge their obligations and rights to the scheme. They do not have a tradition of saving and buying shares: they just want to borrow. Whenever their loan applications are not accepted for not being valid, they complain that they are discriminated against and that SACCOs are benefiting a few rich people. Mobilisation of resources through membership has therefore been difficult owing to the prevailing negative attitudes of the people. In general, SACCO credit for poorer farmers is slim. For instance, in Kirando, the SACCO is considered 'a place for the rich and businessmen'.

In contrast, burial societies and other women's rotating savings and credit associations (ROSCAs) were found to work very well in providing not merely finance to cover crisis costs but also capital for agricultural investment. Burial societies are common in Kalesa, where members contribute resources in the form of cash as well as labour, which they can draw on later to meet the costs of the burial ceremony of another member or close relative. This same society can also be used to finance investments related to agriculture and other agreed economic and social activities. About 20 per cent of women in a village are members of ROSCAs. Some female ROSCAS are linked to SACCOs through their treasurer, who is a SACCO member on behalf of the group. This system works well and could serve as a model for increasing the capital available to poor farmers. Building on this link between SACCO membership and burial societies and other well-running ROSCAs could enhance the capital available to poor farmers, to be invested in new technology—oxen, seeds, fertilisers and pesticides.

Prioritising risk management while increasing productivity

The final cluster of proposals for agricultural policy relates to the recommendation that investments in productivity be filtered through a risk lens. For poor, vulnerable, rural households, the priority may not be to increase productivity but rather to ensure a greater emphasis on risk management. In this regard, output markets may represent a better starting point for poverty reduction than working on increasing productivity through input markets. One constraint facing poor and remote farmers, for instance, relates to cartels of private traders who act as barriers to access to external markets. Meanwhile, in local markets, traders tend to agree on prices each morning beforehand. The relative success of the Warehouse Receipt Scheme (WRS), which began in 2007 under the Agricultural Marketing Systems Development Programme, illustrates the potential gains available from focusing on output markets. This scheme has played a catalytic role, not only by improving the marketing of agricultural products but also in terms of improved agricultural production, confidence among farmers, producer price stability and technological uptake.

The WRS was the government's way to ensure a fair and stable market, and specifically to enable farmers to store their harvest in a warehouse for sale at a later date when prices are more attractive. This system operates through primary societies and SACCOs. The primary society pays farmers 70 per cent of the price (less the price of the next year's subsidised inputs and community charges). The produce is weighed and graded and a farmer is issued a receipt in triplicate. Farmers retain the receipt and, after storage and sale at auction by the warehouse administrator several months later, are given the remaining 30 per cent plus any bonus (less costs of storage, interest, transport and administration). The system also aims to stabilise producer prices, improve technological uptake through the provision of subsidised inputs and link to farmer credit (through SACCOs).

The WRS also stimulates competition by introducing liquidity, which reduces the anti-competitive behaviour of large buyers. Prior to its introduction, large, anti-competitive exporters and processors with access to bank finance were the main sources of cash in the cashew marketing system. They provided local private traders (agents or middlemen) with money, which the latter used to purchase cashews from primary societies and cooperative unions. Since there were relatively few large exporters and processors with the ability to pre-finance cashew purchases, there were opportunities for monopsonistic behaviour. Local traders did not compete with each other, as they were agents of large players, and agents tended to extract a substantial commission for themselves. Now, though, primary societies and cooperative unions have access to independent bank financing. The WRS has also reduced the anti-competitive behaviour of the large exporters and processers by forcing them to purchase cashews through auction instead of directly from cooperative unions and traders.

Is the system working for farmers? Evidence from the operations of the WRS in cashew nut and paddy districts (through agricultural marketing cooperative societies and SACCOs, respectively) reveals that the WRS has been a useful marketing tool which has benefited members in terms of market outlets, price stability and better prices. Farm gate prices have risen in line with export prices, but not fully. For example, in Newala district, Mtwara, farm gate prices rose from TZS 500 to TZS 700 with the introduction of the WRS in 2007 (a rise of 40 per cent). Farmers also benefited from inputs at 75 per cent of their cost. In Tandahimba district, producer prices for cashew nuts have improved from a range of TZS 150–410 per kilogram to a range of TZS 710–850 (almost double); this latter range also shows a drastic reduction in price fluctuations between the two periods.

In Iringa and Mbeya, the WRS works through SACCOs. The warehouse buys paddy from farmers and pays them 50 per cent of the prevailing market price as an initial payment. The average price during harvesting is TZS 50,000 per 100kg bag of paddy, meaning an initial amount of TZS 25,000 for farmers through their respective SACCO. Thereafter, the stocked paddy is sold by the warehouse administrator at an average price of TZS 75,000 off season. The second instalment is normally paid after deductions of the loan, input costs and interest. The total price paid to farmers has on average been TZS 40,000 per 100kg bag of paddy. Farmers are assured of a market, farm inputs and a stable and relatively high price.

The WRS has not been without problems. Most interviews with farmers began with complaints, although they always finished with a positive appeal—that they would like to see it reformed and extended to other crops, such as cassava, maize and pulses, as soon as possible, because traders are not reliable. Among the complaints about the WRS were that some farmers do not want to receive their payment in two instalments. They want 100 per cent at harvest in order to pay off pressing labour costs, school fees and other essentials. Other farmers demanded much greater farmer representation at price-setting for urns and auctions; clearer audits and increased internal controls to limit the opportunities for corruption; and more information on when the second payment will be made and if/when a bonus will be paid (in one year it was not paid).

The cooperative union itself (in Tandahiba and Newala, Mtwara) felt the institution faced two problems: interest rates on bank loans are very high and there are some places where the WRS is not linked to SACCOs (with lower interest rates) and perhaps should be; and the WRS still depends on buyers—large-scale processors and exporters—who might start bidding late. This delay can delay the bonus and the quality of stored cashews. The union also wants to begin processing cashews. This will not only help control the timing of purchases, but also stimulate local off-season female employment, keep value-added local rather than in big cities and increase market opportunities.

Overall, though, farmers appreciate the WRS, and the fact that they would like it, or something similar, extended to other crops reflects the great difficulty they have in adjusting to the seasonal volatility of prices. Both of the two traditional crop export markets (cashews and cotton) are beset with institutional failures, in terms of the state and the market. However, it is in the food crops that involve smallholder producers the most (maize, rice and cassava) where improvements in output markets are most urgently required. This can be achieved through local purchase and/or storage schemes which help to moderate seasonal fluctuations and lessen the growing proportion of the consumer food price represented by transport costs. For example, instead of selling excess cassava to merchants who might or might not arrive, it can be stored and/or milled locally for later sale. This would enable regional stocks if necessary and retaining some local food locally would reduce inflation. At the moment, many food-poor households cannot create the effective demand that is necessary to keep food in these regions, and so food crops like maize in Rukwa and even cassava in Mtwara are exported. MKUKUTA II talks about strengthening the WRS; this could be through achieved extending it. Certainly, the improved producer response in cashews resulting from higher prices and the WRS is an indication of its potential. In other countries, improvements in such markets have been associated strongly with poverty reduction.

Selling traditional cash crops, particularly cashew nuts and cotton, can frequently be affected by delays in crop-buying. Sometimes, the money to pay farmers is not there. For example, in Newala district, the cashew nut buying season starts on 1 October and ends on 31 January. In 2009/10, primary cooperative societies started buying three weeks late; buying went on for two weeks; then there was no cash for three weeks. This compelled farmers to sell to private buyers who used deceitful measurements to cheat them. The delays also denied farmers access to subsidised inputs, which they would ordinarily obtain through cooperative societies using cash deducted from their sales. As a result, farmers received smaller margins during the year and during the subsequent year also. In order to contain this problem, it is recommended that preparation for a cash crop buying season be done well in advance in terms of logistics and finances. Buying relevant cash crop products should start on time and funds should be available throughout the buying season.

One reason why liquidity and the ability to purchase on time may be difficult is that the WRS can sometimes rely on the caprice of foreign buyers and on high financing costs. For instance, in Newala in 2008 farmers did not receive bonuses. The reason given by a cooperative union official for this delay was that the harvest was very early (in October 2008) and the large foreign crop traders who participate in the auction and buy from the warehouse were waiting for the price to come down before bidding. They did not buy until February and did not come forward to finish bidding until April. Moreover, during this time, interest accrued on the microfinance loan to the union.

If cooperative unions can begin to process cashews, they will be freed from dependency on the vagaries of foreign monopolistic traders. Another solution is to reduce the interest rate on loans. In Newala, the union loan is from a microfinance institution at 18 per cent. By linking the union to the local SACCO they may be able to reduce this. A third solution is to ensure some stability in cashew prices by using dollars rather than shillings.

Ideally, farmers should be paid all their money at once so they can repay debts incurred during production, such as payments to labourers and for inputs. In 2008, in a village in Newala district, the price of cashew nuts was TZS 700 per kilogram, but farmers were paid 70 per cent of the price—TZS 490 per kilogram. The remaining 30 per cent, TZS 210, was paid after three months—but it ended up at TZS 110 after the following deductions, which were made without the farmers being informed beforehand: TZS 50 for inputs (sulphur) to be supplied during the next season; TZS 20 for roads; TZS 20 for water; and TZS 10 for education. Measures should also be introduced to ensure that deductions from farmers' sales are not allowed without informing farmers at the time of contracting.

The deceitful measurement by private buyers of farmers' agricultural products, mentioned above, involves a bowl known as a *kangomba*, which weighs 1.25–1.8kg when full of cashew nuts. This 1.25–1.8kg is bought for the price of 1kg. Meanwhile, some individuals who are agents for cotton buyers distort weighing bridges, for example recording 90kg for an amount of cotton that is actually 100kg. Later on, they readjust the weighing bridge, reweigh the cotton and take 10kg for their own benefit. Standard weights and measures are needed to counter under-recording of crops, so that no container or any other measuring tool or equipment other than a weighing scale or spring balance is used to weigh agricultural products. Another issue is that, after farmers became aware of this deceit, they also cheated, by adding water or white sand to cotton before selling it to compensate for the amount of cotton the agents were stealing from them. Any buyer or seller caught under or overweighing any goods should be punished as a deterrent to others.

In addition to risks relating specifically to agricultural production and the sale of agricultural products, poor people live in a context characterised by risks in the form of both shocks and stresses. People complained that the price of food and other essentials in local markets had risen very rapidly over the past five years, out of keeping with the very minor rise in the price of their cashews and wages (see Chapter 7). This rise has made it impossible to afford much food of high quality, such as fish, chicken, beef, milk and some vegetables. It has also coincided with a rise in the number of people dependent on the market for food, as farm sizes have declined. Addressing this rapid inflation in essentials is therefore crucial. It could be approached by exploring ways to cap inflation on essentials and enabling freer cross-border trade to encourage the import of lower-priced essentials from over the border (such as from Mozambique). Reducing transport costs and increasing the value-added on primary products through local processing could be other important measures.

Overall increases in the cost of living were also widely reported (see Chapter 7). Rising costs of services, education, water and hospital fees mean reduced money available for agricultural investment. For example, school fees are supposed to have been abolished for primary and set at TZS 20,000 for secondary schools, but these and rising supplementary contributions still represent a problem for poor families, with teachers telling children to go away if they cannot pay. Inability to pay for uniforms is very common. For the most part, it is only non-poor families whose children are in school, especially in the case of secondary school. In every region, parents found the supplementary costs for education crippling, and the poorest could not afford to keep their children in school. Members of a focus group discussion in Nkangala conveyed this: 'we do everything possible to send our children to school! But the poor and destitute cannot meet the payments for fees, uniforms and supplementary costs and so are turned away.' There needs to be greater exploration of ways to reduce additional local fees on service use and outgoings on schools and uniform. We suggest that uniforms, including set shoes, be abolished, as the cost deters too many parents from sending their children to school.

Conclusions

Currently, agricultural markets are not sufficiently competitive. They are dominated by a few private traders who are free to practise unfair competition, thus burdening and penalising smallholder farmers. The WRS is one instrument which can be used to correct these market distortions. The scheme can be organised in such a way that it enables farmers to sell indirectly to external markets. To scale down the effect of inflation, support services need to be directed to the production of food crops in order to ensure food security, improve farmers' income and reduce food inflation, which is too high.

Some weaknesses within the current WRS can be addressed by promoting strong farmer-based organisations, such as Umoja wa Wakulima wa Korosho Tandahimba and Umoja wa Wakulima wa Korosho Newala, which operate in Tandahimba and Newala districts, respectively. These organisations offer an alternative market channel, buying cashew nuts from their members and depositing the consignment at the WRS. They are said to be more transparent and accountable to their members than primary societies. They are also demand driven, meant to serve the interests of farmer members, and have strong bargaining power. Demand for such organisations is growing in other districts, especially Newala and Masasi.

A diversified set of interventions is needed to address a range of barriers to agricultural growth and therefore poverty reduction: low land productivity; delays in the supply of inputs; limited capital and access to financial services; inadequate technical support services; and poor rural infrastructure hindering effective rural–urban linkages. Efforts must be made to ensure the timely delivery of agricultural support services and to improve the rural road network, increase credit availability and ensure farmers have a higher level of education and skills. Farm input delivery and crop purchasing efficiency also needs to be enhanced and, if cooperatives are to be involved, they need adequate and timely liquidity.

---

1   United Republic of Tanzania (2009b); L. Msambichaka et al. (2009).

2   See, for example, World Bank (2001)

3   United Republic of Tanzania (2007)

4   Ministry of Agriculture, Food Security and Cooperatives (2003)

5   Most of the pesticides are sold in bulk (e.g. 50 litres) by exporting countries, and are thus too expensive for individual farmers to afford—particularly as they normally require a very small fraction of the pesticide (say 0.5 litre). AMAGRO purchases in bulk and sells to members in smaller units without adding any mark-up to the cost.

Part 3

Governance and Social Contract

Chapter 9

Poverty Mobility in Tanzania and Linkages with Governance

Kim Abel Kayunze, Oswald Mashindano and Festo Maro

Introduction

This chapter identifies the governance issues that matter for poverty mobility in Tanzania, using data collected through key informant interviews, focus group discussions and individual life histories in Rukwa, Mwanza and Mtwara regions from September to November 2009 as part of a bigger study titled 'Chronic Poverty and Development Policy in Tanzania'. The first National Strategy for Growth and Reduction of Poverty, widely known by its Kiswahili acronym, MKUKUTA I, guided Tanzania's poverty reduction efforts from July 2005 to June 2010. MKUKUTA I saw governance as a key ingredient in attaining the Tanzania Development Vision 2025,[1] which entails eradicating absolute poverty by 2025.

MKUKUTA I emphasised economic growth to ease poverty reduction. One of its main concerns was to ensure that improvements at the macro level were translated into micro-level economic achievements. It adopted an outcomes approach, which counted on the contribution of all sectors towards growth and poverty reduction, through three clusters: growth and the reduction of income poverty, improved quality of life and social well-being, and good governance and accountability.[2] It prioritised stimulating private investment, infrastructure and human resource development in the context of building a competitive economy and an efficient government. In doing this, it also paid attention to discriminatory laws, customs and practices affecting the economic and human development of vulnerable social groups (children, youth, girls, women, persons with disabilities, the elderly and retired people), as well as giving greater attention to mainstreaming crosscutting issues, including HIV and AIDS, gender, environment, governance, employment, children, youth, the elderly, disability and settlements. In spite of the efforts of MKUKUTA I, though, poverty, as measured using various different methods, is still prominent in Tanzania.

Cluster III of MKUKUTA I, on governance and accountability, was designed to provide the bedrock for achievements in Clusters I and II.[3]

However, there are many cases of decision-making on, and implementation of, economic and social development activities being handled inefficiently, corruptly (at least circumstantially), with a lack of transparency and/or unequally—or at least inequitably. Various factors evidence the existence of such bad governance. For example, the MKUKUTA Annual Implementation Report of 2008/09 reveals that, between 2007/08 and 2008/09, 706 cases associated with corruption were investigated.[4]

This chapter assesses why bad governance elements occur in Tanzania, which groups of people are more affected by such elements and how they affect poverty mobility. It recommends that MKUKUTA II (2011–15) give more weight to governance issues, as poor governance is currently exacerbating poverty and slowing progress towards the attainment of the Tanzania Development Vision 2025.

Overview of governance and poverty

One well-known definition of governance is 'the manner in which power is exercised in the management of a country's economic and social development'.[5] Although widely varying usages of the term in the literature show that governance means different things to different people, it is generally agreed that the differences in its meanings crystallise along two separate lines, one regarding its substantive content and the other its character in practice.[6] With the first line, governance is viewed as being concerned with the rules of conducting public affairs; with the second line, governance is seen as steering public affairs.

In view of the above two prongs of the term governance, Hyden and Court define it as 'the formation and stewardship of the formal and informal rules that regulate the public realm, the arena in which state as well as economic and social actors interact to make decisions'.[7] Regardless of specific definitional issues, though, governance has to be good so that it can enhance economic and social development and help poverty reduction efforts. Good governance is conceived from the process perspective, with an emphasis on the rule of law, accountability, participation, transparency and human and civil rights.[8] Olowu also contends that good governance results from the activities of public sector institutions as they work with other societal organisations to formulate public policies and programmes, which are implemented to improve the people's welfare, reduce poverty and realise other public and societal goals.[9]

Classical analyses of governance

There are various ways to analyse governance and how it is linked to poverty and social and economic development. Hyden and Court outline basic governance principles according to the World Governance Survey, which reflect the emerging global consensus on what should and could constitute good governance: (1) participation—the degree of involvement and ownership of affected stakeholders; (2) fairness—the degree to which rules apply equally to everyone in society regardless of status; (3) transparency—the degree to which decisions made by public officials are clear and open to scrutiny by citizens; (4) decency—the degree to which the formation and stewardship of rules are undertaken without humiliation of or harm to the people; (5) accountability— the degree to which public officials, elected and appointed, are responsible for their actions and responsive to public demands; and (6) efficiency—the degree to which rules facilitate speedy and timely decision-making.[10]

Hyden and Court also give six dimensions, each with five indicators, based on the World Governance Survey: (1) socialising—whose indicators are freedom of expression, freedom of peaceful association, freedom from discrimination, opportunity for consultation and public duties; (2) aggregating— representativeness of legislature, political competition, aggregation of public preferences, roles of legislative function and accountability of elected officials; (3) executive—freedom from fear, freedom from want, willingness to make tough decisions, political–military relations and attitude to peace; (4) managerial—scope of policy advice, meritocracy, accountability of appointed officials, transparency and equal access to public services; (5) regulatory— security of property, equal treatment, obstacles to business, consultation with the private sector and international economic considerations; and (6) adjudicatory—equal access to justice, due process, accountability of judges, incorporation of international human rights norms and predisposition to conflict resolution.[11] Although these dimensions and indicators are useful for analysing good governance and its linkages with poverty and others, however, they are challenged in the context of 'good enough governance'.

'Good enough governance'

Grindle argues that, as much as good governance *per se* is desirable, countries with a long list of things 'to be done' to reduce poverty should sort out their governance issues with a view to addressing a reasonably small number of them that are the most important, hence the term 'good enough governance'.[12] Grindle defines this as 'a condition of minimally acceptable government performance and civil society engagement that does not significantly hinder economic and political development and that permits poverty reduction initiatives to go forward'.[13] Based on World Development Reports from 1997 to 2002/03, Grindle puts forward a list of 178 items that development-oriented governments should adopt and practise, and also a list of dimensions of poverty and governance.[14]

Governance in MKUKUTA I

Following the 1997 World Development Report on governance, Tanzania put more emphasis on good governance as an ingredient in poverty alleviation. For example, the previous poverty reduction strategy paper (the National Poverty Eradication Strategy) underscored the need to increase transparency and accountability, as well as financial support for sectors deemed key to poverty alleviation.[15] MKUKUTA I, on the other hand, stipulated a number of issues related to governance, including use of public resources (financial, informational and natural), management systems, personal security, tolerance and inclusion. Participation in decision-making was to be achieved through local government reform processes, school committees, cooperatives and farmers' associations, with representative and accountable governance structures and systems. MKUKUTA I also emphasised human rights, the need for a functioning and fair justice system and the war against corruption, as well as transparency of information on policies, the legal framework, laws and public finances. Public access to information was underlined as a human right as well as a key means to facilitate effective policy implementation, monitoring and accountability. Effective public administration was also advocated to ensure that systems of government were managed openly and in the interests of the people they served.[16]

Likewise, it is the objective of MKUKUTA II to facilitate the development process by ensuring good economic governance which encompasses policies and institutions for economic management, market regulation and governance of public goods. Thus, the strategy calls for a stronger role of the state in ensuring policies are designed in a participatory manner, implemented efficiently, and that critical decisions are made in a transparent manner and play a critical role in basic services delivery. To make that happen, the strategy directs efforts to building capability for implementing such policies and initiatives effectively through deepened implementation of core public reforms[17].

The information reviewed above was instrumental in developing the conceptual framework presented below for this chapter.

Conceptual framework for this chapter

The main variable of focus (dependent variable) in this chapter is poverty mobility, which is the change (increase or decrease) in income and in education, health and water services. Changes in these indicators of the dependent variable are contingent on changes in the independent variables, which are the six elements of governance put forward by Hyden and Court, the elements of good governance by Grindle, and the elements of good governance presented in MKUKUTA I and II, particularly the indicators of the elements of good governance. For the conceptual framework, it is hypothesized that the dependent variables affect poverty mobility through intermediate outcomes, which are also regarded as secondary independent variables. These are policy choices and public behaviour, equitable access of citizens to productive resources, agricultural and non-agricultural productivity, contribution of citizens to formulation of better policies, and citizens' contributions in kind and cash to community development activities, all of which enhance the attainment of poverty mobility. In view of this conceptual framework, the empirical findings reported below were obtained.

Empirical findings

This section presents the findings of the research in light of the analytical framework presented in Figure 9.1. Since both good and bad elements of governance were found during the research, the section presents cases of both good and bad governance. We also analyse the linkages between governance variables and poverty variables.

Figure 9.1: Analytical framework of linkages between governance and poverty mobility in Tanzania

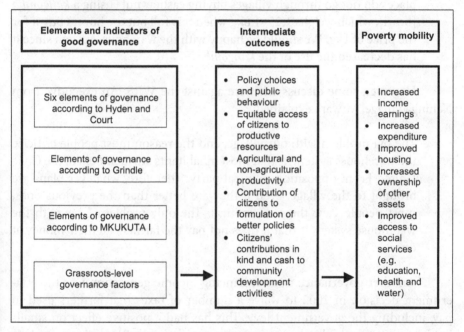

Findings with respect to growth and the reduction of income poverty

Agriculture is the main economic activity in all the three research sites. Some people are also involved in other activities, such as trade, manufacturing, casual labour and salaried employment, to mention a few. Therefore, we report on governance issues that enhance and those that constrain improvements in both farm and non-farm activities.

<u>*Governance issues enhancing income generation*</u>

In relation to agriculture, the Warehouse Receipt System (WRS), introduced nationwide in 2006, is present in all communities. In Mwanza, the system is already working well, but in Mtwara and Rukwa people remained sceptical about it. The WRS was designed to enable farmers to store their crop products so they can wait for prices to increase. Beforehand, traders bought crop products during the harvesting period at low prices, stored them and, later on in the same agricultural season, sold them at high prices, sometimes back to the same farmers.

In one focus group discussion in Newala district of Mtwara, discussants agreed with the following statement that one of them gave:

> The warehouse system is better than the private buyers system because the price is stable [the same from the beginning to the end of a buying season]; there is no cheating in the measurement of the amount of cashew nuts one sells at the buying centre; and private traders from distant places do not go through villages buying cashew nuts using a *kangomba* [bowl], which weighs 1.25–1.8kg when it is full but the buyers buy it for the price of 1kg. We should be happy with the warehouse system since it has decreased the use of the *kangomba*.

However, some discussants were against the WRS. An executive from Nchinga village, Mtwara explained:

> The big problem with our village, and the reason most people criticise the warehouse system, is that most inhabitants are members of the Civic United Front opposition political party. Therefore, whatever plans are brought to the village, even if they are better than the previous ones, most people view them as political. The only problem I see with the warehouse system is that it does not pay the farmers all their money at once.

Another governance issue enhancing income generation was the government decision in 2002 to waive a number of taxes that farmers used to pay, including the government levy. This has had a positive effect on smallholder farmers' and other low-income earners' opportunities to increase their income. In one focus group discussion in Nchinga, discussants agreed unanimously with the following statement:

> Our poverty increased in 1983, when people were sleeping in forests running away from being forced to pay the development levy. Agriculture declined a lot because many people were not cultivating; they were hiding. We are happy that paying the development levy has been waived and transformed into deductions from the cashew nuts we sell. Such deductions are better than us being required to pay the development levy because we get time to do our economic activities and pay according to the amount of income from cashew nuts sold or

other sources, unlike the development levy, which was paid at a flat rate regardless of whether one had an income or not, and regardless of the amount of income obtained from economic activities.

This is linked to pro-poor budget priorities and reforms for service provision, as put forward by Grindle. Some poor people have benefited from the implementation of this decision, and the government has still obtained sufficient revenue through other sources.

In some villages, there was good use of the Opportunities and Obstacles to Development (O&OD) planning approach. For example, a focus group discussion in Wazabanga village, Mwanza, revealed that good governance had prevailed in the community because of this method, with villagers assessing obstacles to, and opportunities for, development and deciding together how to plan development interventions. O&OD had been used to plan the construction of classrooms and dispensary buildings and participation in water projects. Under the Health, Sanitation and Water Programme, the people of the village had used O&OD to decide that each of the five hamlets of their village should have one well and that the hamlet that was more populous should have two. This element of good governance is related to freedom of expression and equal access to public services, as put forward by Hyden and Court. It is also linked to the local decision-making institutions element of good governance put forward by Grindle and the participation element of good governance put forward in MKUKUTA I.

In Nkasi district of Rukwa, the necessary authorities are in place to facilitate trade between Tanzania and its neighbouring countries of Burundi, the Democratic Republic of Congo and Zambia across Lake Tanganyika. For example, there is an immigration office to facilitate entry into and exit from Tanzania and a Tanzania Revenue Authority office to educate taxpayers and ensure traders pay proper taxes. The presence of these services facilitates community members' endeavours to reduce poverty through cross-border trade. This is linked to the international economic considerations element of good governance put forward by Hyden and Court.

There was good news for traders too: in 2005, annual licence fees were removed, to be replaced by permanent business licences. Now, only those with an annual turnover of TZS 20 million or more pay for a licence yearly, at a rate of 10 per cent of turnover. However, all must pay income tax annually. One key informant interviewee in Wazabanga of Mwanza—a successful businessman—praised the reform as 'very likely to help most people perform better in non-farm activities and reduce poverty more effectively'. This finding, like the previous one, is linked to Hyden and Court's obstacles to business element of good governance.

Land is the most important factor in agricultural production, which is the main economic activity of most community members. In terms of positive findings in this regard, in Kalesa village of Rukwa, the Mwandima ward agricultural and livestock development officer reported how he had participated in resolving a conflict over land between Sukuma pastoralists and Fipa sedentary farmers:

> In 1995, the conflict over land between the Sukuma and Fipa was escalating. I reported it to the district agricultural and livestock development office and was instructed to summon representatives of both parties [pastoralists and crop producers] to discuss the conflict. Officials from the district came, and we discussed the problem and agreed that anyone who owned more than fifty cattle and did not want to reduce the number to at most fifty should relocate to another place. Therefore, many Sukuma people left the area with their cattle. In 1995, there were about 16,000 cattle, while the carrying capacity of the ward was estimated to be 5,000 cattle.

Land conflicts have been resolved at village and ward levels too. For example, in 2005, the uncle of James Mwamwezi (nineteen years old) of Kalesa village, Rukwa, migrated to a distant place, leaving behind a farm. Someone took the land as if it had been his by right. James went to the Mwandima ward office in Kalesa to claim the land, despite the second man's threats. Eventually, in 2008, he received his land. He produced rice on it in 2008/09 and harvested 20 bags in 2009, which he sold to make money to establish a kiosk business. Land conflict results are linked to Grindle's conflict resolution institutions item of good governance, whereby amicable conflict resolution is desirable for poverty reduction.

In some communities, savings and credit cooperative organisations (SACCOs) provide services to poor community members. The manager of one SACCO in Mwanza Region said that its clients praised it because, previously, moneylenders lent at interest rates of 100–200 per cent of the amount borrowed. During the research, interest rates at the SACCO were 21.6 per cent per year for a salary loan; 25.2 per cent per year for agricultural, trade and house construction loans; and 60 per cent per year for emergency loans. However, a focus group in one village in Rukwa region revealed that, although some farmers had obtained credit, some people were sceptical about applying for fear that their farms might be confiscated if they failed to repay the loan in a timely manner.

All six communities where the research was conducted had SACCOs, rotating savings and credit associations (ROSCAs), and associations for helping one another with difficult manual activities. Such associations helped people improve their welfare. Wilium Semiono, forty-eight years old and chair of Mwandima SACCO in Kalesa, Rukwa, estimated that 10–20 per cent of women in the ward were members of a ROSCA. The presence of such organisations is linked to the microcredit/savings item of good governance, as put forward by Grindle.

Collaborative farm work, called *luganda* in the Kisukuma language, is a notable kind of peaceful association whereby people form an association for the purpose of working on the farm of one of the members and then move to another one's farm until all the members are covered by the rotation. Members are chosen based on the neighbourhood or age cohort and; as members of the *luganda*; undertake primary tillage, planting, weeding, harvesting and brick-making. The group may have between ten and thirty members. Discussants in Wazabanga village of Mwanza estimated that about 600 households out of 987 were members of *luganda*. These associations exist as a result of good governance among central and local governments, and are helping people exit poverty.

Governance issues constraining income generation

Although agriculture is the main economic activity, agricultural extension services are so inadequate that some farmers do not even know whether they exist. For example, in a life history interview, a farmer in Nkangala village, Mtwara, did not know of agricultural extension services provided by the government. This limited awareness is mainly caused by an extreme shortage of agricultural extension workers. In the 1970s, Tanzania aimed to have one officer for every village but, following structural adjustment in the mid-1980s, some agricultural extension workers were retrenched from the civil service. This was followed by a reduction in the number of extension workers trained, which has led to the extreme shortage today. Ward agricultural and livestock extension officers in the three districts where the research was conducted underlined the shortage. In Newala district, a Ward Agricultural and Livestock Officer said, 'I am the only agricultural officer for all the seven villages of the ward. I was posted here two years ago. I have neither a motorcycle nor a bicycle to visit farmers.'

Low prices of cash crop products and cooperatives' use of instalments in paying farmers for crop products also constrain community members' poverty alleviation. For example, a focus group discussion in Nkangala village in Mtwara said:

> The price per kilogram of cashew nuts is too low, TZS 700, in comparison with the costs of producing them; the price should be TZS 1,500 per kilogram. Yet, when we sell cashew nuts through the primary cooperative society, we are given 70 per cent, that is, TZS 490 per kilogram. The other TZS 210 on every kilogram of cashew nuts is paid after two to three months.

In another focus group discussion in the same village, discussants said, 'we are selling cashew nuts on credit unwillingly. We would not do so if the leaders were not oppressing us.' This finding implies lack of effective markets, which is a governance element according to Grindle.

Deducting cash from farmers' sales of agricultural products without informing them in advance and without good explanation is another governance issue. Village focus group discussion respondents in Nchinga, Mtwara, said:

> From the TZS 210, they deducted TZS 50 for inputs [sulphur] that was to be supplied during the subsequent season. They also deducted TZS 20 for roads, TZS 20 for water and TZS 10 for education. They paid us TZS 110 instead of TZS 210. When we complained about so many deductions without having informed us in advance, they told us: 'Just go on complaining.'

This finding implies lack of transparency on the part of district leaders. This governance element is talked about extensively in Hyden and Court, Grindle and MKUKUTA I.

Poor access to justice by women and poorer community members is another governance problem constraining poverty alleviation. Divorce results in women losing most of the wealth items they own and have control over. Women are not allowed to inherit land (unless they get it through daughters, if they have no sons), so after separation they have no land, house or extra income—yet are fully responsible for child maintenance (Chapter 4).

Another shortfall in law enforcement was reported in Mwanza region. A fifteen-year-old boy found guilty of stealing TZS 500,000 from a shop was imprisoned for only two days and did not return the money. Community members strongly believed that the village leaders who handled the case shared the money with the boy. This case comes under the legal and regulatory framework, fair justice systems, human rights and access to justice elements of governance in Hyden and Court, Grindle and MKUKUTA I.

With respect to land, there were more cases of bad than of good governance. For example, the father of James Mwamwezi, nineteen years old and from Kalesa, ran away from his mother in 1993. Following the separation, someone took the farm on which his father used to produce rice and claimed it was his. James asked the village office over and over to help him recover the farm, but he received no assistance from them until 2008, by which time he was despairing of getting the land. Access to this land would have helped him exit poverty through rice production. Also, Andrew Mahai (forty-nine years old, also of Kalesa village), said in a life history interview, 'if you don't have money you can't get your rights'. He himself had lost part of his farmland to his neighbour, with officials not bothering to follow up on the case despite several reminders.

In some cases, opportunities for generating income through trade across borders have been taken away as a result of a lack of facilitation by upper levels of governance. In Nchinga village, Mtwara, facilities are not available to promote cross-border trade. The ward's acting executive officer in a key informant interview said:

> In brief, trade between Chikota ward, Mtwara and Mozambique is poor because there is no reliable way to cross; we normally cross using local canoes which are operated manually since they don't have engines. Goods to trade are few, and the Tanzania Revenue Authority is not there to streamline trade between Chikota and Mozambique.

The little trade that goes on involves the following goods from Tanzania to Mozambique: second-hand clothes, mattresses, sardines and cashew apples, called *kochoka*, which are used to make local spirits. From Mozambique to Tanzania, the following are traded: iron sheets for roofing houses, petroleum, gin and sugar. However, only an estimated 10 per cent of traders in Newala district of Mtwara are involved in cross-border trade. It was also emphasised that those involved in trade are those at district headquarters who know the way and 'how to talk with the police and officials'. This implies bribery.

'Artificial' scarcity of land for production of more valuable crops is another governance issue constraining poverty reduction. In Kalesa village, Rukwa, some community members are creating land scarcity by hoarding land for rice production. As a result, renting 1 acre of land for rice production is TZS 100,000 per agricultural season—a very large amount of money. One key informant, Josephat Mpama (sixty-two years old), said, 'it is high time land for rice production was reformed so most people have equitable access to it. If land ownership and access are not reformed, the future is likely to see bloodshed owing to wrangles over it.' However, Mwandima ward's agricultural and livestock extension officer Christopha Kipoya (forty-seven years old) was of the opinion that, although newcomers owned about 60 per cent of the land, natives should not complain because the former had obtained it through legal means that prevailed when they obtained it.

Another bad governance element is the uncompensated demolition of buildings in unplanned areas of towns. John Doglass (forty-one years old, from Ndite, Mwanza) lost his kiosk and the shoes he was selling in such a demolition. The incident completely grounded him, leaving him no option but to start working as a casual labourer. The problem of demolition of houses is linked to the land use planning element put forward by Grindle.

The logistics involved in supplying fertilisers and seeds represent another governance problem constraining mobility out of poverty. Focus group discussants in Nkasi district said:

> The delay in receiving fertilisers is a big problem. Fertilisers arrive late when crops have already been planted. Even if you have the money to

purchase fertiliser, it arrives too late to be useful. In 1986–97, when Sasakawa Global 2000 was operating in this area, everyone received fertilisers on time [through loans] and agricultural education was provided. There were really good harvests. The problem was there was no market in which to sell the produce, and therefore many people could not repay the fertiliser loan.

Elsewhere, fake seeds are supplied. For example, in Wazabanga, Mwanza, farmers receive fake cotton seeds from private cotton buyers—unlike Nyanza Cooperative Union, which always gave them good seeds. Some traders supply farmers with expired chemicals which are not effective against cotton pests and diseases. This is related to the enforcement of contracts and penalties for dishonesty and fraud as put forward by Grindle.

Inadequate supervision of agriculture is characterised by use of poor technology and low productivity. Focus group discussion respondents in Kayumbe village, Rukwa, said, 'you can grow maize on 10 acres and harvest only 10 bags of maize instead of 300. Farmers need seminars on good planting techniques as part of agricultural education. Farmers are farming, but they are not doing it wisely.'

There are eight small hand-operated tractors in the ward where this village is located, supplied through an initiative of the prime minister. The problem is that they do not work on the dry land of the ward. The discussants criticised this initiative, saying 'it would be much better to use cattle for farming because they can be controlled. The hand-operated tractors need a lot of manpower, hence using them is very tiring. Some are privately owned; others have been given to particular groups.' It costs around TZS 18–20,000 to hire a power tiller for 1 acre. This finding is related to the appropriate technology aspect of good governance put forward by Grindle.

There are also biases in the way tractors are lent to people. In a Wazabanga village focus group discussion, respondents reported that tractors taken to the district in 2009 to lend to farmers under the Kilimo Kwanza strategy were lent to people who were not farmers. The ward councillor (in a focus group) explained as follows:

> Some people paid bribes in order to get tractors, even though they were not farmers, so that they could hire them out to get money. Tractors were lent to people who had land title deeds in town; one person got three tractors by writing his true name in one case, a fake name in a second case and his wife's name as a person from a different family in a third.

This issue of lack of transparency in the distribution of tractors applies to some other resources. For example, life history interviewee Abdulrahman

Mnyachi (forty-four years old, from Nchinga village, Mtwara), complained that presidential funds for entrepreneurship were disbursed on grounds that were not transparent. After Jakaya Kikwete became president in 2005, he disbursed money to every district to lend to small entrepreneurs. However, nobody in Nchinga village received a loan and intended beneficiaries were sidelined. There were similar complaints in Kayumbe village, Rukwa.

Cases of elected leaders not being accountable to the people who elected them were noted from the village to the district level. Abdulrahman Mnyachi, a member of the Chama cha Mapinduzi ruling party and the local branch secretary, had this to say of the local MP (also a ruling party member):

> The Honourable MP seems to have forgotten the people of this constituency, while it is they who elected him. Since he was elected in 2005, he visited the area only in September 2009, which suggests he was there to ask for votes in the 2010 elections. During his visit, people complained to him about water shortages, high water prices, fluctuating sulphur prices and the system of selling cashew nuts through the warehouse system, which farmers found disadvantageous. He didn't seem to care about people's complaints, and just bragged that he was the Minister for Sports hence didn't have the mandate to address the problems facing them.

To the villagers, this was arrogance; their expectation was that, since their MP was in the government hierarchy, he was in a good position to channel their complaints to the responsible organs. Had these words been said by someone in the main opposition political party in the area, one might have thought they were generated by party differences. However, they were not, and it therefore seems likely that the MP was not accountable to the people. Such allegations did not come out so strongly anywhere else.

In some communities, usury is constraining movement out of poverty. James Cleopa, (fifty-three years old), agricultural and livestock extension officer of Kalage ward, Wazabanga, Mwanza, clarified this:

> Some rich people make the poor poorer through usurious lending to them; they lend money to them at usurious conditions, especially when they need to buy agricultural inputs. Some of them lend TZS 10,000 and ask to be repaid TZS 20,000 or TZS 30,000. Others lend TZS 10,000 and ask to be paid a bag of rice, while the value of such a bag is TZS 40,000.

This finding is linked to the microcredit/savings governance element of good governance put forward by Grindle.

Shortage of rural financial institutions is also a governance problem, since only a few people can access microfinance services. For example, there was only one microfinance facility in Kalage ward, Mwanza, and one in Mwandima ward, Rukwa. Little knowledge of the way financial facilities work leads some people to complain when they fall to meet minimum conditions for getting credit. Most people do not know of or acknowledge their obligations and rights under a credit scheme; they do not have a history of saving and buying shares and just want to borrow. Whenever their loan applications are rejected as a result of lack of qualifications, they complain that they are discriminated against.

Unlike in Wazabanga village, where villagers are benefiting from a ward SACCO, Kayumbe village, Rukwa, has had a bad experience. The National Microfinance Bank (the only banker involved in Makazi's SACCO) has stopped providing loans to the SACCO because its leaders have misused its funds. The SACCO is allowed to operate a bank account but very few farmers have these. Therefore, members are no longer getting credit from the SACCO.

In some communities, freedom of expression is inadequate. One instance of this was in 2009 in Wazabanga village in Mwanza region, when an MP had a meeting with villagers. At the meeting, life history interviewee Robert Kashinje (thirty four years old), asked village and ward leaders to clarify why people who had paid TZS 10,000 as a contribution to the construction of Wazabanga Primary School had been given receipts showing TZS 5,000. Instead of answering the question, the ward councillor said furiously, 'the one who has asked a trouble-making question does not even have a home here, yet he is talking nonsense.' When asked about the TZS 5,000 and 10,000 contributions, another life history interviewee, Joseph Masanja, previous head teacher of Wazabanga Primary School, said:

> Definitely the leaders squandered the money. It appears the district commissioner had already reprimanded them without the villagers knowing. That is why when they were asked about the issue during a meeting with the MP the ward councillor silenced the questioner; it was a secret which the leaders did not want to leak to the villagers and to other leaders like the MP.

This case shows low transparency in the collection and use of cash contributions from community members. Where such problems occur, the chances of people moving out of poverty are slim. This particular incident is in line with the freedom of expression and voice for the poor elements of governance put forward by Hyden and Court and Grindle.

Findings with respect to education

Governance issues enhancing education

The government has expanded schooling opportunities at the primary and secondary education levels through the nationwide Primary and Secondary Education Development Programmes, which started in 2001 and 2004, respectively. James Cleopa, (fifty-three years old, from Wazabanga, Mwanza), praised the government for having increased schooling opportunities through these programmes, charging only TZS 20,000 per secondary school day student per year. However, he said that the materials needed to get a student enrolled in a public secondary school were at least TZS 127,000, in addition to the TZS 20,000 'school fees'. This finding comes under the girls' education element of governance advocated by Grindle in the sense that the programmes have increased opportunities for girls' schooling.

At some schools, there is transparency in the expenditure of school money. For example, respondents in a village focus group discussion in Nkasi district, Rukwa, told of a notice board showing expenditures, although most people were not interested in reading it. Whether or not community members read the information on the notice board, the leaders had fulfilled the accountability downwards item of good governance put forward by Grindle. The discussants added that parents also participated actively in school meetings. This finding is related to the participation element of good governance. More parents participating in school activities can enhance the system thereby improving education in the community.

In Nkasi and Magu districts, girls getting pregnant while pursuing primary education were being allowed to resume studies after delivery. One teacher in Wazabanga village of Mwanza described this move as being a personal decision on the part of some teachers—that is, it is not yet legally permitted. Nevertheless, it is a positive step; for example, forty-one-year-old Hilari Ndasi's daughter passed her primary school examinations after delivering a child and was allowed into Kalage Secondary School in 2010.

Governance issues constraining education

Although school fees in a day government secondary school are only TZS 20,000 per student per year, some parents are too poor to pay, especially because of the other costs mentioned above. The government has stipulated that students whose parents are very poor should be exempted from paying, but some children from such households are not assisted in accessing this opportunity. This happened with nineteen-year-old James Mwamwezi of Kalesa village, Rukwa, who completed primary education in 2008 and was selected to enter Mwandima Secondary School, but his mother, who was divorced, was unable to find the TZS 20,000 to pay. Another boy of the same village, name withheld, completed primary school in 2006 at twenty-two years old, having started at the age of sixteen, after primary school fees were abolished. He was selected to enter Kipili Secondary School in 2007 but could not go for the same reasons as those James Mwamwezi experienced.

Biased implementation of some rules and policies is another bad governance element constraining poverty reduction through education. For example, unlike in Magu and Nkasi districts, girls in Newala district are not being allowed to resume studies after delivering a child, although some education leaders regretted this. For example, Burhan Rajabu from Nchinga village, education coordinator of Chikota ward, Newala district, said:

> Policymakers are reluctant to pass a bill stating that pregnant girls be allowed to resume their studies after delivery because they are afraid it will lead to an increase in pregnancies among school girls. However, in my view, the fear is unfounded. It is high time the bill was passed to become law because some girls are engaged in sexual intercourse only once even unwillingly or through rape and become pregnant. If such girls were allowed to resume studies after delivery some of them would perform well academically and continue with higher education. The current fear is marginalising potential pupils by denying them chances to continue with secondary education up to higher education.

This and the previous two cases are related to the non-distortionary policy element of good governance put forward by Grindle.

Poor governance delayed construction of classrooms in Kalesa and Wazabanga villages of Rukwa and Mwanza, respectively. For example, former head teacher Joseph Masanja of Wazabanga said that he had resigned his school headship because people wanted to involve him in corruption. According to him,

> The process to construct classrooms, teachers' houses, toilets, laboratories and other school buildings is that the teachers identify what needs to be built and send this list to the school committee. The committee confirms the needs and writes a summary of items to be purchased and activities to be done. Unhappily, before the ward education officer or district education officer signs, he/she asks the school committee members to give him/her 'something'. If they give him/her nothing, he/she does not sign to approve their purchasing requests, hence their intent to purchase materials for school construction is frustrated. After signing, they decide where to get the money for the bribe, normally selling construction materials. This results in substandard construction, since they use fewer materials than recommended (e.g. the ratio of cement to sand). An education officer may approve TZS 18 million and tell the head teacher that TZS 12 million of the money is his and that the head teacher will know what to do with the remaining TZS million.

Bribery was also reported in posting and retaining primary school teachers. Joseph Masanja said:

> New teachers are allocated to schools whose head teachers bribe the district education officer. New teachers are also supposed to stay at their new stations of work for at least three years before they can be allowed to ask for a transfer, but it is common to see some teachers, especially ladies in rural remote schools, teaching at a new school for one month and leaving for another school in town. Some of the money used to bribe education officers is obtained from monthly contributions by pupils to pay voluntary teachers.

Given the acute shortage of teachers, community leaders in collaboration with head teachers have been given the mandate to employ people who have secondary education but no professional qualifications. Therefore, TZS 300 is charged per pupil per month to pay 'voluntary teachers' but is also used to bribe ward and district education officers to allocate new teachers to schools and retain new ones to ensure they teach there for a long time. These issues relate to the transparency element of good governance, advocated by many.

Conflict between political parties constrained the construction of a secondary school in one village of Nkasi district. The Secondary Education Development Programme's main objective is to have at least one secondary school constructed in every ward. Elsewhere in Tanzania, such schools started operating in 2005. However, in Mwandima ward, Rukwa, this did not occur until 2009. The delay was caused by antagonism between members of the ruling party and those of an opposition party to which most people in Mwandima adhere. People associated the Secondary Education Development Programme with the ruling party hence refused when they were told to contribute in kind or in cash to the construction of the school. This meant the pace of construction of the school was sluggish. This result comes under the tolerance element of governance in MKUKUTA I.

Findings with respect to health services

In some communities, health facilities are working well. For example, in Kalesa village, Rukwa, Selina Ngungulo (thirty-nine years old) reported in a key informant interview that at Mwandima Health Centre there were always medicines, especially against malaria. The health centre is five minutes away on foot from her home.

Elsewhere, though, bad stories were given about health services. For example, in Kayumbe village, Rukwa, Didas Magangu (forty-five years old) said that community members contribute TZS 10,000 per household per year and become members of a community health fund. With this contribution, eight members of the household are eligible for free health care for one year. However, very few households have joined the fund, mainly because medicines are not there in most cases. Those who are not community health fund members can pay at the service delivery point. The cost is TZS 1,000 per head at a dispensary and TZS 2,000 per head at a health centre, for consultation and medication, but sometimes people are asked to buy drugs from private pharmacies because of the shortage of medicines. Women and children under five years old are exempted from paying for health services, although in reality they do pay since most of the time drugs are not available; they get only consultation and prescriptions free.

Corruption is also reported in the health sector. For example, in 1999, a water tank was being constructed at Wazabanga Health Centre in Mwanza, but the cement used was being sold to the ward councillor and other village leaders. As a result, too little cement was used to make the cover of the tank, so it was weak and broke, and also the tank itself, which then leaked. So the tank has never held water since it was built. This is related to the anti-corruption element of good governance, a concern of MKUKUTA I and Grindle.

Understaffing at dispensaries was reported in some places. A rural dispensary is supposed to have five workers, but there were only two at one dispensary in Chikota ward, Mtwara. This was reported by Burhan Rajabu, Chikota ward education coordinator. This is related to the health services item of good governance advocated by Grindle.

Citizens aged sixty years and above are supposed to get medical treatment free of charge. However, this hardly ever happens. According to life history interviewee Jasmine Nandonde (sixty-three years old) of Nchinga village, Mtwara:

> We are told that the elderly like me get free medical treatment, but in our village that is not the case; even the community health fund does not work. In April 2009, I was suffering blood pressure problems; I spent my TZS 15,000 for treatment in the district hospital and that money will not be refunded.

Such a case was also found in Mwanza region. Edson Mndevu (sixty-nine years old) revealed that he was suffering from diabetes but was not receiving any free medicines. However, he was lucky because he was being sent remittances by his children who were working for a mining company, and he was using this money to get treated. This is related to the non-distortionary policy item of good governance given by Grindle.

Findings with respect to water services

Unfortunately, in all the six communities, there were no good stories about linkages between governance and water supply.

Unrealistic and unaffordable solutions were suggested to community members to solve the problem of shortage of water for domestic use. Mr. Rashidi of Nkangala, Mtwara, said:

The government has been campaigning and lobbying for rainwater harvesting for decades; this can never be a solution to such a serious issue in our area. After all, who can afford the cost; one needs to have not less than TZS 2 million to have a well just outside one's house, then there is the whole issue of treating the water. This is a complicated process which even those with money won't be able to afford. We need to address the real issue here. Just walk around the village, you will see the wells outside the houses and some of them have become traps into which people fall at night because they are not covered.

This suggests that plans to solve the problem of water shortage are not participatory. This is therefore linked to the governance elements of freedom of expression and opportunity for consultation put forward by Hyden and Court. Newala district has very high scarcity of water supply for domestic use. Abdul Idrisa, acting executive officer of Chikota ward, Mtwara, reported that bribery in supplying water was affecting other people's access to water. He added, 'every time we ask them to supply us with water, they tell us, "it's coming"'. Focus group discussants in Nchinga village of the ward elaborated on this issue:

The tap water supply in this village was adequate from 1957 to 1985, but in the late 1980s it started declining. For the past six years, water availability has become so scarce that it is fetched mainly by men from 7km away in Makota. But the problem of water is compounded by workers of the Water Department: there are water pipes in this village taking water from Makonde Water Supply Centre to Mihambwe. Members of the Water Department distribute water to better-off people who have good water wells. As for common people, like those in our village, they supply water when national leaders are coming or when the Uhuru Torch is about to pass through our village. This problem is constraining our efforts to reduce poverty since we spend a lot of time fetching water.

The shortage of water supply for domestic use is also a problem in Nkasi district, but here it is attributed to lack of accountability of village leaders. According to Novath Nanzalalila of Kalesa village, Rukwa:

The leaders of this village are not responsible, and this is contributing to ineffectiveness in poverty alleviation. Tap water was introduced in 1977, and during the handover of the project district-level officials insisted that the villagers be responsible for maintenance of the taps through their contributions. However, owing to poor follow-up by village leaders, tap water is no longer available, since maintenance of the taps has not been done. In the early 1990s, wells using pumps were established but only a few of them are working; others have become dysfunctional due to poor maintenance.

This is related to the safe water and investment in basic social services and infrastructure elements of good governance explained by Grindle.

Conclusions and Recommendations

CONCLUSION 1: It is evident from the empirical findings of this research that many conventional indicators of governance are important as far as explanations of poverty are concerned. Moreover, the findings imply that negative governance points are more applicable than the positive ones. Interviewees were able to explain the negative and positive ways in which the indicators of governance affected them. In this regard, classical approaches to analysing governance are useful to assess linkages between governance indicators and indicators of poverty.

> *Recommendation 1*: This approach should therefore be given the attention it deserves in analysing the relationships between governance indicators and poverty indicators.
>
> *Recommendation 2*: The government and other key stakeholders in Tanzania need to take governance issues more seriously at the grassroots levels by disseminating information more effectively and involving communities more actively in development plans, from conception to evaluation. Use the O&OD approach to identify obstacles and opportunities and prioritise interventions.

CONCLUSION 2: Pro-poor reforms implemented by the government of Tanzania since 1999, when local government reform started and the Tanzania Development Vision 2025 was promulgated, have enabled some people to make strides towards exiting poverty. For instance, the removal of the development levy and the yearly payment for a business licence has had a positive impact for some people in terms of improved livelihoods. Meanwhile, in one ward of Nkasi district, government facilitates cross-border trade well, although in another ward of the same district and in one ward of Newala district there is limited facilitation of cross-border trade. This constrains communities' ability to exit from poverty.

CONCLUSION 3: Under the National Poverty Eradication Strategy and MKU-KUTA I, some commendable progress has been made, such as increased coverage of schools, health facilities and water services. However, a great deal still needs to be done: most schools still have shortages of teachers, books, libraries and laboratories; health facilities lack experts, medicines and equipment; and improved water sources are still inadequate.

> *Recommendation 3(a):* There is therefore a need to continue and heighten the nationwide pro-poor reform programme and explore more opportunities for pro-poor growth policies. Areas in MKUKUTA I that have not yet been improved adequately should be carried forward in MKUKUTA II, but without forgetting new priority areas for MKUKUTA II. For example, improve education but incorporate the tertiary system which absorbs secondary school leavers.

> *Recommendation 3(b):* Further promote and facilitate cross-border trade for poverty reduction.

CONCLUSION 4: Although a booklet in Kiswahili summarising MKUKUTA I was circulated, dissemination has been inadequate. Low publicity of national and local programmes, projects, policies and strategies constrains implementation of the same since potential implementers are not aware of their importance. This partly explains the low implementation of some priorities of MKUKUTA I, as in Mwandima ward, Nkasi district, where some community members boycotted participation in government-run community activities.

> *Recommendation 4:* The government needs to ensure capacity Strengthening and intensive dissemination at lower level namely districts and community levels.

CONCLUSION 5: If community members are well educated, mobilised and involved, in all stages of interventions, from problem identification to prioritisation to implementation, community development can achieve a great deal. Participatory use of O&OD further heightens impacts, particularly if the government or other sources can inject financial resources to obtain materials that are not available locally.

> *Recommendation 5:* Make it possible for communities to participate in all stages of planning and implementation, and enable them cast votes of no confidence in leaders at any point, to make them and subsequent leaders more responsible towards citizens.

CONCLUSION 6: Unfair distribution of tractors for Kilimo Kwanza, biased provisioning of presidential funds for entrepreneurs and lack of transparency in issuing credit in some ward SACCOs show that, in some cases and places, economic resources meant for specific groups of people for poverty alleviation do not reach them. This constrains poverty alleviation efforts among those people and at large.

CONCLUSION 7: The number of SACCOs has increased in rural areas and at workplaces recently, which is promising for poverty alleviation. However, some SACCOs do not work well, putting people off joining and leading them to go back to moneylenders who loan money at very high rates. In addition, some community members have poor knowledge of the methods of microfinance

Recommendation 6(a): Generate objectively verifiable indicators for the provision of government resources such as tractors so it is easier to convict corrupt officials who violate such criteria

Recommendation 6(b): Work towards stemming corruption and formulate mechanisms to punish officials who breach regulations, such as the rule that children from very poor households be exempted from paying the annual secondary school contribution.

Recommendation 6(c): Strengthen existing institutions like warehousing, extension, cooperative societies, community banks and SACCOs, so agriculture can contribute more to poverty alleviation. New institutions could be established to develop agricultural technologies.

CONCLUSION 8: Agricultural extension services are one of the most important institutions in the sector, but in some areas in the research sites there is only one agricultural and livestock extension officer for many villages, with neither a bicycle nor a motorcycle to visit farmers. This means the sector's vital contribution to overall poverty reduction is weakened. This situation is exacerbated if farmers have poor or no access to financial services for agriculture and if markets for agricultural products are poor.

Recommendation 7: More Extension Officers must be trained to meet the existing demand. In addition, there is also a need to establish funds to finance small- and medium-scale farmers to buy basic inputs without going through moneylenders. Precede such lending by providing farmers with education on how to use credit profitably and on the conditions of the credit. Enable farmers to form SACCOs so financial institutions can serve them more easily.

CONCLUSION 9: Before the WRS was introduced in 2006, the price of cashew nuts could vary greatly within one agricultural season, because traders were taking advantage of the loopholes that existed in the marketing system. The government did well to interfere by introducing the WRS. However, some farmers go on selling their cashew nuts using a *kangomba*, despite the government having outlawed this practice and despite its negative impacts.

Recommendation 8: Introduce the WRS all over the country for major crop products. At the same time, look for markets for the products to be stored in warehouses

CONCLUSION 10: Land suitable for the production of high-value crops is in such high demand it is a potential source of serious conflict, which will undermine poverty alleviation efforts. In some places, leaders have experience of solving land conflicts, which could help them in the future.

Recommendation 9: Work towards the prevention of land conflict by abiding strictly by land use plans and land laws. Review land laws regularly with a view to increasing access to land by various groups of citizens, especially the poor, women, orphans and widows. Give special attention to such groups in relation to access to the legal system too.

CONCLUSION 11: There are some primary school teachers who allow female pupils to resume their studies after delivering children. This is positive, although it would be preferable if a bill were passed to legally allow such girls to resume their studies, so as to improve progress towards attainment of Millennium Development Goals 2 and 3 on education and gender equality, respectively.

Recommendation 10: Legally allow school girls who have delivered children to resume their studies to speed up progress towards attainment of Millennium Development Goals 2 and 3.

CONCLUSION 12: Community health services are not good in almost all sites. Rural people depend mainly on public health facilities, unlike in towns, where incomes are higher and private health facilities are more numerous. Nevertheless, much needs to be done to improve health facilities in both rural and urban areas. Shortage of water is a big problem in all communities.

Recommendation 11: Ensure that efforts to improve health facilities are more equitable between rural and urban areas. Furthermore, the elderly must obtain free medical treatment and that those who are entitled to pension payments receive them more frequently.

---

1   United Republic of Tanzania (1999a)
2   United Republic of Tanzania (2005)
3   Ibid.
4   United Republic of Tanzania (2009b)
5   World Bank (1994), in D. Olowu (2003)
6   G. Hyden and J. Court (2004)
7   Ibid., p. 16
8   D. Olowu (2003)
9   Ibid.
10 G. Hyden and J. Court (2004)
11 Ibid.
12 M. Grindle (2002)
13 Ibid., p. 1
14 Ibid.
15 United Republic of Tanzania (1998)
16 United Republic of Tanzania (2005)
17 United Republic of Tanzania (2010b)

Chapter 10

Taking the Plunge on Social Assistance in Rural Tanzania—Assessing the Options

Andrew Shepherd, Flora Kessy, Lucy Scott and Eliab Luvanda

Introduction

Poverty barely reduced in Tanzania between 2000/01 and 2006/07, especially in rural areas, despite economic growth. A large number of households lived just below the poverty line and there was a widely perceived decline in living standards, according to the results of the Household Budget Survey. During the period, many people depended on agriculture and the poorest had the least diversified livelihood portfolios. Average productive asset ownership, including of livestock, was low and declining. This suggests significantly increasing vulnerability, as livestock represents savings which act as buffers against shocks. The major improvement in quality of life came through enhanced access to education, including for the poorest, as a result of continuous high levels of public investment. This is a large achievement, although there is still a way to go in terms of achieving quality education as well as health services.

In 2006, the major correlates of avoiding poverty included the possession of many assets and the monetisation of economic activities through involvement in markets, credit society membership and access to bank loans. Farming was generally associated with poverty, with two caveats. First, the quantity of land owned could mitigate this association. Second, farm households engaged in commercial crops have done better than others: there has been a big increase in the production of commercial crops compared with stagnation in food crops.[1] Additional important determinants of poverty status include age and education level of the household head, and of spouses in urban areas; household size and dependency ratios; and being on the electricity grid.

Our qualitative research in Mwanza, Rukwa and Mtwara, combined with the evidence from national Household Budget Surveys, suggests that persistent poverty is the overwhelming issue for most Tanzanians. The critical issue is how to promote more pathways out of poverty. We know that escaping poverty involves taking risks, such as educating children, investing in a business, diversifying and so on. Having some protection against destitution, such as through social protection, would make it easier to take such risks.

The Kagera Health and Development ten-year panel survey (1991–4/2004) compared people who escaped poverty with those stuck there.[2] Each additional year of education was associated with significant additional assets, which were the survey's welfare measure. The same effect was obtained by having a migrant child remitting. On-farm diversification was critical to income growth, and lack of it was associated with stagnation and/or decline. The biggest success stories included off-farm diversification, especially through trading. Social networks, which include apprenticeships, were also important, and relatively independent of a person's starting position. However, network-based options were not accessible in remote areas. Poor markets, with exploitative buyers, and poor infrastructure also prevent income growth, especially in remote areas.[3]

There are also broader influences. In the 1990s, stagnant crop prices led to sales of smallholdings and a scramble for non-farm work, pushing wages down to bare survival level.[4] Many are trapped in casual labour and unable to re-enter the land market, given high land prices—a consequence of population growth and income inequality. While the supply of labourers has increased, demand has not, as a result of the low level of private sector job creation.[5] It is extremely important to support agriculture and fishing, since income growth in these sectors will have the biggest effect on poverty,

Insecurity and vulnerability are widespread in Tanzania. While there is 'generalised insecurity',[6] with vulnerability to shocks stretching far up the income distribution, there is significant regional variation in the incidence of shocks, and also among households in terms of their ability to cope. Fieldwork recorded a number of common covariant and idiosyncratic shocks which had impoverishing effects across the communities studied. Idiosyncratic shocks are widespread, but not yet well addressed through policy. In particular, women have to cope with property-grabbing, male alcoholism and serial polygamy. Table 10.1 presents the principal reasons behind moving into poverty over the course of people's life histories. Divorce was cited the most often (nearly all women reported this, as did many men). Failure of non-farm business was the next most prominent. Any social protection response would need to be able to address these vulnerabilities.[7]

Table 10.1: Reasons behind moves into poverty in the study areas in Tanzania

Cause	Total
Divorce	12
Failure of non-farm business	6
Drought/El Niño season	4
Illness/accident and associated medical and caring costs	4
Death of family member	3
Closure of non-farm business by government	2
Unpaid labour	1
Division of family assets	1
Rising costs of living relative to income	1
Loss of salaried job	1
Inheriting dependants after a family member dies	1
Husband takes on more wives	1
Pregnant out of wed-lock	1
Failure of agriculture/fish farming	1
Theft of assets	1
Alcohol	1
Livestock disease	1

Note: These numbers are in no way statistically representative—they derive from qualitative life history interviews carried out with 120 households in six Household Budget Survey clusters. They give a qualitative indication of the kinds of factors which propel people into poverty. The National Panel Survey will eventually be able to validate this picture. The figures are low, as relatively few entries to and exits from poverty were found overall.

Source: Higgins (2011)

Agriculture clearly emerges as a risky business, with many and varied sources of risk. This is true for labourers as well as farmers and fishers. A major problem widely identified by the majority of our informants is the inaffordability of important agricultural inputs such as fertiliser—which are key to resilience and upward mobility.

In addition to the aforementioned sources of vulnerability, to which rural people appear universally vulnerable, there are also significant life-cycle risks (particularly associated with old age and childhood). Children are vulnerable in many situations: 41 per cent of mainland children are found to be deprived on at least three counts in the 2004/05 Demographic and Health Survey.[8] While child survival indicators have improved significantly and progress is 'on track', child malnutrition is still widespread and children are vulnerable to shocks.[9] Children rely on parents to feed them, so their nutrition depends on getting a good level of care from them or other relatives, and child malnutrition is closely related to maternal education levels. While most families prioritise the needs of children and older people when there is not enough to eat, sometimes children lose out as a result of a poor level of care.

There has been a general improvement in dietary energy consumption, but hunger is still widely experienced, especially in rural areas and in the hungry season, with hunger deepening for the poorest quintile. Food insecurity and consequent malnutrition have detrimental short- and long-term consequences, affecting child physical and cognitive development as well as the risks of developing chronic illness.[10] Malnutrition also impedes labour productivity and in turn food security, since payment for casual waged labour is often at a piece rate.

There are many causes of hunger, macro and micro, of which two can be singled out. One major issue is high market prices, especially important for the urban poor but also for rural households dependent on wage labour or selling products and services. Food price inflation has also eaten into household budgets. For the poorest, this has led to lower nutritional levels.[11] In a recent opinion poll, 52 per cent of respondents identified high food and other commodity prices as a major economic problem.[12]

A second major cause of food insecurity is the saturated rural wage labour market. Wages are low and uncertain and there are poor returns to farming, despite the price of purchased food, on which many are heavily reliant. Temporary, insecure labour contracts near villages are especially short in duration. For households where work is the major source of cash/food, there are no or few buffers against food price (or other) shocks. According to respondents, casual labour is 'not enough for a day's food' and so further work is required, on top of their twelve-hour work days. This exhausting toil drains hungry bodies, making them vulnerable to ill-health, which is costly. Assets are sold to pay for health expenses and income-generating work is disrupted to make time to care for sick family members. Many remain trapped in casual labour and only eat one meal a day—the 'destitute' and the 'very poor' in the well-being classification used in the fieldwork.[13] The destitute can usually eat in other people's houses at the expense of their dignity. Poor but not destitute people will often not do this to preserve their dignity.

Jobs may bring a relationship with employers, who may be called on in times of difficulty for a loan or for food. Relatives may also help. But such support cannot be relied on. In some cases, food insecurity is caused by old age and exacerbated by lack of support from spouses, children or other relatives. Aggregate figures show that 70 per cent of older people (sixty years or older in 1993) reported declining welfare (especially in terms of health) after 1993, as well as dwindling respect and status.

In conclusion, poverty, food insecurity and vulnerability are all 'mass' phenomena in Tanzania. There is a state of 'generalised insecurity', and vulnerability to shocks reaches far up the income ladder. The absence of buffers against shocks lower down the ladder means that the risk of impoverishment, chronic poverty and destitution is high.

Poverty in Tanzania is widespread and not reducing quickly, especially in rural areas, despite economic growth. This owes partly to the pattern of growth, but also to the increasingly structural nature of poverty. The draft 2009 National Social Protection Framework has committed the country to a stronger approach to social protection, including social transfers. However, additional efforts to transform the situation are clearly called for. This chapter examines further the decisions that need to be made in this regard.

Social assistance—what can it do?

Poverty reduction in Tanzania will come mostly from growth. It is important that social transfers enable poor people to participate more fully in growth by allowing them to take advantage of investment and business opportunities, wage employment and education. Growth is now reasonably stable but poverty has reduced little, especially in rural areas where there has also been less economic growth. Growth has been most rapid in mining and urban construction, hence has not benefited poor rural people much. Incidence of urban poverty, especially in Dar es Salaam, has been on the decline.

Agriculture is recognised as a major part of the problem. The already large sector has grown, but most smallholders depend on food crops and livestock, and these sub-sectors have not grown much.[14] It is difficult to make a good income in small-scale farming. Lacking the resources to make their smallholdings productive, many resort to casual wage labour and petty trading. Working in these saturated markets rarely enables the accumulation of assets or even food security, given rising commodity prices. These are some of the reasons growth has not reduced income poverty faster. Meanwhile, several human development indicators have improved as a result of high government expenditure on health and education.

Social transfers contribute positively to growth, especially its inclusiveness, as well as to poverty and vulnerability reduction. This is achieved by protecting and enhancing human capital and labour productivity, as well as productive assets, since these need not be sold as a response to crisis.[15]

Social transfers can protect chronically poor people from shocks and reduce vulnerability by smoothing consumption. Transfers can also promote livelihood development by helping to conserve people's limited assets, and thereby enable people to take investment risks. Ultimately, they can transform socioeconomic relationships and improve long-term well-being prospects.[16] We know that regular transfers over substantial periods can improve nutrition, health and education outcomes for poor children, facilitate the rebuilding of household and community assets and enable inclusive economic growth— and they can reach the extreme poor. They can also be an important part of a transformative approach to development which can interrupt the exclusion and adverse incorporation which characterises current patterns of development.

The options for social transfers

It is important to be clear what decisions need to be made when putting a programme of social transfers in place. There are choices to be made about objectives, then about how much to continue to rely on informal social protection, and whether any new formal approaches should strengthen the informal. Finally, questions are raised about the sort of programme that would be appropriate. This chapter focuses on social transfers (cash transfers), given that social insurance is unlikely to be feasible for poor households. However, experiences with community health funds suggest that an insurance approach may be useful, so this is also discussed in the analysis.[17]

The government of Tanzania has decided that informal systems of protection are no longer working adequately and need to be supplemented with formal social protection, according to the National Social Protection Strategy. Research by the Chronic Poverty Research Centre illustrates this concern, through findings that women who return home after divorce or widowhood are, in many cases, no longer welcomed and protected by their parents or brothers.[18]

While social protection includes a broad range of measures (social security, social insurance and social transfers, and in some cases labour market regulation), social transfer schemes have been shown to be one of the most effective strategies for developing countries to address widespread poverty.[19] Formal employment-related social security or social insurance is limited as most employment is informal.

One option is to develop tailor-made social transfer or insurance schemes that address each specific major risk separately—as suggested by the National Social Protection Framework. However, our research suggests that the poor are trapped by a multitude of risks over the course of their lives. It may be difficult for top-down efforts to predict and effectively respond to the risks encountered by a multitude of individual households. Elsewhere, social transfer programmes have been shown to enable the poor themselves to respond effectively to prevailing insecurities and to plan accordingly. Furthermore, it may not be cost effective for the government to establish a labyrinth of separate agencies to address different sources of vulnerability through the same medium of social protection. The National Social Protection Framework suggests that several schemes might be needed. However, for the moment, one well-run and wide coverage programme addressing many risks might be better than several patchy and less well-run programmes addressing different sources of risk.

There is an argument about the universal entitlement to social protection. Free health services at the point of delivery are widely accepted by many governments as a right, whether funded from tax revenue or from insurance premiums. An employment guarantee, as in India, is universally available in theory but self-targeted in practice: it is usually taken up only by those who need it. While in principle a right to social protection may be accepted as a long-term goal, in practice it is also accepted that, in the short to medium term, some targeting may be necessary for financial sustainability reasons.

In Tanzania, income poverty is widespread (three or four people out of ten) and increasing. However, many of the poor live at a level not far under the poverty line. Social protection could plausibly prevent the depletion of their assets on negative shocks and promote asset accumulation, thereby providing a pathway out of poverty. One policy option would be to protect the population in stages, first reducing the vulnerability of the poorest, then of the poor, then of the remaining vulnerable, progressing equitably towards eventually achieving near-universal coverage. This would mean starting with a manageable commitment and increasing that commitment as the fiscal envelope expands.

Most frequently, social transfers are targeted at those who need it most, or at those whose situation will be most transformed by them. A combination of a universal and targeted approach is also possible. Thus, certain poor or highly vulnerable regions/localities can be targeted, within which universal provision can be made. Again, this could be a first stage before universal provision nationwide.

If it is decided that targeting is desirable, then further decisions about adopting a categorical or non-categorical approach need to be made. The advantage of categorical targeting (such as of children or of older people) is that it is usually easier and cheaper to do than targeting by income or well-being category. The disadvantage is that categorical targeting often misses too many poor or vulnerable people (exclusion errors); if the category is very broad—such as all children or all older people—it can reach too many non-poor (inclusion errors).

A growing number of schemes are using income/poverty targeting, however. Research in Tanzania, as well as elsewhere, has found that local focus groups are very good at categorising households in terms of poverty/well-being (Box 10.1). This could be a less bureaucratic basis for non-categorical or poverty targeting. However, it could be that communities, if they knew that resources would follow, would be less accurate at identifying the poorest households or individuals. This would mean there would need to be supportive systems for verification, which could be expensive.

Box 10.1: Example of focus group-based wealth ranking in the study areas in Tanzania

Focus groups identified six well-being classifications ranging from destitute (1) to rich (6).

These sought to take into account assets, income, levels of consumption and vulnerability to risk:

1. Destitute = *maskini hohehahe*

- Depend on others for basic needs
- Cannot work
- Tend to be socially excluded

2. Very poor = *maskini sana*

- No clear livelihood source
- No significant productive assets
- Dependent on selling labour/scavenging
- Erratic income and food access
- Very vulnerable to becoming destitute with shock

3. Poor = *maskini*

- Have access to limited productive assets (e.g. land and livestock)
- Cannot earn enough from farming or trade to take family provisioning through whole year and so will reduce family food consumption
- Cannot save much in good years
- Must sell assets in order to cope in a crisis
- Vulnerable to downward mobility to 'very poor' category but not to 'destitute' category

4. Vulnerable but not poor = *tete ila siyo maskini*

- More productive assets which takes family through the year
- During good times can save
- During bad times will reduce family consumption
- Vulnerable to downward mobility with a significant shock

5. Resilient = *tajiri kiasi (mwenye uwezo)*

- Sufficient capacity (e.g. assets, social networks) to prevent significant downward mobility relative to overall productive wealth
- May employ small amounts of labour on farm or be involved in small-scale trade

6. Rich = *tajiri*

- Significant assets and local power
- Involved in large-scale trade or employment of labour
- Own large-scale non-farm assets
- May lend money

Source: Adapted from Higgins (2010)

Latin American conditional cash transfers have been able to raise political support among elites and middle classes. This support stems largely from the imposition of conditions on recipient households—usually that children attend school or pregnant women and young children attend health clinics regularly. While these conditionalities may address taxpayers' fears that poor people need an incentive to improve their human capital, evaluations suggest that unconditional provision works just as well in terms of achieving these development objectives.[20] Gender roles and inequality may also be reinforced if, as in Latin American, government programmes identify women alone as responsible for taking their children to school and health checkups, as a condition for grant receipt.[21] Additionally, it is administratively costly to monitor and enforce compliance with conditions.

There is a clear trade-off between the coverage of a social transfer scheme and the size of the benefits it can distribute. The more people covered, the smaller the transfer can be. The smaller the transfer, the less significance it will have for the recipient and the smaller the effects in terms of consumption smoothing as well as poverty reduction and growth. However, strict financial constraints should not be assumed, since it is possible to find additional money if there is political momentum. There is now plenty of experience in other countries indicating that relatively small transfers can make a big difference to a significant proportion of the population.

If people are to feel secure to save, invest and accumulate assets, they must know that any transfer will be regular. Regularity means that the household budget can be planned around the knowledge that the transfer will be available. Children can be kept in school and small savings and investments in farming and business can be made in the knowledge that the household will not go short of food. Although social protection should be predictable, it could still be seasonal, as for example with a well-timed public works programme or an off-season employment guarantee or cash transfer.

Governments worry about creating dependency and typically want to see people 'exit' (leave off receiving transfers) or 'graduate' (move onto a more commercial basis of support such as microfinance) programmes. However, the evidence for dependency in developing countries is very limited. Transfers, generally too small to become dependent on, tend to support poor people's existing strategies to escape poverty through small savings, investments and education. They also strengthen the informal social protection networks provided by families and kinship groups.[22]

Some transfers that have definite cut-off points: transfers targeted at the elderly, school-going children or neonatal and under-five children. Otherwise, it can be difficult for a programme to determine when a participant should exit or graduate. Here again community-based targeting has value—a local community knows when a household is doing significantly better. The discussion would then be whether the improvement is sustainable or whether withdrawing a transfer would simply put a household back where it was. Graduation may involve the introduction of other services, financial or vocational.[23]

Where political commitment to social transfers is hesitant, as it often is—for reasons of affordability or worries about dependence—it may be advisable to 'go with the political grain': if politicians are keen on a certain sort of transfer they should be supported to implement their initiative, which they may decide to revise over time in light of emerging assessments. Programme sustainability crucially requires government commitment and ownership, which may be lacking if donors pursue their preferred strategy. This may not be in the long-term interests of the poor.[24] Social transfers can quickly become a core part of the social contract between state and citizen, so these are important political decisions.

Existing policy and practice on social assistance in Tanzania

This research suggests the need for a social protection programme which is part of Tanzania's development strategy and not mere relief. By protecting consumption and enabling more people to participate in economic growth, social protection would boost poor people's demand for basic foodstuffs and in turn strengthen agricultural growth. Boosting effective demand for education and health services would also have beneficial outcomes in terms of human capital, as shown by long-term monitoring of Mexico's Oportunidades programme. In these ways, the cost of social protection can be more than offset by greater and more inclusive economic growth and human capital development.[25]

The policy context

Tanzania's first and second National Strategy for Growth and Reduction of Poverty (MKUKUTA I (completed in June 2005) and MKUKUTA II (finalised in 2010)) are sympathetic to the idea of social protection. MUKUKTA II states that,[26]

> The main objective of social protection is to prevent unacceptable levels of socioeconomic insecurity and deprivation [...] The strategy underscores developmental role that social protection can play – in preventing poverty traps, reducing household insecurity, and encouraging investments in poverty-reducing assets (physical, human, social and financial) that can strengthen people's resilience and capacity for self-sufficiency [...] Social protection interventions will focus on: orphans and vulnerable children; people with disabilities; the elderly; people living with HIV and long term illnesses; vulnerable women and youth; former inmates, and people disabled by accidents, wars and conflicts.

The two operational targets associated with this goal are an increase in the proportion of vulnerable children, including children outside family care, persons with disabilities and eligible adults covered by social protection measures and an increase in the proportion of eligible elderly people reached with minimum social pension.

MKUKUTA II puts forward a range of strategies to meet these objectives and targets. These include specific schemes for the economically non-active poor (persons with disabilities, orphans and vulnerable children, elderly people living with HIV) such as strengthening systems and institutions for effective access to a minimum social protection package, through exemption and waiver schemes for children and other vulnerable groups and increasing access to civil registration systems for older people, orphans and vulnerable children and persons with disabilities. Another group of strategies relates to providing support to carers. This includes continuing the provision of care and support to people living with HIV and those indirectly affected, including home-based care, social security schemes and food safety nets; and supporting the capacity of poor households to care for vulnerable members. In relation to the economically active poor, MKUKUTA II proposes to promote their economic empowerment, along with that of vulnerable groups, through measures such as start-up kits on income-generating activities and cash transfers.

More generally, MKUKUTA II's objectives and targets relating to social protection would be pursued through revising policy and regulations to ease access to financial services and exemptions applicable to vulnerable groups; and mainstreaming the provision of social protection measures in the plans of state and non-state actors and promoting and coordinating the involvement of the government, development partners, non-governmental organisations, faith-based organisations, the business sector and communities. MKUKUTA II envisages a role for private sector initiatives in implementing social protection measures, including through promoting corporate social responsibility as a means to support social protection interventions.

In addition, Goal 2 of MKUKUTA II is to improve public service delivery to all, especially the poor and vulnerable. One target for this is to introduce mechanisms for targeting the poor and vulnerable groups (to cover 65 per cent of the poor and vulnerable groups currently excluded from public service delivery). A strategy to achieve this includes promoting social protection interventions which recognise the potential of each individual, to ensure security for all and to minimise the risks affecting the most vulnerable, including the unemployed, pensioners, women, children, the elderly and victims of disasters.

However, both MKUKUTA I and MKUKUTA II indicate that many questions remain to be resolved, especially about what the objectives should be, who should be targeted and what sort of targeting system to use. The draft 2009 National Social Protection Framework, another component in the national effort to eradicate poverty, discusses these issues further. Its goal is to reach the most vulnerable and to enable them to engage in productive activities and become beneficiaries of the wider process of economic growth. It notes that there is a range of existing social protection mechanisms, but that the challenge is to extend their reach, especially to the informal sector. The National Social Protection Framework aims to address both the state of generalised insecurity mentioned above, preferably through universal approaches, and also the vulnerability of the poorest through targeted approaches.

The framework is cognisant of the potential public expenditure implications. While external assistance can be helpful, it is also unpredictable (which is highly problematic for social protection support)—and Tanzania is already highly aid dependent. At the time of writing (early April 2011), the framework had not yet been approved, and this remains the case in early 2012.

Social protection pilots

There are several social protection pilot programmes in operation, which this section summarises. While different in objectives and focus, they share some common features. All are targeted. All are extremely small in scale, although the National Costed Plan of Action for Most Vulnerable Children is now scaling up. The results of these schemes are currently being evaluated, and lessons should be drawn from these evaluations to inform the development of a national programme. For example, the effects of imposing conditions could be assessed or the various approaches to targeting could be compared.

Tanzania Social Action Fund community-based conditional cash transfer pilot[27]

Funded by the government of Tanzania, the World Bank and the Japan Social Development Fund, the Tanzania Social Action Fund covers 80 villages and 2,500 households in 3 districts. Households that qualified for the programme are very poor, not receiving similar benefits in kind or cash from another programme and include an elderly person (over sixty years old) or an orphan or vulnerable child. Beneficiaries were selected using 'verified community-based targeting', which involved community-based pre-selection of the most vulnerable 50 per cent of households in the community. A proxy means test questionnaire was then applied and the 50 per cent of households were ranked according to vulnerability. Finally, the most vulnerable 15 per cent of households (according to the proxy means test formula) were enrolled in the programme subject to a second round of public validation. This process required around seven days to implement in each village. Beneficiaries are required to comply with education and health conditionalities, which involve regular attendance at primary schools by vulnerable children and occasional visits to the health centres by the elderly and children under five years old. Households were targeted in December 2008, the pilot was officially launched in September 2009 and the first transfers were received in December 2009. Those who are eligible will receive benefits for a maximum of 20 months. The Tanzania Social Action Fund is implemented through local government authorities.

The Kwa Wazee project[28]

This unconditional cash transfer programme aims to reduce the vulnerability of chronically poor households and combat the malnutrition of children. It targets poor and vulnerable people over the age of sixty, including those caring for children without parents. Initially, Kwa Wazee used village leaders to target poor households, with verification carried out by a questionnaire conducted by project staff. Accurately targeting around ninety beneficiaries was reported to take up to two months (ten or eleven days in each village). However, up to 60 per cent of households selected by community leaders were ineligible and the methodology had to be abandoned. The project has since attempted to use a community-based targeting approach. Although faster than the original methodology, in one out of three pilot villages it later came to light that local leaders had predetermined who should be targeted—again resulting in inclusion errors. In order to achieve its objective of targeting the very poorest, village-level coverage of the Kwa Wazee project needs to be scaled up significantly—from supporting less than 5 per cent to over 30 per cent of older people in any one community.

Each household receives a monthly grant of TZS 6,000 with an additional monthly grant of TZS 3,000 for every child. By 2007, nearly 600 older people were receiving a regular monthly pension.

The National Costed Plan of Action for Most Vulnerable Children[29]

This programme supports especially vulnerable children, not just those with HIV and AIDS, to avoid stigmatising the latter. This is a United Nations Children's Fund-supported pilot now expanded nationally, with support from the Global Fund, the President's Emergency Plan for AIDS Relief and the United Nations Children's Fund. Its objectives are to identify the most vulnerable children, protect them from harm and give them access to essential services. Village and ward committees identify vulnerability criteria and take some responsibility for all children identified. Civil society organisations support the provision of essential services and the Department of Social Welfare is the coordinating agency.

By 2009, 410,000 most vulnerable children had been identified across at least one ward in each of sixty-two districts, as the programme was being rolled out nationally. There are estimated to be one million most vulnerable children in mainland Tanzania.

The Respect Study[30]

This research project used conditional transfers to encourage the prevention of sexually transmitted diseases, that is, transfers given to adults not to have unsafe sex. It gave payments of up to $60 per person over 12 months to those who tested negative for a group of common sexually transmitted diseases. The project was funded by the World Bank, its Spanish Trust Fund for Impact Evaluation and, through the non-profit Population Reference Bureau, the William and Flora Hewlett Foundation. Research was conducted in Tanzania (Kilombero and Ulanga districts) because its infection rate is about average for Africa. Residents in the district are aware of HIV, partly because it is close to a major highway and sugar producing factory, so migration and mobility have made it a major pathway for HIV transmission in Tanzania and East Africa.

The programme enrolled 2,399 people from 10 villages in these districts. Most participants were between eighteen and thirty years old. Medical teams were sent to each village every four months, for about one week at a time.

One team introduced the participants to the project, obtained consent, took samples and conducted interviews; another gave out the lab results two weeks later in private, face-to-face interviews. All samples and results were marked with bar codes, instead of names, to protect privacy. All participants received free treatment, such as antibiotics, and counselling. But only those who tested negative in the cash group (as opposed to the control group) received payments.

After twelve months, 9 per cent of participants eligible for the $60 award tested positive for one, or more, of six infections (Chlamydia, gonorrhoea, Trichomoniasis, Mycoplasma genitalium or syphilis). The rate was 12 per cent for a control group who did not receive payments. But half of the cash-eligible group was eligible for $30 a year and the other half $60: the study found that the $30 group had the same infection rate as the control group. Meanwhile, not surprisingly, the programme is more effective for people from poorer and rural areas.

Save the Children pilot cash transfers in Lindi district[31]

In a programme launched in November 2007 (but now closed), cash transfers were given to HIV and AIDS orphans and their care-givers. The goal was to significantly reduce vulnerability, increase household income and improve children's nutritional status. Cash transfers were given to households in three villages, benefiting 198 children in 60 families. Households received a monthly grant of TZS 6,000. An additional monthly grant of TZS 3,000 was provided for every orphaned child living in the household.

Eligible households were selected using data from a recent Save the Children study on extreme poverty in Lindi rural district. These households were typically smaller than average, that is between one and four people; had the least able-bodied labour (50 per cent had no active male labour, 47 per cent of households had no active labour and 33 per cent had one active person regardless of gender); were dependent on remittances from elsewhere (e.g. family members working in urban areas—40 per cent); had the highest dependency ratio (2.2 children and older people dependants for every 18–59-year-old adult working); often faced labour shortages owing to ageing, sickness and divorce; or had a very small annual cash income of between TZS 60,000 per month (older woman-headed households) and approximately TZS 150,000 per month (active couple profile). The pilot was endorsed by the village government and approved by the village assembly.

Social transfer options

This section discusses the options for a nationwide social transfer programme in Tanzania. It puts forward some suggestions in light of the decisions which need to be made when putting a programme of social transfers in place. It does this while incorporating research findings and analysis about poverty, vulnerability and hunger in the country.

Objectives

Should the government address the generalised insecurity of the mass of poor people, or emphasise protecting the most vulnerable, reducing the deepest poverty? It is suggested that the first be the ultimate objective, but it might make sense to start small and build capacity in terms of revenue and administration over a reasonable period of years before attempting the larger objective. Generalised insecurity can also be addressed by actively promoting community health funds; working out how to raise resources to cover waivers; and also continuing to invest significantly in improving the quality of health services so that people feel these are worth the pre-payments. Ensuring that existing fee waiver systems in education and health work well is another measure. A number of other policies already legislated for will also help in addressing generalised insecurity.

Specific risks, such as in agriculture, which contribute hugely to generalised insecurity should be addressed through sectoral policies. Social protection should not be expected to take on all risks. However, any national programme should acknowledge that it is small farmers (and fishers and pastoralists) and casual labourers who are especially vulnerable to chronic poverty. Social transfers should be able to support the risks poor people have to take to improve their livelihoods, escape poverty and contribute to growth. Transfers should also be capable of addressing the main reasons for impoverishment, which include divorce and business failure.

One social transfer programme or several?

The many sources of risk and widespread vulnerability together with the affordability and capacity contexts create two difficult choices—between running one versus several programmes of social transfers and between categorical and non-categorical targeting. Given the generalised state of insecurity among the poor, and even some of the non-poor, it might be sensible to develop a programme which starts small but is capable of extending to a wider group as it develops. One programme could be designed so that it addresses all the major vulnerable groups and also builds a platform that can be expanded over time. Focusing on one scheme to address multiple vulnerabilities avoids making difficult choices between categories of beneficiaries.

Developing separate schemes to address the insecurities of different vulnerable groups is also possible, and may be politically more desirable, in the sense that naming each group can lend political legitimacy to the programme. This would also facilitate targeting. But this would almost certainly take more administrative effort, since several schemes would be necessary to reach the different vulnerable groups. Going to scale with several schemes at the same time may be more difficult than focusing on one.

Targeting choices

The choices are categorical transfers; employment guarantee/public works schemes; and poverty-targeted transfers. Employment based transfers are by nature self-targeted and conditional on people turning up to work. The others can be conditional or unconditional. As mentioned above, there are no strong technical reasons for making transfers conditional, although there may be political reasons in a given context. Whether this is the case in Tanzania is not known. Another question is whether grants are awarded to individuals or households. A universal cash transfer pilot programme in Namibia makes each person rather than each household eligible. However, with Tanzania's lower fiscal resources, it is likely that the household would be targeted.

Modelling exercises elsewhere have indicated that growth can be differentially affected by social transfers, depending on who is targeted. In Cambodia, modelling suggests that the growth and poverty reduction effects would be greatest if the economically active, and especially those depending on selling labour to others, were targeted, because they will use the transfers to build their productive assets and thus participate more and better in growth.[32]

There is clearly a head of steam behind a pension, as a solution to a widely recognised need. Any general transfer would have to acknowledge that older people are vulnerable and support their position. However, despite current inclinations towards categorical targeting, such strategies may not achieve the government's goals of reaching all the poorest, since the elderly are not a homogenous group. For example, poverty in households with only elderly people and children is only slightly higher than among the population as a whole,[33] so for this targeted policy to reach all the chronically poor it would need to be complemented by other categorical transfers—to families with many children, the disabled, etc.

Transfers to orphans are likewise not a good proxy: these constitute only 10 per cent of all children[34] and only in the small proportion of cases where both parents are deceased are their enrolments rates lower than those of the rest of the population. The best-researched of these categorical schemes, a universal pension, would reach over 40 per cent of orphans and vulnerable children and 72 per cent of most vulnerable children. But, according to the Ministry of Labour, Employment and Youth Development study, only 23 per cent of households have a person over sixty (30 per cent of the poorest 30 per cent of households).[35]

The implication of this analysis is that one categorical scheme would not be enough. There would need to be several to provide social protection to all chronically poor people.

In Uganda, it was demonstrated that the most technically effective approach in terms of reducing the poverty gap would be a transfer targeted to the poorest households, with supplementary payments for each especially vulnerable member of the household (older people, people with disabilities, children). This was the measure which would most effectively bring the biggest number of people below the poverty line up to the poverty line. Given that levels of poverty and many other conditions are similar in the two countries, the same effects might be predicted for Tanzania. This is a scheme which can start by targeting the poorest and over time gradually expand as resources and administrative capacities develop. It could also begin in the poorest districts and gradually expand to achieve countrywide coverage. The critical calculation which underpinned this decision is given in Figure 10.1 below. A similar calculation for Tanzania (Table 10.2) gives the following results. Raising the standard of living of the average household in the lowest decile up to the level of the 11th percentile would require a transfer of TZS 3,121, say a round TZS 3,000. This would cost about 1.8% of GDP in the Tanzanian case, and has a significant effect on the poverty gap (P1) and the severity of poverty (P2). In other words the poorest households become a lot better off, although this measure alone will not take them out of poverty. If you add in supplementary payments, the impact is even greater, and includes a reduction in the incidence of poverty, but it probably goes way of the scale of what is probably politically affordable at this point in time, however desirable it would be from a poverty angle. Unless the political leadership is willing to go from next to nothing spent on social protection to spending a very significant amount, this presents a difficult choice for the Tanzanian government. It could be that it could make the basic payment itself and mobilise the donor community to contribute the supplementary payments for a period of time, until a larger GDP is able to absorb them in years to come.

The weakness of this approach is that the poorest households may not be easy to identify correctly, especially when receipt of a transfer hangs on this, providing a substantial incentive for inclusion. Can a proxy be developed? One suggestion is to target a transfer to households with nine or more people, a dependency ratio of over 120, a household head over fifty years old and a thatched roof. Almost four out of five such households are likely to be poor, based on the Household Budget Survey for 2007, representing a high degree of potential targeting accuracy.[36] Alternatively, verified community-based targeting could be relied on to identify the destitute and very poor (see Box 10.1 above) or as practised in the Tanzania Social Action Fund.

Figure 10.1: Estimated impact on the poverty gap in Uganda of allocating 1 per cent of gross domestic product in different ways

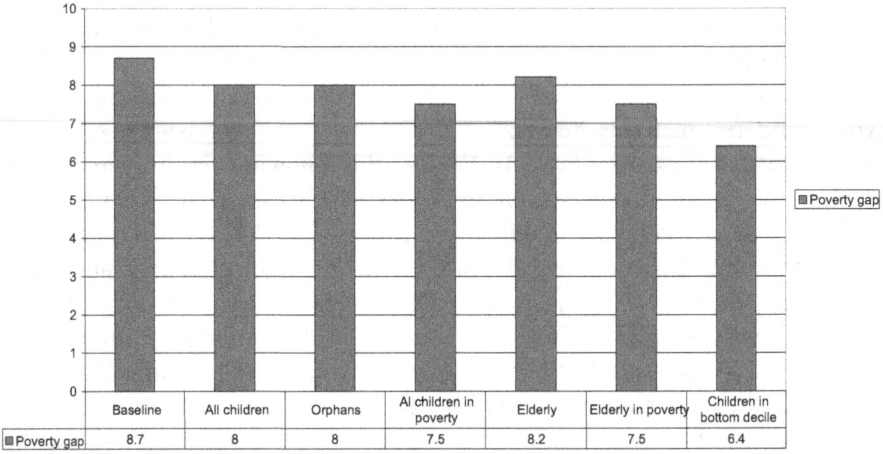

	Baseline	All children	Orphans	Al children in poverty	Elderly	Elderly in poverty	Children in bottom decile
Poverty gap	8.7	8	8	7.5	8.2	7.5	6.4

Note: Simulations assume that perfect targeting is costless and that beneficiary households share transfers equally among household members.

Source: Social Protection Task Force, Ministry of Gender, Labour and Social Development, Uganda (2007)

Table 10.2: Predicted poverty reduction impact of the cash transfer programme

	Mean CPAE (2001 constant prices)		Poverty measures			Cost (mill. TZS)	As % GDP
	All	Decile 1	P0	P1	P2		
Base scenario, without cash transfer	131,730	46,530	33.4	9.9	4.3		
Basic household transfer	133,103	52,820	33.4	5.9	1.6	1,068	1.8
Basic household transfer plus supplementary transfers	133,432	54,541	30.6	4.7	1.1	3,245	5.4

Source: Calculations based on the proposed CT options

Note: CPAE refers to consumption expenditure per adult equivalent, in TZS

Also note that figures in columns 2 and 3 are multiples of 4.4, the overall average household size to arrive at the household expenditure.

Gender sensitivity

Whichever approach is taken, it must take into account gender relationships, given the vulnerabilities of poor women. What does this mean in practice? Gender relationships need to be understood and their implications should be taken into programme design. Monitoring and evaluation systems need to investigate what effects programmes have on gender relationships. Finally, programme implementation needs to address three critical issues:[37]

First, it is vital to develop tailored and ongoing capacity-building about gender-related programme aims, including reducing women's time poverty and finding collective solutions to care work responsibilities – for male and female programme participants and programme implementers alike. Poor training undermines the potential for benefiting from the programme's linkages. Support from women's ministries or agencies may be necessary.

Second, in the case of public works and asset and cash transfer programmes, there is scope to make better use of the regular interactions that social welfare officers/local implementation officers have with local communities on payment days, to initiate community dialogues on ways to address gender inequalities such as gender-based violence, early marriage, the costs of child labour, especially for girls' human capital development, and gendered forms of social stigmatisation.

Programmes with strong and well-coordinated linkages to complementary services are more likely to have a notable impact on women's practical gender needs and their more strategic gender interests by tackling their vulnerabilities in a more holistic fashion. Good linkages are needed, for example across health and reproductive health services, credit access and employment training.

Given the prominence of divorce (and probably separation and widowhood) as causes of impoverishment in life history accounts of changing well-being, and the evidence that many female-headed households are poor and extremely poor, while it is important to include such vulnerable women as a deserving category for social transfers it is also vital to revisit the inheritance and marriage laws and practices which result in these outcomes.[38]

An employment guarantee?

Many poor Tanzanians depend on thin wage labour markets where supply exceeds demand, wages are very low and jobs are insecure and seasonal. Other countries faced with similar situations have instituted massive public works schemes or an employment guarantee. The lessons from programmes in India, Ethiopia and South Africa are many, but include the following:

(1) Self-targeting, which is a feature of works programmes, ensures inclusion of the poorest households that have able-bodied members who can work, but may not pick up the less able-bodied, for whom social transfers would be required.

(2) Creating a right to work (as in India) does provide additional security, but also requires a big political commitment from government.

(3) Both household and community productive assets can be enhanced through public works schemes.

(4) The conditional nature of the programmes may be attractive to taxpayers who feel they are getting something in return.

Tanzania has limited experience running public works schemes, but is about to expand the Tanzania Social Action Fund in this direction. The scope for delivering widespread social protection through this in the near future would need to be assessed. While Tanzania's Agricultural Sector Development Programme considers public works a possible strategy to address food insecurity,[39] a simple cash transfer might be easier to implement. Forethought must also be given to the pro-poor value of the public assets created as well as the resilience of labourers' livelihood options on exit.[40] As noted in a recent international conference hosted in Tanzania, ensuring women's participation in planning public works programme can help ensure a selection of projects that reduce their time burdens.[41]

Politically, categorical transfers (a pension, a child allowance, a disability allowance) combined with an employment guarantee might be most attractive—simple to understand and easier to target. But, given the likely scarcity of financial resources for the long-term commitments which are required, as well as implementation capacity limitations, one programme addressing many risks and funded from tax revenues would be optimal.

Beyond social transfers

It should be clear to policymakers designing a social transfer programme what this can and cannot do. Social protection is not a panacea, and other policy responses to vulnerability and risk are also needed. These include measures against food price inflation; decent crop payment systems; some progressive norms and (possibly local) regulations (bylaws) on casual wage contracts; and the implementation of provisions giving land rights to women. In this sense, social protection is complementary to inclusive growth, social services for the hard to reach, an inclusive demographic transition and institutional development to modernise agriculture.

To protect against farming risks, insuring small farmers against risk would be a good start. Tanzania can learn from Kenya's pilot weather insurance, for example. To protect against health risks, community health funds are already in existence. Making these work requires improving the quality of health services such that people feel they are worth pre-paying for and determining how waivers for older people and others are to be financed.

In terms of the objectives for social transfers, which are most relevant in Tanzania? Chronic poverty appears to be widespread; a staged approach could start by protecting people experiencing the most extreme forms of poverty which are likely to keep their families poor for generations. Social transfers for this group will help to prevent the intergenerational transmission of poverty. This is simply a start, though: others are also vulnerable. On the big choices, the above analysis would tend to favour unconditional social transfers targeted by local communities at the poorest people as a starting point. The evaluation of the Tanzania Social Action Fund programme, which has used this approach, will be of great interest.

However, political dynamics may favour conditional and/or categorical transfers, perhaps combined with a public works scheme to reach the able-bodied poor. If there is a strong political preference in this direction it would be a mistake to prolong the debate too much. Moving forward would involve a public debate, then beginning to implement a programme while monitoring its performance and the outcomes it generates. Further public discussion can then be fostered on the basis of this information.

There are regional and local variations in poverty, vulnerability and food security. An element of local input into programme design as well as implementation is probably justified, so that any national programme can be adjusted to local realities. This means leaving scope for local actors to determine aspects of the programme's approach to suit local conditions.

In terms of the way forward, the different options need to be costed. Once decisions are taken, it is important to make a quick start and refine the approach and targeting procedure, using new data sources as they become available—for example the National Panel Survey—to evaluate impact and further refine targeting.

1   National Bureau of Statistics (2010), p. 32; K. Pauw and J. Thurlow (2010)

2   De Weerdt, (2010)

3   Ibid

4   D. Bryceson (2002)

5   National Bureau of Statistics (2010), p. 27, p. 33

6   United Republic of Tanzania (2009c), p. 7

7   How this relates to quantitative analysis needs to be explored.

8   National Bureau of Statistics and ORC Macro (2005)

9   Research on Poverty Alleviation et al. (2009)

10 K. Bird (2007)

11 National Bureau of Statistics (2010)

12 Synovate (2009)

13 A. Shepherd et al. (2011a)

14 K. Pauw and J. Thurlow (2010)

15 Barrientos (2008)

16 Chronic Poverty Research Centre (2008)

17 P. Kamuzora and L. Gilson (2007)

18 L. da Corta and J. Magongo (2010)

19 Chronic Poverty Research Centre (2008)

20 A. Barrientos and Nino-Zarazua (2010)

21 M. Molyneux (2007)

22 A. Shepherd et al. (2011b)

23 S.M. Hashemi and W. Umaira (2011)

24 M. Niño-Zarazua et al. (2010)

25 A. Barrientos and M. Niño-Zarazua (2010)

26 United Republic of Tanzania (2010a), p. 92

27 Information on the first two pilots comes from their websites and also Ministry of Labour, Employment and Youth Development in collaboration with HelpAge International (2010)

28 Regional Psychosocial Support Initiative et al. (2008)

29 Research on Poverty Alleviation (2009)

30 http://go.worldbank.org/YVMPZBKC00

31 C. Watson and J. Gibson (2009)

32 Chronic Poverty Research Centre (2008); S. Levy (2007)

33 Ministry of Finance and Economic Affairs (2009)

34 United Republic of Tanzania (2010b)

35 Ministry of Labour, Employment and Youth Development in collaboration with HelpAge International (2010)

36 J. Hoogeveen and R. Ruhunduka (2009)

37 R. Holmes and N. Jones (2010)

38 L. da Corta and J. Magongo (2010)

39 United Republic of Tanzania (2006), p. 58

40 A. McCord (2010)

41 World Bank and Tanzania Social Action Fund (2010), p. 39

Chapter 11

Conclusions and Policy Implications

Flora Kessy, Andrew Shepherd and Lucy Scott

Introduction

Poverty has remained persistent in Tanzania, especially in rural areas. The National Bureau of Statistics in the 2007 Household Budget Survey identifies a worrying trend of households remaining clustered at or below the poverty line over time (2000–7); in other words, the majority of Tanzanians are stagnating in poverty, despite rapid economic growth which has remained above 6 per cent per annum.[1] Results from the National Panel Survey 2008/09 are close to those in the 2007 Household Budget Survey. They show that poverty has remained unchanged in mainland Tanzania as a whole, with food poverty rising (insignificantly) from 16.6 per cent in 2007 to 17.4 per cent in 2008/09 and basic needs poverty from 33.6 to 34 per cent.[2]

Qualitative research findings from a subsample of National Bureau of Statistics and National Panel Survey households, as presented in this book, reveals similar results, with very few households moving out of poverty over the 1999–2009 period. Thus, the chapters presented in this book address the key policy question in Tanzania: why has modest economic growth not translated more rapidly into reduced poverty, especially in rural regions, where the majority of the poor still live? The chapters draw on new, largely qualitative data based on life histories, focus group discussions and key informant interviews across several regions (see Chapter 2), complemented by analysis of national household and panel survey datasets.

Manifestation of vulnerability

In the study areas, poor people's vulnerability is manifested in the form of a limited number of meals per day (a measure of food insecurity) and several covariant and idiosyncratic shocks. The major covariant shocks identified include food price inflation; weather/climate-related shocks; agriculture-related shocks such as crop pests and a lack of the necessary agricultural inputs including land; witchcraft; and the theft of agricultural produce while still on the farm (mentioned strongly in Newala). Property-stripping and property-grabbing, alcoholism, old age, divorce, serial polygamy and selling labour on credit are major idiosyncratic shocks.

Vulnerability differs by groups of community members, with destitute and very poor people facing two types of vulnerability: reduced consumption and reduced production. While elderly and disabled people often lack the capacity to produce, alcoholics and people living in despair frequently lack entrepreneurial or development ambitions. Thus, addressing the vulnerability of poor community members requires different policy interventions based on the type and nature of the vulnerability. For instance, the elderly might need social assistance to smooth consumption, whereas the able-bodied destitute and very poor might also need social transfers to boost their productive capabilities.

Number of meals per day

Qualitative findings from the six research clusters produced a varied picture of experiences of hunger. In all cases, individuals and households in the poorest two categories ('destitute' and 'very poor') were likely to have difficulty ensuring sufficient food intake from day to day. With the exception of one cluster, where the majority of the households ate one meal per day, most households survive on two meals per day (although in one cluster the same number of households survive on two meals a day as on just one per day). While detailed information on the type of meals was not collected, during additional discussions it was apparent that sometimes this meal comprises just cassava stiff porridge and tea, maize porridge or sorghum/maize porridge. Destitute people might have one meal a day—boiled, with no salt or oil and which 'doesn't taste good'. The poor but not vulnerable group and the rich were said to consume diverse food, including 'food from industry', for example bread, soft and hard drinks and meals containing 'delicacies' such as milk and 'delicious foods'. Being able to consume such foods placed these households in a higher well-being classification.

On the basis of Participatory Poverty Assessments,[3] it has been argued that the real concern of the poor is not their lack of income, consumption or assets, but rather insecurity, that is, the imminent likelihood, or actual experience, of a sudden sharp reduction in any one of these. Members of focus group discussions confirmed the insecurity facing the destitute and very poor in terms of being able to eat a certain amount of food each day and knowing where their next meal will come from. In contrast, for resilient households, the issue is not about how many meals they can afford per day but whether they can eat well.

There is no one, or dominant, cause of episodes and experiences of hunger. Focus group participants identified four sets of factors as leading to food insecurity: (1) covariant shocks such as weather and disease; (2) effects of policies such as villagisation and food security policies, including a ban on maize exports; (3) structural economic imbalances (e.g. wage/price relationships); and (4) more idiosyncratic but still widespread factors such as divorce, property-stripping, theft, sickness, old age, etc.

Covariant shocks

Food insecurity is related to food price inflation and the rising costs of basic essentials, which have eaten into household budgets. Respondents noted that, since 2005, money has not been available, incomes have been low and the prices of goods have risen. Consumer price indices for selected products have been rising gradually since 2002, and rapidly since 2005, in all areas, most notably food, followed by fuel. Of particular import in this regard has been the global food price crisis, which began in 2006. Expenditure on food increased from 2000/01 to 2006/07 (constant 2007 prices) even in poor households whose nutritional levels worsened (Chapter 7, Figure 7.8). Meanwhile, alongside this, low prices of agricultural crops and trade entitlement failures can result in a lack of income to buy food, and drought may lead to hunger.

Increasing the number of meals households take per day requires measures that address the whole agricultural production and market chain (as discussed below). As well as these overall measures, policies and interventions must also address the specific risks which have far-reaching consequences for individual households and which may not be generalised in terms of policy and interventions.

Some aspects of food security policies may have negative consequences for some households. For example, maize export bans remain a sensitive policy issue. Government policy is to allow the export of maize only when all regions of the country are said to be food secure. In practice, however, there is almost always a problem of food security somewhere in the country, particularly in the semi-arid central region. This means that maize exports are banned on an almost continual basis. The effect of this policy is to make the price of maize in the southern highlands—the main maize surplus regions—not just lower but also more volatile than they would otherwise be, so harming the livelihoods of maize farmers[4] and also making it more difficult for poor households to plan.

Many smallholders also despair about perennial limitations to their agricultural productivity, which impede their escape from food insecurity. These include poor land quality; unaffordability of improved agricultural inputs such as fertiliser, pesticides, herbicides, improved seeds and mechanisation; endemic livestock and human diseases; and adverse agro-climatic conditions. These shocks are both idiosyncratic and covariant, the latter often on a small scale—for example floods knocking out a small irrigation scheme. We tend to think of covariant shocks as being big droughts or floods affecting large areas, but smaller-scale events like the above can also have devastating effects, especially as very few smallholders have access to insurance against such shocks. Price and market uncertainty also mean the prices producers receive for commodities may be less than the costs incurred in production. Market prices do not necessarily adjust to compensate for risks, given the many (including international) influences involved.

Witchcraft (*uchawi* in Kiswahili) is another covariant shock, one that featured strongly in Nkasi district. Witchcraft is part of daily life in all social settings throughout Tanzania. Although its specific manifestations vary, *uchawi* and witches display certain characteristics and attributes that allow for intelligibility between the various traditions. Discourses on witchcraft in Tanzania consistently address themes of envy, greed, consumption, cannibalism and death (although some studies represent witchcraft as a path to accumulation: traditional healing, for instance, can be a significant source of rural economic growth).[5] Despite witchcraft being rampant, it has not been debated as a policy issue because of the difficulty involved in proving acts of witchcraft. Respondents pointed out three major components of the witchcraft–poverty nexus;

- Witchcraft may prevent risk-taking, entrepreneurship development and displays of wealth (people have to leave a community if they become too wealthy and people in town never come back to the village to visit after getting rich).
- Witchcraft may impoverish households that are 'doing well': the majority of households reported that school children, in particular those at secondary school, are a target (as they are considered a future path out of poverty). Households become impoverished through the sale of assets carried out to make it possible to access care from witchdoctors for a 'bewitched' child. In most cases, these children either die or develop psychiatric problems.
- Witchcraft is used as revenge in cases of conflict between households; this can have far-reaching consequences such as the death of human beings and livestock.

The major covariant risk pointed out in Nchinga and Nkangala clusters in Newala district was the theft of cashew nuts while they are still on the farm. Thieves invade the farm at night or very early in the morning and collect all the fallen cashew nuts, meaning households are deprived of the long-awaited harvest. This is a community-wide problem to which no solution has been found: people have to spend time guarding their farms instead of participating in productive activities. The widespread but localised nature of this risk suggests that a collective 'farm watch' scheme might have great advantages.

Idiosyncratic shocks

Widowhood was not necessarily associated with a downward spiral in well-being, except in cases where relatives grab property, leaving widows to raise their family without the means to do so. Meanwhile, though, in patriarchal systems, land passes through the male line and women rarely own land in their own right. Property-grabbing after the death of the husband was reported in a few instances in Wazabanga cluster. Property appropriation by the husband after separation or divorce is common and was reported in every research site. This was attributed mainly to women not being informed about divorce laws, which do protect women. Divorce and separation are caused by several factors, including husbands finding another wife and women's infertility.

Property-grabbing has been reported elsewhere in Tanzania.[6] Some widows have lost property to their in-laws and have been asked to leave their nuptial home. Those who cannot leave succumb to the levirate system by accepting being 'inherited' by one of their in-laws. For most widows, being inherited is not a matter of choice but rather one of convenience—they agree to it in order to safeguard their property and be able to take care of their children. Despite the good intentions of the levirate institution (wife inheritance) as a social security system, its impact must be examined closely in the context of HIV and AIDS and amid the rapidly changing societal values and norms fuelled by globalisation.

Linked to divorce and separation is serial polygamy. This was very evident in Kalesa, Nchinga, Nkangala and Wazabanga clusters, where it had resulted in family disintegration and loss of family property. The motivation of second wives often is to obtain economic security. Because of this, many are attracted to men with off-farm income-generating activities, including ownership of a kiosk, fishing or fish-mongering or cultivating a large amount of cashew nuts. The life histories showed cases of men replacing their first wife for a new one but returning to their first wife after becoming bankrupt or when their second wife had left them.

Alcoholism was mentioned in every cluster. Making local brew was seen to have positive and negative aspects. Some women were able to make local beer-brewing a profitable venture. However, for most households, alcohol has brought harm, including bankruptcy and misery, driving people into poverty and contributing to the intergenerational cycle of poverty. Alcoholism was associated with the erosion of household resources, including a failure to send children to school (low investment in human capital which can lead to the intergenerational transmission of poverty) and a failure to give the family a decent life (stagnation or moving into poverty). In particular, community members were concerned about the numbers of people using staple food grains after harvest to make local brew, thus putting the food security of their family at risk. Some community members were also selling their grains to buy local brew. In some cases, people leave home to go to the farm but on the way change their mind and end up in the local bar, leading to delays in tillage, planting and weeding and thus low harvests.

Alcoholism was also associated with family disintegration and divorce. Husbands who drink excessive alcohol are frequently violent and hit their wives. This violence often extends beyond the household, contributing to instability in the community. In Wazabanga cluster, the village authorities have had to establish a police post to deal with conflicts arising every afternoon and evening when many men were drunk. Husbands also sometimes migrate for long periods of time without supporting their family. Excessive drinking was also associated with multiple partners and increased incidence of HIV infection. The growing number of households dependent on wage labour is particularly vulnerable to a range of risks. In general, rural and agricultural growth has been uncertain; where it has been strongest, poor people have participated as labourers in oversupplied labour markets in areas such as petty trade, casual labour, brewing and subsistence foods, where returns are low. The worst form of 'un-decent labour' is where the worker provides their labour on credit, an arrangement based on trust with no formal contracts—labourers work under the agreement that they will get paid after harvest. If the harvest is poor, they are not paid. Poor labourers have to enter into these arrangements through necessity, but such setups are possible only where the labour market is oversupplied and under-regulated.

Summing up

Vulnerability limits economic growth in that households cannot accumulate sufficient assets to consume and reinvest. Well-designed social protection measures can mitigate risks and vulnerability and can contribute directly to economic growth and poverty reduction through redistributive transfers that raise the incomes and smooth the consumption of the poor. This would also allow them to engage in moderate risk-taking and to protect rather than erode their assets when confronted by livelihood shocks.[7]

Poverty and gender dynamics

One important reason for the widespread persistence of poverty has been the effect of the pattern of unequal rural growth on perverse changes in gender roles, responsibilities and rights, which has served to deepen poor people's inability to move out of poverty. Traditional gender relations are being fiercely contested in the context of the scramble for jobs, increasing land scarcity and rising costs of accessing basic needs. Men and women are contesting who does what work, who has what share of responsibility for family maintenance and who has what rights over assets, power and social protection in kin networks. The shift in responsibility for family provisioning onto women in the context of rapidly rising costs relative to earnings, and their falling rights in relation to assets and to kin social protection, is intensifying their own poverty and that of their dependants. This does not augur well for intergenerational escapes from poverty.

Changes in gender roles are coupled with changes in trade patterns. For example, in fishing communities, men used to have a prominent role in buying fish from the lake and selling it in the village but such business has been hijacked by big traders: 'we see fewer and fewer local fish traders in the village because sometimes they make a trip to the lake and come back empty-handed because all the day's catch is purchased by big traders'. As such, men are losing their traditional employment and do not have a suitable replacement. In Magu district, the declining fish stock in Lake Victoria was cited as a reason for many people turning to paddy and sugarcane production. In Nkasi district, Fipa fisherman in Kalesa along Lake Tanganyika were trying to farm paddy but needed support in this transition, as they were struggling to learn new techniques, especially training oxen to drive ploughs. In Newala district, the fish trade from nearby River Ruvuma and imported from the coast had died in recent years, as no one could afford the high cost of fish. Many of these (male) ex-fish traders are now unemployed.

The study also found a rise in prevalence of effectively female-headed households as a result of male chronic illness (usually resulting from HIV and AIDS-related diseases); despair (resulting from chronic underemployment and from rising barriers to escape poverty), often promoting refuge in alcohol and mistresses; and semi-permanent migration, with remittances not sent home (preceding abandonment). Although female headedness is rather difficult to capture, given its fluidity—women drift in and out of marriage through successive divorces and widowhood—it seems their responsibility for provisioning is constant: for the most part, women are responsible for supplying food and clothing, primary school educational costs, health costs for themselves in pregnancy and for young children and water costs. Meanwhile, as we have seen, when chronic illness ends in widowhood, or semi-permanent migration results in permanent abandonment and divorce, this can lead to a women's loss of the family farm and dispossession of assets, including her children.

Our key argument is that this major rise in women's responsibility for maintaining the family is located within a context where women are finding it increasingly hard to provide for their dependants and therefore it may promote intergenerational poverty:

- Following divorce and widowhood, women are dispossessed of productive capital (by husbands or their male kin) and other property (farms, homes, livestock, etc.). This situation has been more ruthless in the 2000s because of the high value of land and because of poverty in general. A significant number of women are serially dispossessed (divorced then widowed).
- Enforcement of women's statutory rights to marital property is wholly inadequate given provisions on the dominance of customary law.
- Women's own traditional male sources of support are less dependable: fathers and brothers do not always welcome widows and divorcees back and women are forced to rely heavily on their female networks. Traditional responsibilities to provide social protection are being actively contested.
- With little land, many women juggle income-earning from small farms and an increasing reliance on agricultural labour, petty trade and prostitution—all in flooded markets.

- For the newly single mother, land is expensive and costs of essentials and services (especially education and water) are becoming unaffordable.

As a consequence, the very agents responsible for managing household poverty—women—are suffering the most in terms of their ability to do so.

With these forces rallying against women's ability to provide for their families, what is working? A lucky few have become involved in trade, although, for most poor women, their income is based on a rise in casual farm labour and petty production as well as trade. Women have also increasingly been organising themselves into organically grown, highly disciplined and largely female networks based on social support, credit, petty production and sale. The rise of such groups has enabled women to contest unfair gendered relations safe in the knowledge that they have the support of both unorganised and highly organised female networks (production and credit groupings).

Women forge and rely on female networks throughout their lives. They report that the only support they can depend on comes from male (father) kin and females (mothers, sisters, daughters and friends). While fathers often help out, they die younger than mothers and may well have divorced them. Brothers do help out sometimes, mostly under pressure from mothers, but this is not secure. In most life histories, we found women providing land, a home, food and crucially day-to-day labour to support other women. Quite often, women in their fifties and sixties were shouldering the responsibility for feeding their daughter's children.

That female networks work so well for women might be one reason for the success of rotating savings and credit associations (ROSCAs) in the past ten years. Women organise themselves into all-female economic groupings (for credit, production and marketing), which affords them a greater chance of controlling income earned and forging a new, socially empowered identity. Most women fund their monthly deposits of TZS 1,000 through agricultural labour. The society empowers women through the capital they accumulate and through the social support they receive.

Women have also coped by borrowing from savings and credit cooperative societies (SACCOS). It is often argued that credit is scarce in Tanzania, particularly for women in rural areas, where banks and microfinance institutions have made little progress by way of finding cost-effective ways of lending.[8] This is compounded for the poor by administrative barriers (e.g. having to write up a business plan) and security barriers (need for collateral in the form of titled assets or a full-time salaried job). Moreover, private banks do not like giving unsecured loans, so are less likely to lend to microfinance non-governmental organisations or SACCOS whose clients are poor. In two regions, savings and credit cooperative societies (SACCOS) have more female than male members—through their linkages with ROSCAs—thus money capital is becoming an un-gendered terrain.

Movement out of poverty

The focus group discussions ranked the well-being of the twenty-four Household Budget Survey households in 1999 and 2009. In 1999, of the six well-being classifications, the 'poor' classifications were overwhelmingly the most cited. Further, 'non-movers' were the most prominent group identified in the poverty dynamics analysis; this reflects that, between 1999 and 2009, there was little socioeconomic mobility across the research sites. In 2009, the 'poor' were again the most cited classification but the 'vulnerable but not poor' category was the most cited in the ranking by women in Kayumbe. These findings are in line with other documented poverty trends in mainland Tanzania which highlight the stubbornness of poverty despite sustained economic growth and better human development indicators nationally. In the minority there were cases of households experiencing upward mobility and poverty escape. While 43 'upward mover' cases were identified in total, this constituted just 32 households (in 11 cases households were identified as 'upward movers' by both women and men focus groups discussion; in the remaining 21 cases only one of the two focus groups identified the household as an 'upward mover'). A total of 17 'poverty exiter' cases were identified. In the case of three households, both the focus group discussions identified the households as 'poverty exiters'. In the remaining 11 cases, only one of the focus groups identified the household as a 'poverty exiter'.

Through systematic analysis of the qualitative dataset, agriculture emerges as a key factor in supporting upward mobility. But, critically, it is non-farm business, the accumulation of physical assets (such as land and housing), salaried employment and favourable marriage (defined as marrying up or marrying someone with a better level of well-being)—some of which agriculture plays a role in supporting—which are most effective at triggering the move out of poverty. Where salaried employment was identified as a key contributor to upward mobility and poverty escape, it was linked with educational achievement, particularly that in post-primary education, which was highly valued for this very reason. Families which are unable to accumulate assets and appear to be stuck in poverty traps are in turn extremely vulnerable to negative shocks. Arguably, it is not the shocks themselves which cause poverty or hunger but the absence of 'buffers', or strategies, institutions and safety nets, to prevent the shock having an impoverishing effect.

Analysis of the 2007 Household Budget Survey yields similar results.[9] Owning multiple assets and being involved in monetised economic activities (e.g. incorporation in markets, credit society membership and access to bank loans) are correlates of moving out of poverty. Level of education of the household head, number of dependants and being on the electricity grid are also important correlates of moving out poverty. When it comes to agriculture, the story is more complex: farming is generally associated with poverty, although the quantity of land owned could mitigate this association (only in rural areas), and farm households engaged in commercial crops have done better. Large agricultural households with high dependency ratios and older household heads with lower education levels are especially prone to remaining poor.

Hoogeveen has suggested a path for enabling diversification: investment in human capital and enabling poor households to build physical capital, so as to enhance on- and off-farm income-generating activities.[10] His analysis highlights the instrumentality of education—and higher levels of education— in moving out of poverty, findings this book supports. Mkenda et al. found the difference in poverty indices between primary and higher education considerable.[11]

Upward mobility trends identified in the life history interviews do indicate differences between rural and urban sites. In rural areas, agriculture and fish-farming are the most common cause of upward mobility, followed by non-farm business, land purchase, house purchase/construction and favourable marriage. Perhaps unsurprisingly, in urban areas like Ndite community, non-farm business was the most commonly cited reason for upward mobility. This was followed by salaried employment, agriculture and fish-farming and the purchase or construction of a house.

Despite being one of the major drivers of upward mobility, agriculture has not been able to move people out of poverty. Agriculture is clearly a risky business. A major problem widely identified by respondents was the unaffordability of important inputs which are key to resilience and upward mobility. The cost of agricultural capital—land purchase or rental, oxen purchase or hiring in a plough driver and his oxen—has also become very high in the past ten years, erecting an increasingly robust barrier between the poor and the non-poor. Poor people find it very difficult to expand acreage or to intensify production using new technologies. Renting could be an affordable alternative to buying, but again the supply is low. People are reluctant to rent out their land as they are concerned that renters will damage soil fertility and/ or subsequently claim the land as their own on the basis of customary land law. The lack of markets to dispose of agricultural produce, which leads to low prices and wastage, is also critical.

Good governance: does it matter?

Several agriculture sector-related governance factors have an impact on whether households can move out of poverty. First, low prices for cash crop products and cooperatives' payment to farmers in instalments; farmers having to sell cash crops, notably cashew nuts, on credit; and cooperatives deducting cash from sales of farmers' products without informing them in advance and without good explanation were mentioned as governance issues that constrain communities' poverty alleviation. Farmers in Newala, for instance, were unhappy with the Warehouse Receipt System (WRS) for storing crop products because payments come in instalments. This was mentioned as being especially detrimental to farmers with little to harvest. However, the WRS, introduced in 2006 nationwide, was also said to have enhanced income generation in the sense that farmers do not have to sell at low prices during the harvesting period because they lack storage facilities: the system is designed to enable farmers to store their crop products so that they can wait for prices to increase. Beforehand, traders bought crop products during the harvesting period at low prices, stored them and, later on in the same agricultural season, sold them at high prices, sometimes back to the same farmers.

Meanwhile, in 2005, annual licence fees were removed, to be replaced by permanent business licences. Now only those with an annual turnover of TZS 20 million or more pay for a licence yearly, at a rate of 10 per cent of turnover. In this regard (and as noted above), off-farm activities in the form of petty trading have contributed significantly towards moving households out of poverty and maintaining some at resilience level. These findings are strongly supported by findings from analysis of the Kagera Health and Development ten-year panel survey (1991–4/2004), which found that movement out of poverty was enabled by the diversification of income-generating activities, both on and off the farm. More specifically, on-farm diversification was critical to income growth, and lack of it was associated with stagnation and/or a decline in well-being. Diversification into non-farm activities (e.g. trading crops, having a shop or owning plots of timber trees) was found to have strong explanatory power when it came to understanding movements out of poverty.[12] Thus, removal of nuisance taxes is very likely to have helped small traders perform better in non-farm activities and to have reduced poverty more effectively.

In some communities, SACCOS and ROSCAs have been formed to make up for the shortage of rural finance services providing services to poor community members. There are also associations whereby people help one another with difficult manual activities. Such societies help people improve their welfare. For example, the manager of one SACCOS in Nkasi district said that its clients praised it because, previously, moneylenders lent at interest rates at 100–200 per cent of the amount borrowed. During the research, interest rates at the SACCOS were 21.6 per cent per year for a salary loan; 25.2 per cent per year for agricultural, trade and house construction loans; and 60 per cent per year for emergency loans. However, a focus group in one village in Nkasi district revealed that, although some farmers had obtained credit, some people were sceptical about applying for fear that their farm might be confiscated if they failed to repay the loan in a timely manner.

Turning to the negative, there have been issues related to dishonesty in business practices. Fake seeds have been supplied to farmers in some cases. For example, in one village of Magu district, farmers have received fake cotton seeds from private buyers of cotton. Some private traders have supplied farmers with expired agrochemicals which are then not effective against cotton pests and diseases. In addition, although agriculture is the main economic activity, agricultural extension services are so inadequate that some farmers do not even know whether they exist. In the 1970s, Tanzania aimed to have one extension officer for every village but, following structural adjustments in the mid-1980s, some were retrenched from the civil service. This was followed by a reduction in the number of extension workers trained.

Poor access to justice by women and poorer community members is another governance problem constraining poverty alleviation. As pointed out above, divorce results in women losing most of the wealth items they own and have control over. As women are not allowed to inherit land (unless it goes through daughters if there are no sons, or they purchase it), after separation they have no land, house or extra income— yet full responsibility for child maintenance.

Policy implications of the findings

Overall, this book suggests both important macro- and micro-level causes of the persistence of poverty in Tanzania. The latter, on which the book is focused, centre around a negative dynamic affecting a large number of poor households in which a widespread failure to provide for household food security undermines gender relationships and reduces the possibility of saving and asset accumulation which is necessary for escaping poverty. This results in very low upward mobility. Vulnerability is widespread and resilience against shocks minimal, even for many who are not absolutely poor. What can be done to make growth more inclusive, and what are the implications for governance and the state–citizen social contract?

Income generation

Continue to prioritise agricultural development

The majority of poor people in Tanzania are farmers, and supporting agricultural growth—as articulated in Tanzania's Kilimo Kwanza strategy— should remain a priority. There is an urgent need to develop and implement effective agriculture programmes which support and transform smallholder agriculture and increase agricultural growth. Input and output markets are critical and improvements here could potentially have a bigger impact on poor farmers. For poor, vulnerable rural households, the priority may not be to increase productivity but rather to put a greater emphasis on risk management. In this regard, output markets may represent a better starting point for poverty reduction than working on increasing productivity through input markets. Contract farming can have significant advantages, especially where access to seeds and agrochemical inputs is a major barrier for poor farm households, as in cotton.

Local purchase and storage schemes such as the WRS help to moderate seasonable fluctuations, as well as supporting local food security by reducing food price inflation. However, there is an urgent need to address some weaknesses within the current WRS by promoting strong farmer-based organisations as an alternative market channel through the WRS—to collect (buy), for instance, cashew nuts from members and deposit the consignment at the WRS. These organisations are said to be more transparent and accountable to members than primary societies, as demand-driven farmers' organisations which have strong bargaining power and meant to serve the interests of their members.

New farmers' associations could be built through integrated producer schemes which develop the capacities of smallholders through the provision of a wide range of extension services. Contracts under these would include price information, to make prices available to all farmers to serve as the basis of decision-making. Alternatively, a new generation of agricultural cooperatives could be developed, designed in such a way as to ensure that they can respond to the needs of members, and with a trained and educated leadership.[13]

Pay greater attention to rural industrialisation

Rural industrialisation would support business and employment growth through local, national and foreign investment. This is in line with Ellis,[14] who has argued that promoting non-farm employment and sustainable urban growth is a sounder option than promoting a 'green revolution' in the liberalised agricultural market context of sub-Saharan Africa. It is also important in order to create more jobs for vulnerable youth and to maintain the machinery envisaged under Kilimo Kwanza, which includes irrigation systems and agro-processing. Any programming in this regard requires infrastructural investment, particularly in roads, transport and energy (low levels of electrification are a significant constraint for businesses in rural Tanzania).

Promote asset accumulation

Asset accumulation—particularly the accumulation of land—is central to poverty escape in rural Tanzania. Policy needs to support such processes by ensuring people can access land and ensuring equitable distribution. The interests of the poor and women also need to be protected. Women in particular remain significantly disadvantaged when it comes to land access and ownership, as a result of entrenched customary law practices and cultural norms. Local employment must be stimulated through land redistribution; credit to enable access to productive assets like land, oxen or power tiller rentals; farming and marketing extension, especially to improve productivity, given land shortages; and reforms to the land law to stimulate land rental.

Ensure the economic empowerment of women

The economic empowerment of women through participation in off-farm income-generating activities is important to cushion against shocks such as abandonment, divorce and serial polygamy. It can be achieved through access to and ownership of land and by enhancing access to capital for investment in agriculture and off-farm income-generating activities.

Support business development

Policies need to facilitate and support, rather than impede, entrepreneurship and business development needs. Programmes that enhance the marketing and business skills of micro-entrepreneurs should be encouraged.

Promote access to credit

Loans—from family or social networks or through institutions such as credit societies and banks—help people to enhance productivity, both in agriculture and non-farm business, but can also represent a source of significant risk. As a result, people are reluctant to borrow. Improving financial literacy and reducing the risk associated with loans may increase demand for credit and support agricultural and business expansion. Shepherd proposes adding a small premium to insure against defaulting as one way to address this, if the costs can be spread widely enough.[15]

Support secondary and vocational education

Post-primary education is considered by many as the key to a salaried job—which, as our evidence suggests, can be a route out of poverty. As life histories showed, upwardly mobile families are prioritising the post-primary education of their children, in the hope that their children will not have to struggle as farmers. But this is an unattainable option for most poor households. Finding ways to increase access to secondary and vocational education—through bursaries, discounts on fees and more schools (which would lower transport and accommodation costs) would in the short term increase access to post-primary education.

Introduce employment guarantee schemes

The decline of village work opportunities for men since liberalisation has created a vacuum which women have had to fill. Men abandon the mothers of their children because they are stressed when they have no work and may fall into alcohol or depression. Policy to promote women's rights, knowledge, power and assets must be linked to a solution for poor men. There are those who are loath to afford men any more rights, power and assets in a situation which has remained so unequal for so long, but we urge them and policymakers to explore ways to enable poor men to recover a space for responsibility in family provisioning in order to help them to contribute towards engineering a future for their children. Such ideas may be preferable to those which make support, such as cash transfers, conditional on children's uptake of services, which exacerbates women's time poverty and can hamper their ability to earn an income.[16]

Employment can be stimulated through employment guarantee schemes which can simultaneously teach men new skills, such as in construction, mechanical work or even farming (e.g. plots which can be used to supplement school lunches). Such employment will enable dry season work, preventing sales of land in that period; encourage men to stay local; push employers to adhere to basic levels of facilities (drinking water, shade, medical services, etc.); and help with the accumulation of the necessary savings to invest in new technology which might serve to release men from underemployment or scavenging activities that are harmful to the environment, such as charcoal production. A key feature of such schemes is that they tend to bolster local wage levels and labour standards.[17] They can also be used as a forum to discuss gender relations.

Public works programmes have been promoted under the Tanzania Social Action Fund, and significant experience has been accumulated. However, it may be that public works programmes are not the most efficient way to deliver social protection because of self targeting.

Governance

Disseminate legal rights, such as those related to selling labour and leasing out land

Knowledge about legal contracting is needed to make people aware of their rights when they are selling labour on credit. One latent resilience avenue which needs to be activated relates to the leasing out of land. The traditional land tenure system needs to be formalised so that people can lease out their land without the fear of losing it. Currently, many of Tanzania's poorer farmers can afford to cultivate only a portion of their land but they are unwilling to lease out the other part because of the lack of legal security. Farmers fear leasing productive land as those who cultivate it may later claim it as their own.

Raise awareness on, enforce and expand women's legal rights to land

While women have rights under the 1999 Land Policy, awareness among women, the judiciary and local leaders on these remains low. Meanwhile, women are estimated to own only about a fifth, or 19 per cent, of titled land in the country, and their plots are less than half the size of those of their male counterparts.[18] Insecure land rights discourage women from making the necessary investments in their land to increase its productivity and economic value. Ellis et al. recommend reforms, which include,[19]

- Reviewing laws on inheritance to create one uniform law on this issue;
- Stipulating that courts should follow the customs of the community to which parties to divorce belong, as long as these are not inconsistent with the Constitution. In order to be able to recognise unvalued work, the court could be required to assess the extent of contributions made by each party to the marriage and to the care of the family;
- Bringing property laws related to the death of the spouse in line with the Constitution;
- Amending the Marriage Act to stipulate that property acquired during marriage belongs to both spouses;
- Simplifying and disseminating knowledge on existing land laws and enforcing them;
- Simplifying the Land Law to aid dissemination;
- Educating magistrates, customary leaders and communities on case law which establishes women's entitlement to property and support.

Control food price inflation

Controlling food price inflation should be a top priority, since most poor and food-insecure people in Tanzania rely on purchased food. Food stocks and market interventions are part of the story, as is enabling the modernisation of smallholder farming. The latter implies measures to enable land markets, including rental markets, as well as a focus on mechanisation and agricultural inputs markets. One priority area of intervention is the expansion and development of rural roads to link rural producers in remote areas with urban consumers and to reduce food prices linked to high transport costs.[20]

The removal and decline of cooperative societies since the late 1980s has meant that private traders now operate as middlemen in food crop marketing, operating to maximise their profit by paying the lowest price at the farm gate and selling for the highest possible price to the final consumers.[21] In this regard, mobile phones can play an important role in providing both producers and consumers with information on market rates.[22]

Reconsider the maize selling ban policy

Government is seen as having an important role to play in agriculture: structuring markets (e.g. cashew, maize) and protecting livestock against disease, but the consequences are not always good. It would appear that aspects of food security policies themselves (control of the maize market, export bans) may have negative consequences for some. The effect of the maize ban policy is to make maize prices in the southern highlands not just lower but also more volatile, thereby harming livelihoods and making it more difficult for poor households to plan their expenditure. This needs a much more thorough investigation than was possible based on the limited data we have. Certainly, sorting out crop payment systems so that farmers know what they are going to get, and then get it, would be advantageous. Further, the government should promote and facilitate cross-border trade for poverty reduction.

Introduce school feeding to reduce child hunger

The survey's analysis of number of meals taken a day may not be as important in determining food insecurity as an analysis of the quality of those meals, when this relates to distinguishing between two and three meals a day. However, consuming only one meal a day is a clear indication of distress in almost all cases. In the very short term, one way to ensure that children obtain the necessary nutrients could be through school feeding programmes.[23] Finding new ways, perhaps using modern media, of spreading knowledge about nutrition would also contribute significantly to better nutrition outcomes, especially for children and infants.

Protect assets against shocks through social transfers

Central to upward mobility is *acquiring assets*. But, as Kessy and Tarmo note, *protecting assets* against shocks is also critical—and failure to do so can result in fast and detrimental downward mobility.[24] Shepherd flags social transfers as a policy option to help people to smooth consumption during shocks and to promote livelihood development by enabling people to preserve assets and take investment risks.[25] Some pilot programmes are in operation, and a draft National Social Protection Framework was established in 2009, but progress in making decisions about national programming on social protection has been slow.

Issues relate to whether the government should address the generalised insecurity of the mass of poor people or emphasise protecting the most vulnerable, reducing the deepest poverty? It might be sensible to develop one programme which starts small but is capable of extending to a wider group as it develops. This could be designed to address all the major vulnerable groups as a platform that can be expanded over time. Focusing on one scheme to address multiple vulnerabilities also avoids having to make difficult choices between categories of beneficiaries, so does not stretch limited implementation capacities. Developing separate schemes to address the insecurities of different vulnerable groups is also possible, and may be politically more desirable. However, this would almost certainly take more administrative effort, since several schemes would be necessary.

It should also be clear to policymakers that social protection is not a panacea: other policy responses to vulnerability and risk are also needed. In this sense, social protection is complementary to inclusive growth, social services for the hard to reach, inclusive demographic transition and institutional development to modernise agriculture. Resources are of course limited, and institutional constraints hamper the effectiveness of existing policy in these areas.

While our findings on factors that support upward mobility and poverty escape are not the last word, and it will be vital to continue to identify, explore and act on key policy areas, it is appropriate here to comment on priorities in this regard. Certainly, protecting assets once they have been painstakingly acquired is critical—so moving to a national programme to implement the Nationals Social Protection Framework is a first priority. Second, getting to grips with the problems of access to property faced by poor widowed, separated, abandoned and divorced women (and their children) would make an enormous contribution. And third, there may be specific opportunities to promote asset acquisition: one which the government has in a way recognised already is the mechanisation of small-scale agriculture.

1   National Bureau of Statistics (2008a)
2   United Republic of Tanzania (2010b)
3   United Republic of Tanzania (2004)
4   N. Minot (2010)
5   A. Green and S. Mesaki (2005)
6   F. Kessy et al. (2010)
7   J. Omiti and T. Nyanamba (2008)
8   A. Ellis et al. (2007)
9   E. Luvanda (2011)
10 J. Hoogeven (2008)
11 A. Mkenda et al. (2010)
12 J. de Weerdt (2010)
13 S.A. Chambo (2009)
14 F. Ellis (2009)
15 A. Shepherd (2011a)
16 M. Molyneux (2006)
17 . See, for instance, D. Campbell, 2010)
18 A. Ellis et al. (2007)
19 Ibid.
20 R. Haug et al. (2009)
21 Ibid.
22 E.E. Msuya and A.C. Isinika (2011)
23 R. Haug et al. (2009)
24 F. Kessy and S.V. Tarmo (2011)
25 A. Shepherd (2011a)

References

Bagchi, D.K., P. Blaikie, J. Cameron, M. Chattopadhyay, N. Gyawali and D. Seddon, 'Conceptual and Methodological Challenges in the Study of Livelihood Trajectories: Case Studies in Eastern India and Western Nepal'. *Journal of International Development* 10: 453–8 (1998)

Baregu, M. and J. Hoogeveen, 'State and Markets in Cashew Marketing: What Works Better for Tanzanian Farmers?' (Washington, DC, 2009)

Barrientos, A., 'Social Transfers and Growth: A Review'. Chronic Poverty Research Centre Working Paper 112 (Manchester, 2008)

Barrientos, A. and M. Niño-Zarazua, 'Do Social Transfer Programmes Have Long-term Effects on Poverty Reduction? Lessons from Mexico's Oportunidades and Challenges Ahead'. Chronic Poverty Research Centre Policy Brief 20 (Manchester, 2010)

Baulch, B. and P. Davis, 'Poverty Dynamics and Life Trajectories in Rural Bangladesh'. *International Journal of Multiple Research Approaches* 2(2): 176–90 (2008)

Beegle, K., J. de Weerdt and S. Dercon, 'Migration and Economic Mobility in Tanzania: Evidence from a Tracking Survey'. World Bank Policy Research Working Paper 4798 (Washington, DC, 2008)

Bird, K., 'The Intergenerational Transmission of Poverty: An Overview'. Chronic Poverty Research Centre Working Paper 99 (Manchester, 2007)

Bird, K., 'Using Life History Research as Part of a Mixed Methods Strategy to Explore Resilience in Conflict and Post-conflict Settings'. Conference on 'Ten Years of "War against Poverty": What Have We Learned since 2000 and What Should We Do 2010–20?' (Manchester, 8–10 September 2010)

Bird, K. and I. Shinyekwa, 'Even the "Rich" Are Vulnerable: Multiple Shocks and Downward Mobility in Rural Uganda'. *Development Policy Review* 23(1): 55–85 (2005)

Bird, K., K. Higgins and A. McKay, 'Conflict, Education and the Intergenerational Transmission of Poverty in Northern Uganda'. *Journal of International Development* 22(8): 1183–96 (2010)

Bird, K., K. Higgins and A. McKay, 'Education and Resilience in Conflict- and Insecurity-affected Northern Uganda'. Chronic Poverty Research Centre Working Paper 215 (Manchester, 2011)

BoT (Bank of Tanzania) 'Recent Macroeconomic Development, Directorate of Economic Policy, (Dar-es-Salaam 2010)

Bryceson, D.F., 'African Rural Labour, Income Diversification and Livelihood Approaches: A Long-term Development Perspective'. African Studies Centre Working Paper 35 (Leiden, 1999)

Bryceson, D.F., 'The Scramble in Africa: Reorienting Rural Livelihoods'. *World Development* 30(5): 725–39 (2002)

Bryceson, D.F. and M. McCall 'Lightening the Load: Women's Labour and Appropriate Rural Technology in Sub-Saharan Africa'. African Studies Centre Working Paper 21 (Leiden, 1994)

Campbell, D., 'Decent Work and India's National Rural Employment Guarantee'. Asian Development Bank Board of Governors Meeting (Tashkent 1-4 May 2010)

Chambers, R., 'Editorial Introduction: Vulnerability, Coping and Policy'. *Institute of Development Studies Bulletin* 20(2): 1–7 (1989)

Chambo, S.A., 'Agricultural Co-operatives: Role in Food Security and Rural Development'. United Nations Expert Group Meeting on Co-operatives (New York, 28–30 April 2009)

Chipeta, C., 'The Second Economy and Tax Yield in Malawi', African Economic Research Consortium Research Paper (Nairobi, 2002)

Chronic Poverty Research Centre, *Escaping Poverty Traps: Chronic Poverty Report, 2008–09* (Manchester, 2008)

Coles, C., K Ellis and A. Shepherd, 'Assessment of The Gatsby Charitable Trust Tanzania Cotton Sector Development Programme', (London, 2011)

Coulson, A., *Tanzania: A Political Economy* (London, 1982)

da Corta, L., 'The Political Economy of Agrarian Change: Dinosaur or Phoenix?' *The Comparative Political Economy of Development: Africa and Asia*, eds B. Harriss-White and J. Heyer (New York, 2010)

da Corta L. and K. Bird, 'Comparative Life History Project: Research Questions and Hypotheses'. Chronic Poverty Research Centre Comparative Life History Project Concept Note (Manchester, 2009)

da Corta, L. and J. Magongo, 'Evolution of Gender and Poverty Dynamics in Tanzania'. Chronic Poverty Research Centre Working Paper (Manchester, 2010)

da Corta, L. and Price, L. 'Poverty and Growth in Remote Villages in Tanzania (2004-2008): Insights from Village Voices Film Research'. Chronic Poverty Research Centre Working Paper 153 (Manchester, 2009)

da Corta, L. and D. Venkateswarlu, 'Field Methods for Economic Mobility', *Fieldwork in Developing Countries*, eds S. Devereux and J. Hoddinott (Hemel Hempstead, 1992)

Davis, P., 'Poverty in Time: Exploring Poverty Dynamics from Life History Interviews in Bangladesh', *Poverty Dynamics: Interdisciplinary Perspectives*, eds T. Addison, D. Hulme and R. Kanbur (Oxford, 2009)

Davis, P., 'Moving out of Poverty: Patterns and Causes of Poverty Exits in Rural Bangladesh', Chronic Poverty Research Centre Working Paper 142 (Manchester, 2010)

Davis, P., 'Passing on Poverty: The Intergenerational Transmission of Wellbeing and Ill-being in Rural Bangladesh'. Chronic Poverty Research Centre Working Paper 192 (Manchester, 2011a)

Davis, P., 'Social Exclusion and Adverse Incorporation in Rural Bangladesh: Evidence from a Mixed-methods Study of Poverty Dynamics'. Chronic Poverty Research Centre Working Paper 193 (Manchester, 2011b)

Davis, P., 'Escaping Poverty: Patterns and Causes of Poverty Exits in Rural Bangladesh'. Chronic Poverty Research Centre Working Paper 194 (Manchester, 2011c)

Davis, P., 'The Trappings of Poverty: The Role of Assets and Liabilities in Socio-economic Mobility in Rural Bangladesh'. Chronic Poverty Research Centre Working Paper 195 (Manchester, 2011d)

Davis, P. and B. Baulch, 'Parallel Realities: Exploring Poverty Dynamics Using Mixed Methods in Rural Bangladesh'. *Journal of Development Studies* 47(1): 118–42 (2011)

Department for International Development, Sustainable Livelihoods Guidance Sheets (London, 2000)

Department for International Development, 'Tanzania MDG Progress' (London, 2009)

de Weerdt, J., 'Moving out of Poverty in Tanzania: Evidence from Kagera'. *Journal of Development Studies* 46 (20): 331–49 (2010)

Economic and Social Research Foundation, 'Report on the Study of Growth and Impact of Investment in Tanzania' (Dar es Salaam, 2006)

Ellis, F., 'Agrarian Change and Rising Vulnerability in Rural Sub-Saharan Africa'. *New Political Economy* 11(3): 387–97 (2006)

Ellis, F., 'Strategic Dimensions of Rural Poverty Reduction in Sub-Saharan Africa', *The Comparative Political Economy of Development: Africa and South Asia*, eds B. Harriss-White and J. Heyer (London, 2010)

Ellis, A., M. Blackden, J. Cutura, F. MacCulloch and H. Seebens, *Gender and Economic Growth in Tanzania*, (Washington, DC, 2007)

Fall, A.S., P. Antoine, R. Cisse, L. Dramani, M. Sall, T. Ndoye, M. Diop, B. Doucoure, M. Sylla, P. Ngom and A. Faye 'Les Dynamiques de la Pauvreté au Sénégal' (2011)

Famine Early Warning Systems Network, 'Tanzanian Food Security Outlook, October 2009 to March 2010'. (Washington, DC, 2009)

Farrington, J., R. Slater, and R. Holmes, 'The Search for Synergies between Social Protection and Livelihood Promotion: The Agriculture Case' (London, 2004)

FinScope, 'National Survey on Access to and Demand for Financial Services in Tanzania' (Dar es Salaam, 2006)

Glavovic B. C., R. Scheyvens and J. Overton, 'Waves of Adversity, Layers of Resilience: Exploring the Sustainable Livelihoods Approach', *Contesting Development: Pathways to Better Practice. Proceedings of the Third Biennial Conference of the Aotearoa New Zealand*, eds D. Storey, J. Overton and B. Nowak (Massey, 2003)

Green, A. and S. Mesaki, 'The Birth of the "Salon": Poverty, Modernization, and Dealing with Witchcraft in Southern Tanzania'. *American Ethnologist* 32(3): 371–88 (2005)

Green, M., 'The Social Distribution of Sanctioned Harm: Thinking through Chronic Poverty, Durable Poverty and Destitution'. *Poverty Dynamics: Interdisciplinary Perspectives*, eds T. Addison, D. Hulme and R. Kanbur (Oxford, 2009)

Grindle, M.S., 'Good Enough Governance: Poverty Reduction and Reform in Developing Countries' (Cambridge, MA, 2002)

Harriss-White, B., 'A Note on Destitution'. Queen Elizabeth House Working Paper 86 (Oxford, 2002)

Hashemi, S.M. and W. Umaira, 'New Pathways for the Poorest: The Graduation Model from BRAC'. Centre for Social Protection Research Report 10 (Brighton, 2011)

Haug, R., W. Tessema, T. Lemma, T. Berg, A.R. Phiri, J.W. Banda, E.E. Kaunda, J. Hella, I. Kamile and C. Erik Schultz, 'Global Food Prices—Crisis or Opportunity for Smallholder Farmers in Ethiopia, Malawi and Tanzania?' Noragric Report 48 (Oslo, 2009)

Hickey, S. and A. Du Toit, 'Adverse Incorporation, Social Exclusion and Chronic Poverty'. Chronic Poverty Research Centre Working Paper 81 (Manchester, 2007)

Higgins, K., 'Escaping Poverty in Tanzania: What Can We Learn from Cases of Success?' Conference on 'Ten Years of "War against Poverty": What Have We Learned since 2000 and What Should We Do 2010–20?' (Manchester, 8–10 September 2010)

Holmes, R. and N. Jones, 'Gender-sensitive Social Protection and the MDGs'. Overseas Development Institute Briefing Paper 61 (London, 2010)

Hoogeveen, J., 'Enhancing the Capacity of the Poor to Participate in Growth', *Sustaining and Sharing Economic Growth in Tanzania*, ed. R. Utz (Washington, DC, 2008)

Hoogeveen, J and R. Ruhunduka, 'Poverty Reduction in Tanzania since 2001: Good Intentions, Few Results'. Draft for Research and Analysis Working Group (Dar es Salaam, 2009)

Hulme, D., K. Moore and A. Shepherd, 'Chronic Poverty: Meanings and Analytical Frameworks'. Chronic Poverty Research Centre Working Paper 2 (Manchester, 2001)

Hyden, G. and J. Court, 'Comparing Governance across Countries and over Time: Conceptual Challenges', *Making Sense of Governance*, eds G. Hyden, J. Court and K. Mease (Boulder, CO, 2004)

Isinika, E.E. and A.C. Msuya, 'Addressing Food Self-sufficiency in Tanzania: A Balancing Act of Policy Coordination'. *African Smallholders: Food Crops, Markets and Policies*. Eds G. Djurfeldt, E. Aryeetey and A.C. Isinika (Wallingford, 2011)

Kaijage, F. And A. Tibaijuka, '*Poverty and Social Exclusion in Tanzania*,' Geneva: International Institute of Labor Studies (Geneva, 1995).

Kamuzora, P. and L. Gilson, 'Factors Influencing the Implementation of the Community Health Fund in Tanzania'. *Health and Policy Planning* 22: 95–102 (2007)

Kanbur, R. and L. Squire, 'The Evolution of Thinking about Poverty: Exploring the Interactions', *Frontiers of Development Economics: The Future in Perspective*, eds G. Meier and J. Stiglitz (Oxford University Press, 2001)

Kayunze, K., O. Mashindano and F. Maro, 'Poverty Mobility in Tanzania and Linkages with Governance'. Chronic Poverty Research Centre Working Paper (Manchester, 2010)

Kessy, F., 'Gender Dimensions in the Cut Flower Industry in Tanzania: Implications for Economic and Social Policy' *Tanzania Journal of Development Studies*, Vol 10 Nos. 1&2, 30-57 (2010).

Kessy, F., 'Synthesis of Focus Group Discussion Findings from Rural and Urban Clusters—World Bank Household Enterprises Study' (Dar es Salaam, 2010)

Kessy, F. and S.V. Tarmo, 'Exploring Resilience Avenues for Managing Covariant and Idiosyncratic Poverty-related Shocks: A Case Study of Three Districts in Tanzania'. Chronic Poverty Research Centre Working Paper (Manchester, 2010)

Kessy, F., O. Mashindano, D. Rweyemamu and P. Charle, 'Moving out of Poverty: Understanding Growth and Democracy from the Bottom up: Ruvuma Regional Synthesis Report' (Dar es Salaam, 2006)

Kessy, F., I. Mayumana and Y. Msongwe, 'Widowhood and Vulnerability to HIV and AIDS-related Shocks: Exploring Resilience Avenues'. Research on Poverty Alleviation Research Report 10/5 (Dar es Salaam, 2010)

Kilimo Trust, *Feasibility and justification for a common strategy for food security in EAC*, Report submitted by the Economic and Social Research Foundation, (Dar es Salaam, May 2010

Laderchi, C.R., R. Saith and F. Stewart, 'Does It Matter That We Do Not Agree on the Definition of Poverty? A Comparison of Four Approaches'. Queen Elizabeth House Working Paper 107 (Oxford, 2003)

Leach, V. and B. Kilama, 'Institutional Analysis of Nutrition in Tanzania', Research on Poverty Alleviation Special Paper 09.31 (Dar es Salaam, 2009)

Levy, S., 'Linking Agricultural Growth and Social Protection' (London, 2007)

Likwelile S., 'Measurement of Poverty and Inequality: The Basics of Poverty and Evidence and Trends on Poverty and Inequality Locally and Globally'. Training Workshop on Policy Analysis, Poverty, Inequality and Research Methodology (Dar es Salaam, 2000)

Luvanda, E., 'Analysis of the 2007 Household Budget Survey' (Dar es Salaam, 2011)

Mashindano O. 'Understanding Poverty: The Meaning, Measurements and Indicators'. Training Manual for Workshop on Poverty and Policy Analysis (Dar es Salaam, 2007)

Mashindano, O., K. Kayunze and F. Maro, 'Agricultural Growth, Markets and Poverty Reduction in Tanzania'. Chronic Poverty Research Centre Working Paper (Manchester, 2010)

Mbelle, A.V.Y. 'MKUKUTA and MDGs Costing: Fiscal and Macroeconomic Implications of Scaling up Investments in Achieving the Set Targets'. PER and MKUKUTA Consultative Meeting (Dar-es-Salaam, 2007)

McCord, A., 'The Social Protection Function of Short-term Public Works Programmes in the Context of Chronic Poverty', *Social Protection for the Poorest: Concepts, Policies and Politics*, eds A. Barrientos and D. Hulme (London, 2010)

Miller, R., M. Mathenge, K. Bird, F. Karin, R. Gitau and E.K. Nteza, 'Ascending out of Poverty: An Analysis of Family Histories in Kenya'. Chronic Poverty Research Centre Working Paper 219 (Manchester, 2011a)

Miller, R., F. Karin, K. Bird, E.K. Nteza, R. Gitau and M. Mathenge, 'Family Histories and Rural Inheritance in Kenya'. Chronic Poverty Research Centre Working Paper 220 (Manchester, 2011b)

Ministry of Agriculture, Food Security and Cooperatives, *National Sample Census of Agriculture (2002/03)* (Dar es Salaam, 2003)

Ministry of Agriculture, Food Security and Cooperatives, 'Financing Agricultural Sector Development in Tanzania'. Brief 4 (Dar es Salaam, 2010)

Ministry of Finance and Economic Affairs, 'Poverty and Human Development Report 2002' (Dar es Salaam, 2002)

Ministry of Finance and Economic Affairs, 'Poverty and Human Development Report (Dar es Salaam, 2003)

Ministry of Finance and Economic Affairs, 'Poverty and Human Development Report 2005' (Dar es Salaam, 2005)

Ministry of Finance and Economic Affairs, 'Poverty and Human Development Report 2007' (Dar es Salaam, 2007)

Ministry of Finance and Economic Affairs, 'Poverty and Human Development Report 2009' (Dar es Salaam, 2009)

Ministry of Labour, Employment and Youth Development, with HelpAge International, 'Achieving Income Security in Old Age for All Tanzanians: A Study into the Feasibility of a Universal Social Pension (Dar es Salaam, 2010)

Minot, N., 'Staple Food Prices in Tanzania'. COMESA Policy Seminar on Variation in Staple Food Prices: Causes, Consequence, and Policy Options (Maputo, 25–6 January 2010)

Mkenda, A.F., E.G. Luvanda and R. Ruhinduka, 'Growth and Distribution in Tanzania. Recent Experience and Lessons', Research on Poverty Alleviation Report (Dar es Salaam, 2010)

Molyneux, M., 'Mothers at the Service of the New Poverty Agenda: Progresa/ Oportunidades, Mexico's Conditional Transfer Programme'. *Journal of Social Policy and Administration* 40(2/3): 425–49 (2006)

Molyneux, M., 'Change and Continuity in Social Protection in Latin America: Mothers at the Service of the State?' United Nations Research Institute for Social Development Working Paper (Geneva, 2007)

Msambichaka, L.A., 'Kilimo Kwanza: Challenges and Opportunities'. Tanzania Private Sector Foundation Forum (Dar es Salaam, 2011)

Msambichaka, L.A., M.E. Mwamba and O.J. Mashindano, 'Poverty in Tanzania: Situation, Perception and Escape Routes'. *Tanzania Journal of Population Studies and Development* 12(1): 43–6 (2005)

Msambichaka, L., O. Mashindano, E. Luvanda and R. Ruhinduka, 'Analysis of the Performance of Agriculture Sector and Its Contribution to Economic Growth and Poverty Reduction' (Dar-es-Salaam, 2009)

Msokwa, Z.E., 'Development and Application of National Accounts in Tanzania, 1976–1999: Problems and Prospects'. Degree of Doctor of Philosophy in Economics, University of Dar es Salaam (Dar es Salaam, 2001)

Mwaipopo, R., 'The Impact of Commodity Relations on the Status and Position of Women in Peasant Households: A Case Study of Syukula Village, Rungwe District, Mbeya Region' (1994)

Narayan, D. and P. Petesch, *Moving Out of Poverty: Cross Disciplinary Perspectives on Mobility.* (Washington, DC, 2007)

National Bureau of Statistics, 'Household Budget Survey 1991/92' (Dar es Salaam, 1992)

National Bureau of Statistics, 'Household Budget Survey 2000/01' (Dar es Salaam, 2002)

National Bureau of Statistics, 'Household Budget Survey 2007' (Dar es Salaam, 2008a)

National Bureau of Statistics, 'Disability Survey' (Dar es Salaam, 2008b)

National Bureau of Statistics, 'National Accounts of Tanzanian Mainland' (Dar es Salaam, 2008c)

National Bureau of Statistics, *Trends in Food Insecurity in Mainland Tanzania* (Dar es Salaam, 2010)

National Bureau of Statistics and ORC Macro, *Tanzania Demographic and Health Survey 2004/05* (Dar es Salaam and Calverton, MD, 2005)

Nino-Zarazua, M., A. Barrientos, D. Hulme and S. Hickey, 'Social Protection in Sub-Saharan African: Will the Green Shoots Blossom?' Brooks World Poverty Institute Working Paper 116 (Manchester, 2010)

Nyerere, J.K., 'Leadership and the Management of Change'. Address at the Quinquennial General Conference of the Association of Commonwealth Universities (Ottawa, 17 August 1998)

Obrist, B., C. Pfeiffer and R. Henley, 'Multi-layered Social Resilience: A New Approach in Mitigation Research'. *Progress in Development Studies* 10(4): 283–93 (2010)

Olowu. D., 'Introduction: Governance and Policy Management Capacity in Africa', *Better Governance and Public Policy: Capacity Building and Democratic Enewala in Africa*, eds D. Olowu and S. Sako (Bloomfield, CT, 2003)

Omiti, J. and T. Nyanamba, 'Using Social Protection to Reduce Vulnerability and Promote Economic Growth in Kenya'. Future Agricultures Consortium Policy Brief (London, 2008)

Pauw, K. and J. Thurlow, 'Agricultural Growth, Poverty and Nutrition in Tanzania'. International Food Policy Research Institute Discussion Paper 947 (Washington, DC, 2010)

Platteau, J., A. Abraham, F. Gaspart and L. Stevens, 'Traditional Marriage Practices as Determinants of Women's Land Rights: A Review of Research'. Food and Agricultural Organization, *Gender and Land Compendium of Country Studies* (Rome, 2005)

Rahman, A., *Peasants and Classes: A Study in Differentiation in Bangladesh* (London, 1986)

Regional Psychosocial Support Initiative, World Vision, Swiss Agency for Development and Cooperation and HelpAge International, 'Salt, Soap and Shoes for School: Evaluation Report–Impact of Pensions on the Lives of Older People and Grandchildren in the Kwa Wazee Project in Tanzania's Kagera Region' (London, 2008)

Research on Poverty Alleviation, National Bureau of Statistics and United Nations Children's Fund, 'Childhood Poverty in Tanzania: Deprivations and Disparities in Child Well-being' (Dar es Salaam, 2009)

Revolutionary Government of Zanzibar), *Zanzibar Human Development Report: Towards Pro-Poor Growth* (Zanzibar, 2009)

Sender, J. and S. Smith, *Poverty, Class and Gender in Rural Africa: Tanzanian Case Study* (London, 1990)

Shepherd, A., 'Understanding and Explaining Chronic Poverty: An Evolving Framework for Phase III of CPRC's Research'. Chronic Poverty Research Centre Working Paper 90 (Manchester, 2007)

Shepherd, A., F. Kessy, L. Scott and E. Luvanda, 'Addressing Chronic Poverty and Vulnerability through Social Assistance in Tanzania: Assessing the Options'. Chronic Poverty Research Centre Policy Brief (Manchester, 2011a)

Shepherd, A., D. Wadugodapitiya and A. Evans, 'Social Assistance and the Dependency Syndrome'. Chronic Poverty Research Centre Policy Brief 22 (Manchester, 2011b)

Synovate, 'Poll of Social and Political Opinions (Dar es Salaam, 2009)

Social Protection Task Force, Ministry of Gender, Labour and Social Development, Uganda, 'Design of a Cash Transfer Pilot' (Kampala, 2007)

Tanzania Gender Networking Programme, *Gender Profile of Tanzania: Enhancing Gender Equity* (Dar es Salaam, 2007)

United Republic of Tanzania, *National Poverty Eradication Strategy* (Dar es Salaam, 1998)

United Republic of Tanzania, *Tanzania Development Vision 2025* (Dar es Salaam, 1999a)

United Republic of Tanzania, 'Poverty and Welfare Monitoring Indicators' (Dar es Salaam, 1999b)

United Republic of Tanzania, *Poverty Reduction Strategy Paper* (Dar-es-Salaam, 2000)

United Republic of Tanzania, 'Vulnerability and Resilience to Poverty in Tanzania: Causes, Consequences and Policy Implications'. Tanzania Participatory Poverty Assessment Main Report (Dar es Salaam, 2004)

United Republic of Tanzania, *National Strategy for Growth and Reduction of Poverty: MKUKUTA I* (Dar es Salaam, 2005)

United Republic of Tanzania, *Agricultural Sector Development Programme* (Dar es Salaam, 2006)

United Republic of Tanzania, *Integrated Labour Force Survey* (Dar es Salaam, 2007)

United Republic of Tanzania, 'Guideline for the Development of Next Generation of MKUKUTA and Mkuza' (Dar es Salaam, 2009a)

United Republic of Tanzania, 'MKUKUTA Annual Implementation Report 2008/09: Success amid Turbulence' (Dar es Salaam, 2009b)

United Republic of Tanzania, 'National Social Protection Framework' (Dar es Salaam, 2009c)

United Republic of Tanzania, 'Tanzania National Panel Survey Report Round 1: 2008–9' (Dar es Salaam, 2010a)

United Republic of Tanzania, 'National Strategy for Growth and Reduction of Poverty II: MKUKUTA II' (Dar es Salaam, 2010b)

United Republic of Tanzania, 'Review of the Tanzania Development Vision 2025, Volume I: Main Report' (Dar es Salaam, 2011a)

United Republic of Tanzania, 'Tanzania Five-year Development Plan 2011/12–2015/16: Unleashing Tanzania's Latent Growth Potentials' (Dar es Salaam, 2011b)

US Censors Bureau: International Data Base (1995 – 2010)

van Schendel, W., *Peasant Mobility: The Odds of Life in Rural Bangladesh* (Assen, 1981)

Watson, C. and J. Gibson, 'Save the Children Fund/UNICEF Multi-year, Multi-country Research Programme on the Impacts of Cash Transfers on Children in Eastern and Southern Africa: Tanzania Country Report (Dar es Salaam, 2009)

World Bank, 'Tanzania Turn of the Century: From Reforms to Sustained Growth and Poverty Reduction' (Washington, DC, 2001)

World Bank, 'Investment Climate Assessment: Improving Enterprise Performance and Growth in Tanzania, Regional Programme for Enterprise Development' (Washington, DC, 2004)

World Bank, *Measuring Vulnerability—Poverty Reduction Equity* (Washington, DC, 2011)

World Bank and Tanzania Social Action Fund, 'Making Public Works Work'. Social Protection South South Learning Forum Final Report (Arusha, 14–18 June, 2010)

Wuyts, M., 'Developing Social Protection in Tanzania within the Context of Generalized Insecurity'. Research on Poverty Alleviation Special Paper 06.19 (Dar es Salaam, 2006)